English Poetry
1700-1780

CONTEMPORARIES OF SWIFT
AND JOHNSON

Edited
with an introduction by

David W. Lindsay

LECTURER IN ENGLISH
UNIVERSITY COLLEGE OF NORTH WALES,
BANGOR

DENT, LONDON
ROWMAN AND LITTLEFIELD, TOTOWA, N.J.

© Introduction, selection and commentary,
J.M. Dent & Sons Ltd, 1974

Made in Great Britain
at
Biddles Ltd., Guildford, Surrey
for
J.M. DENT & SONS LTD
Aldine House Albemarle Street London
First published 1974
First published in the United States 1974
by ROWMAN AND LITTLEFIELD, Totowa, New Jersey

This book is set in 9 on 10pt Times New Roman

Dent edition
Hardback ISBN: 0 460 10700 3
Paperback ISBN: 0 460 11700 9

Rowman and Littlefield edition
Library of Congress Cataloging in publication Data

Lindsay, David W   comp.
English poetry, 1700-1780; contemporaries of Swift
& Johnson.

(Rowman and Littlefield university library)
CONTENTS: Pomfret J. The choice. – Philips J. The
splendid shillings. – Wats I. The day of judgement.
[etc.]
1. English poetry – 18th century. I. Title.
PR1215.L5   821'.5'08   74-4240
ISBN 0-87471-547-4
ISBN 0-87471-546-6 (pbk.)

Contents

Textual Note

The texts printed in this anthology have been taken from the following books: J. Pomfret, *The Choice*, 1701; J. Philips, *The Splendid Shilling*, 1705; I. Watts, *Horae Lyricae*, 1706; *The Tatler*, 5-7 May 1709; J. Gay, *Trivia*, 1716; T. Parnell, *Poems on Several Occasions*, 1721; M. Prior, *Poems on Several Occasions*, 1718; A. Ramsay, *Poems*, 1721; D. Lewis, *Miscellaneous Poems*, 1726; *The Gentleman's Magazine*, 1737; E. Young, *Night Thoughts*, 1747; W. Shenstone, *Works*, 1791; J. Byrom, *Miscellaneous Works*, 1773; J. Macpherson, *The Works of Ossian*, 1765; C. Churchill, *The Rosciad*, 1765; C. Smart, *A Song to David*, 1763; J. Cunningham, *Poems*, 1766; M. Akenside, *Poems*, 1772; T. Chatterton, *Poems Supposed to have been Written at Bristol by Thomas Rowley and Others*, 1778; *The Weekly Magazine and Edinburgh Entertainment*, 12 November 1772; J. Langhorne, *The Country Justice*, Part II, 1775. The original spelling and punctuation have been retained, except in the case of obvious misprints; but proper names indicated by initial letters have been spelt out in full. Dedications, epigraphs, prefaces, marginal notes, footnotes and appendices have in most cases been omitted; but they are frequently cited in the commentary.

Select Bibliography

The most comprehensive collection of poetry from the years 1700-1780 is to be found in the twenty-one volumes of Alexander Chalmers' *The Works of the English Poets,* which appeared in 1810. Other editions of the poets represented in this anthology include:

J. Byrom, *Poems,* edited by A.W. Ward, 3 volumes, Manchester 1894-1912.

T. Chatterton, *The Complete Works,* edited by D.S. Taylor, 2 volumes, Oxford 1971.

C. Churchill, *Poetical Works,* edited by D. Grant, Oxford 1956.

R. Fergusson, *Poetical Works,* edited by M.P. Mc.Diarmid, 2 volumes, Edinburgh 1954-6.

J. Gay, *Poetical Works,* edited by G.C. Faber, Oxford 1926.

J. Macpherson, *The Poems of Ossian,* edited by M. Laing, Edinburgh 1805.

T. Parnell, *Poetical Works,* edited by G.A. Aitken, 1894.

A. Philips, *Poems,* edited by M.G. Segar, Oxford 1937.

J. Philips, *Poems,* edited by M.G.L. Thomas, Oxford 1927.

M. Prior, *Literary Works,* edited by H.B. Wright and M.K. Spears, 2 volumes, Oxford 1959.

A. Ramsay, *Works,* edited by B. Martin, J.W. Oliver, A.M. Kinghorn and Alexander Law, 6 volumes, Edinburgh 1951-

R. Savage, *Poetical Works,* edited by C. Tracy, Cambridge 1962.

W. Shenstone, *Works,* edited by R. Dodsley, 3 volumes, 1791.

C. Smart, *Collected Poems,* edited by N. Callan, 2 volumes, 1949.

I. Watts, *Works,* 9 volumes, Leeds 1812-13.

E. Young, *Complete Works,* edited by J. Nichols, 2 volumes, 1854.

A full bibliography of texts and secondary material can be found in the second volume of *The New Cambridge Bibliography of English Literature.*

Introduction

John Dryden and the seventeenth century were buried in Westminster Abbey on 13 May 1700; in a love-letter George Farquhar described the ceremony:

'And so much for Mr. *Dryden,* whose Burial was the same with his Life; Variety, and not of a Piece. The Quality and Mob, Farce and Heroicks; the Sublime and Redicule mixt in a Piece, great Cleopatra in a Hackney Coach.'[1]

The new age, whose dawn had been heralded at Drury Lane in April by the performance of Dryden's *A Secular Masque,* was apparently to be an age whose consistent and controlled ambitions would evade such extremism and incongruity; and that hope, implicit also in the epistle to a Hunting-donshire cousin which Dryden had just published with his *Fables,* was frequently expressed at this time in both public and personal terms.

In a pseudo-Pindaric welcome to the eighteenth century Matthew Prior, having piously likened the victor of Namur to the victor of Jericho, explained what Britain wanted from her constitutional monarch:

> Science to raise, and Knowledge to enlarge,
>> Be our great Master's future Charge...
>> Let Him unite His Subjects Hearts,
> Planting Societies for peaceful Arts;
> Some that in Nature shall true Knowledge found,
> And by Experiment make Precept sound;
> Some that to Morals shall recal the Age,
> And purge from vitious Dross the sinking Stage;
> Some that with Care true Eloquence shall teach,
> And to just Idioms fix our doubtful Speech...
> Through various Climes, and to each distant Pole
> In happy Tides let active Commerce rowl...
> Nations yet wild by Precept to reclaim,
> And teach 'em Arms, and Arts, in WILLIAM's Name.[2]

These lines assert with platitudinous clarity the values which were hence-forth to govern public life: a Lockean concept of monarchy, a desire for national prosperity and civil peace, a Baconian attitude to scientific in-vestigation, a belief that the arts should be morally respectable, a linguistic theory derived from the Royal Society, and a confidence in the

[1] *Love and Business.*   [2] *Carmen Seculare.*

civilizing power of international trade. In a stanzaic ode allegedly written about 1700, on the other hand, Alexander Pope celebrated the ideal of tranquillity through moderation which he had learned from Horace and Claudian, writers educated by civil war:

> Blest! who can unconcern'dly find
> Hours, days, and years slide soft away,
> In health of body, peace of mind,
>   Quiet by day,
> Sound sleep by night; study and ease
> Together mix'd; sweet recreation,
> And innocence, which most does please,
>   With meditation.[1]

This concept of civilized retirement was to maintain its imaginative power throughout the century: its most popular expression was John Pomfret's *The Choice,* but it also contributed (for example) to Gibbon's picture of Diocletian planting cabbages at Salona. Considered as the literal representation of a perfect state, it may be dismissed as *rentier* escapism; but as poetic statement it reflects, in its unhysterical awareness of life's imperfection, the emotional temper which governed the cultural achievements of 1700-1780.

While Dryden, deposed from the laureateship, was translating Virgil and presiding at Will's coffee-house, young Whigs of the professional class like Sir Richard Blackmore and Sir Samuel Garth had been shaping a poetry appropriate to the post-Revolutionary world; and the limited virtues of that poetry were variously manifested in volumes published during the first decade after Dryden's funeral. Writers of that decade drew inspiration from the Greek and Latin poets, from Boileau and La Fontaine, from Marvell, Milton and Cowley, from Butler, Dryden and Oldham; and the forms with which they worked included the hymn and the love-song, the Pindaric ode and the Cecilia's Day ode, the eclogue and the verse-satire, the didactic essay and the mock-epic. The influence of Waller was apparent in the songs and epistles of gentleman-poets like George Granville and William Walsh; and echoes of Rochester and Dorset could sometimes be heard in erotic and satirical lyrics. The predominant non-lyrical verse-form was the heroic couplet; but octosyllabics were used for both satirical and meditative poems, and there were modest experiments with the Spenserian stanza and with neo-Miltonic blank verse. The most distinctive personalities among the poets of this phase are Matthew Prior and Isaac Watts; but there are other writers whose verse occasionally sounds an individual note.

In a disorderly but vigorous satire on the Tory opposition, Daniel Defoe, pours scorn on those enemies of the new order who profess to resent the importing of a monarch:

[1] 'Ode on Solitude'.

These are the Heroes who despise the *Dutch,*
And rail at new-come Foreigners so much;
Forgetting that themselves are all deriv'd
From the most Scoundrel Race that ever liv'd,
A horrid Crowd of Rambling Thieves and Drones,
Who ransack'd Kingdoms, and dispeopled Towns:
The *Pict* and Painted *Britain,* treach'rous *Scot,*
By Hunger, Theft, and Rapine, hither brought;
Norwegian pirates, Buccaneering *Danes,*
Whose Red-hair'd Offspring ev'ry where remains;
Who join'd with *Norman-French* compound the Breed
From whence your *True-Born Englishmen* proceed.[1]

In a 'country diversion' wrongly suspected of political overtones, William King (imitator of Horace in *The Art of Cookery* and of Ovid in *The Art of Love*) celebrates the hospitality offered by a villa on Dublin Bay.[2] And in a blank-verse celebration of the cider industry combining Virgilian and Miltonic techniques, John Philips devised a semi-heroic manner which proved the apposite medium for practical advice:

When swelling buds their odorous foliage shed,
And gently harden into fruit, the wise
Spare not the little offsprings, if they grow
Redundant; but the thronging clusters thin
By kind avulsion; else the starveling brood,
Void of sufficient sustenance, will yield
A slender autumn; which the niggard soul
Too late shall weep, and curse his thrifty hand,
That would not timely ease the ponderous boughs.[3]

Dryden's successor as president of the literary world, however, was Joseph Addison; and Addison's poetry (less vigorous than Defoe, less exuberant than King, and less original than John Philips) reflects the accomplishment and versatility of one for whom Latin verse, the Church of England and the British constitution were aspects of a single intellectual harmony. Visiting Italy in 1701, Addison commented in a polished verse-letter to Lord Halifax on the lost grandeur of Rome and the present liberty of Britain; and three years later he commemorated Marlborough's victory at Blenheim, paying tribute to the general's controlling will in a passage which was much admired:

But O, my Muse, what Numbers wilt thou find
To sing the furious Troops in Battel join'd!
Methinks I hear the Drum's tumultuous Sound
The Victor's Shouts and Dying Groans confound,
The dreadful Burst of Cannon rend the skies,
And all the Thunder of the Battel rise.

[1] *The True-Born Englishman.* [2] 'Mully of Mountown'. [3] *Cyder.*

> 'Twas then Great MARLBRO's mighty Soul was prov'd
> That, in the Shock of Charging Hosts unmov'd,
> Amidst Confusion, Horror, and Despair,
> Examin'd all the Dreadful Scenes of war;
> In peaceful Thought the Field of Death survey'd,
> To fainting Squadrons sent the timely Aid,
> Inspir'd repuls'd Battalions to engage,
> And taught the doubtful Battel where to rage.
> So when an Angel by Divine Command
> With rising Tempests shakes a guilty Land,
> Such as of late o'er pale *Britannia* past,
> Calm and Serene he drives the furious Blast;
> And, pleas'd th'Almighty's Orders to perform,
> Rides in the Whirl-wind, and directs the Storm.[1]

Addison's Whiggish blend of classical and Christian values was expressed with comparable authority in his occasional poems and in his hymns; and the craftsmanship apparent there and in his translations was emulated by the 'little senate' which applauded his *obiter dicta* in Button's coffee-house. A leading member of the Addisonian circle was Ambrose Philips, and Philips' odes and eclogues conveyed not the religio-political dogmas of the new era but its domestic pathos and pastoral idealism:

> O, *Colinet,* how sweet thy Grief to hear!
> How does thy Verse subdue the list'ning Ear!
> Not half so sweet are Midnight Winds, that move
> In drowsie Murmurs O'er the waving Grove;
> Nor dropping Waters, that in Grots distil,
> And with a tinkling Sound their Caverns fill:
> So sing the Swans, that in soft Numbers waste
> Their dying Breath, and warble to the last.
> And next to thee shall *Mico* bear the Bell,
> That can repeat thy peerless Verse so well.[2]

Literary historians can recognize a significantly exploratory element in Philips' emotional response to natural phenomena, and can relate it to his admiration for Spenser; but this gently rococo sentiment, linked as it was with archaism and half-conscious naivety, offered an irresistible target to contemporary writers who did not share the Buttonian sensibility.

Philips' pastorals were collected in 1709; and between then and 1714 the inevitable and necessary critique was effected by Jonathan Swift in a vivid fragment of town-eclogue, by Alexander Pope in a cunningly ironic essay for *The Guardian,* and by John Gay in a burlesque eclogue-sequence entitled *The Shepherd's Week.* These three men, together with a Scottish doctor named John Arbuthnot and an Irish clergyman named Thomas Parnell, constituted a group of Tory wits which met, during the Harley-

---

[1]*The Campaign.*   [2]'The Fourth Pastoral'.

Bolingbroke ministry of 1710-14, to compose the memoirs of an imaginary scholar named Martinus Scriblerus. Despite their very different political views, the members of the Scriblerus Club shared many of the social and cultural values of the Buttonian circle; but the habit of mind revealed in their characteristic work is sharper, more sceptical and less affirmative. Drawing like Addison on the poetic tradition established by Dryden, they developed it as a vehicle for wide-ranging cultural criticism; and in particular they explored the potentialities of literary burlesque and refined the inherited concept of genre. Their more formal poems, for which the usual verse-form was the heroic couplet, included eclogues, georgics, topographical poems, verse-epistles, verse-satires, didactic essays, mock-epics and major translations; and their less formal poems, commonly in the octosyllabic couplet, were predominantly narrative, satiric and epistolary. Their criticism of the Whig ethos was developed not only in verse but also in prose and drama; and it reached its climax, after the death of Anne and the emergence of Walpole, in the publication during the years 1726-8 of *Gulliver's Travels, The Beggar's Opera* and the first version of *The Dunciad.* Until the end of George I's reign at least, the Scriblerian intellect was much the strongest creative force in English poetry; but older traditions continued to develop, and other writers made significant innovations.

In 1710, when Swift's 'A Description of a City Shower' appeared in *The Tatler,* William Congreve published his *Collected Works.* Among the new pieces were love-songs in the courtly manner, whose fusion of satire and sentiment sometimes recalled their author's comedies:

> False though she be to me and Love,
>   I'll ne'er pursue Revenge;
> For still the Charmer I approve,
>   Tho' I deplore her Change.
> In Hours of Bliss we oft have met,
>   They could not always last;
> And though the present I regret,
>   I'm grateful for the past.[1]

In 1712, when Arbuthnot was issuing the satirical pamphlets which made up *The History of John Bull,* a country curate named William Diaper published a series of eclogues set not in Arcadia but in the depths of the ocean. Diaper's sensitivity and wit are apparent both in his idiosyncratic imagery and in the fluid precision of his heroic couplets:

> If *Glaucus* will be kind, and constant prove,
> Let us review those Scenes of former Love,
> And sink embracing to th'Abyss below,
> Where spiry Herbs, and lovely Coral grow;
> The Ocean has its Groves, and gloomy Shades,
> And chrystal Springs below, and cooling Glades.

[1] 'Song'.

> Fond you once thought that nothing here cou'd please,
> But we have fairer Meads, and taller Trees
> Than you on Sun-Burnt, sapless Earth cou'd boast,
> Whose fading Beauties are too quickly lost.
> The Glories of their Spring are soon defac'd
> By miry Storms, and tost by ev'ry Blast.[1]

In 1713, when Gay and Pope were celebrating the English countryside in *Rural Sports* and *Windsor Forest,* and Parnell was examining the doctrine of kinds in *An Essay on the Different Stiles of Poetry,* the Countess of Winchilsea brought out a quietly unfashionable volume entitled *Miscellany Poems.* Alongside lyrical meditations whose rhythms recall now Marvell's 'The Garden' and now Milton's 'L'Allegro', we find here the unpretentious lines which attracted Wordsworth's attention by their independent response to natural phenomena:

> In such a *Night,* when ev'ry louder Wind
> Is to its distant Cavern safe confin'd...
> When in some River, overhung with Green,
> The waving Moon and trembling Leaves are seen...
> Whilst now a paler Hue the *Foxglove* takes,
> Yet checquers still with Red the dusky brakes...
> When the loos'd *Horse* now, as his Pasture leads,
> Comes slowly grazing thro' th'adjoining Meads,
> Whose stealing Pace, and lengthen'd Shade we fear,
> Till torn up Forage in his Teeth we hear...
> In such a *Night* let Me abroad remain,
> Till Morning breaks, and All's confus'd again.[2]

In 1717, when Parnell was translating a pseudo-Homeric mock-epic and the Gay-Pope-Arbuthnot comedy *Three Hours after Marriage* was being performed at Colley Cibber's Drury Lane, Lady Mary Wortley Montagu arrived with her husband in Constantinople. Some months later, from 'the Chiosk of the British Palace at Pera', she reported in verse her impressions of the Turkish capital.[3] In 1720, when Swift in Dublin was starting a new political campaign with *A Proposal for the Use of Irish Manufacture,* Allan Ramsay collected in book form the songs and occasional poems in which he had begun to recreate the Scottish literary tradition. His imitations of Horace, like those written by the Scriblerians in England, evoke the time and place of their composition.

> Gin ony want to ken my Age,
> See *Anno Dom.* on Title Page;
> This Year when Springs by Care an' Skill

[1]*Nereides,* Eclogue I. [2]Anne Finch, Countess of Winchilsea, 'A Nocturnal Reverie'. [3]'Verses Written in the Chiosk of the British Palace at Pera, overlooking the city of Constantinople'.

The Spacious leaden Conduits fill,
An' first flow'd up the *Castle-hill;*
When *South-Sea* projects cease to thrive,
An' only *North-Sea* seems alive,
Tell them your Author's Thirty five.[1]

There is much variety, then, in the poetry of that central Augustan period when Addison and Steele remained as influential as Swift and Pope. The major works of 1710-25 include not only Scriblerian masterpieces like 'Cadenus and Vanessa', *The Rape of the Lock* and *Trivia* but also such ambitious and professional poems as Blackmore's *Creation* and Nicholas Rowe's translation of Lucan's *Pharsalia,* both of which received high praise from Samuel Johnson. Some of Prior's most triumphantly amateurish and unambitious verses appeared for the first time in the 1718 edition of *Poems on Several Occasions;* and a new mode of light verse in anapaestic stanzas was developed by Rowe in 'Colin's Complaint' and by John Byrom in a contribution to *The Spectator.* Other works of these years offer interesting anticipations of a later fashion: a three-volume collection of 'old ballads', which was published in 1723, evoked in 1724-5 melodramatic and sentimental ballad-imitations by David Mallet, Thomas Tickell and William Hamilton of Bangour.

The new developments which began in the later twenties were twofold, stemming partly from a new depth and seriousness in the work of the Scriblerians and partly from the interest of some younger writers in subjects and models which the Scriblerians had ignored. Gay published no verse of major importance after the *Fables* of 1727; but the years of Walpole's supremacy evoked from Swift and Pope a series of masterpieces ranging from *An Essay on Man* to *On Poetry: A Rhapsody.* Although Pope in *The Dunciad* lamented the destruction of literary culture by commercial values, a young bookseller's hack named Samuel Johnson re-affirmed Popean standards in 1738 with an imitation of Juvenal entitled *London.* The years of Pope's greatest achievements, however, were also the years in which James Thomson developed, through the successive instalments and revisions of *The Seasons,* a philosophico-descriptive poetry in which neo-Miltonic blank verse was unironically matched by a large and imaginative response to the Newtonian universe. *The Seasons* is indicative of cultural change, not only in its commitment to a new world-picture and a new apprehension of man's physical surroundings, but also in what its non-allusive manner implies about relations between the writer and the reading public.

These works by Swift, Pope, Thomson and Johnson are the commanding heights in the poetic landscape of 1726-43; but other authors offer not only analogous poems but also poems whose essential character is entirely

[1]'The Conclusion, After the Manner of Horace, ad librum suum'. Ramsay is alluding here to the new Edinburgh water-supply, the South Sea Company and the North Sea Fishery.

different. The songs in *The Beggar's Opera* may be considered the last masterpieces of the Restoration lyrical tradition, which had lingered not only in Congreve and Prior but also in minimal poets like Elijah Fenton. In their uncourtly energy and confidence, however, they belong equally to the eighteenth-century lyrical movement whose triumphs include 'The Vicar of Bray' and Henry Carey's 'The Ballad of Sally in our Alley'. From the thirties onwards, this new fashion in song-writing is reflected not only in love-songs and patriotic songs but also in hunting-songs, burlesque cantatas and songs celebrating food and drink. While readers of Pope were marvelling at the bad taste of Timon's villa, audiences at the Haymarket Theatre were applauding the hearty vulgarity of one Henry Fielding:

> When mighty rost Beef was the *Englishman's* Food,
> It enobled our Hearts, and enriched our Blood;
> Our Soldiers were brave, and our Courtiers were good,
> > Oh the Rost Beef of Old *England,*
> > And Old *England's* Rost Beef!
> Then, *Britons,* from all nice Dainties refrain,
> Which effeminate *Italy, France,* and *Spain;*
> And mighty Rost Beef shall command on the Main.
> > Oh the Rost Beef of Old *England,*
> > And Old *England's* Rost Beef![1]

Even in the three non-lyrical forms characteristic of the major writers, lesser poets could sometimes make an individual contribution. The heroic couplet, for example, is used by Christopher Pitt for a new version of the *Aeneid,* by rural clergymen like James Bramston and James Miller for satirico-didactic epistles in the Horatian manner, and by admirers of Newton for philosophico-scientific treatises like Henry Brooke's *The Universal Beauty.* Among other pieces in this form, however, one finds an erratic and enthusiastic work by Johnson's friend Richard Savage entitled *The Wanderer: A Vision;* and there are also historical curiosities like Stephen Duck's first-hand account of life as a farm-labourer:

> Divested of our Cloaths, with Flail in Hand,
> At proper Distance, Front to Front, we stand:
> And first the Threshal's gently swung, to prove
> Whether with just Exactness it will move;
> That once secure, we swiftly whirl them round;
> From the strong Planks our Crab-tree Staves rebound,
> And echoing Barns return the rattling Sound...
> In briny Streams our Sweat descends apace,
> Drops from our Locks, or trickles down our Face.
> No intermission in our Work we know;
> The noisy Threshal must for ever go.
> Their Master absent, others safely play;
> The sleeping Threshal does itself betray.

[1] *The Grub-Street Opera*

> Nor yet, the tedious Labour to beguile,
> And make the passing Minutes sweetly smile,
> Can we, like Shepherds, tell a merry Tale;
> The Voice is Lost, drown'd by the louder Flail.[1]

In the many poems of these years which use the other Scriblerian form, the octosyllabic couplet, one can distinguish three principal traditions. The Hudibrastic tradition of satiric and epistolary verse is maintained not only by Swift but also (in a softened form) by Gay, Ramsay and Somerville; and the tradition of narrative verse, derived by Prior from the *Fables* and *Contes* of La Fontaine, is continued not only in Gay's comic and pathetic beast-fables but also in numerous ribald anecdotes which often claim to be 'imitations of Chaucer'. The octosyllabic tradition of meditative verse, derived from Marvell and Milton by Lady Winchilsea and Parnell, is combined in John Dyer's *Grongar Hill* with the Denham-Pope tradition of topographical poetry; and we find another mutation of it in Matthew Green's civilized and witty prescription for the spleen:

> If spleen-fogs rise at close of day,
> I clear my evening with a play,
> Or to some concert take my way.
> The company, the shine of lights,
> The scenes of humour, music's flights,
> Adjust and set the soul to rights...
> Sometimes I dress, with women sit,
> And chat away the gloomy fit;
> Quit the stiff garb of serious sense,
> And wear a gay impertinence,
> Nor think nor speak with any pains,
> But lay on fancy's neck the reins:
> Talk of unusual swell of waist
> In maid of honour loosely laced,
> And beauty borrowing Spanish red,
> And loving pair with separate bed,
> And jewels pawned for loss of game,
> And then redeemed by loss of fame;
> Of Kitty (aunt left in the lurch
> By grave pretence to go to church)
> Perceived in hack with lover fine,
> Like Will. and Mary on the coin:
> And thus in modish manner we,
> In aid of sugar, sweeten tea.[2]

During the first quarter of the century, non-dramatic blank verse had re-mained, despite the experiments of John Philips, a manifestly eccentric form closely associated with Miltonic burlesque. The success of *The*

---

[1] 'The Thresher's Labour'.   [2] *The Spleen.*

Seasons, however, established blank verse as one of the staple forms for serious non-dramatic poetry; and some ambitious blank-verse poems appeared even before Thomson's masterpiece achieved its final shape. David Mallet, whose literary career was closely associated with that of Thomson, defined the new world-picture enthusiastically in a discursive poem of 1728:

> But how shall mortal wing
> Attempt this blue profundity of heaven,
> Unfathomable, endless of extent!
> Where unknown *suns* to unknown *systems* rise,
> Whose numbers who shall tell? stupendous host!
> In flaming millions thro the vacant hung,
> Sun beyond sun, and world to world unseen,
> Measureless distance, unconceiv'd by thought!
> Awful their order; each the central fire
> Of his surrounding stars, whose whirling speed,
> Solemn and silent, thro the pathless void,
> Nor change, nor error knows.[1]

Thanks to John Philips, blank verse was considered especially suitable for didactic poetry. William Somerville employed it, therefore, for the informative poem about hunting which he published in 1735; and though he later produced a revised version in heroic couplets, it was the blank-verse text of *The Chace* which survived as a popular classic until the nineteenth century. Another manifestation of changing social and literary attitudes is Richard Glover's blank-verse epic *Leonidas,* which celebrates the Whig concepts of patriotism and liberty by describing the Thermopylae campaign. The poems of Mallet, Somerville and Glover reflect the gradual emancipation of neo-Miltonic blank verse from mock-heroic inhibitions; and in the early forties the developing form becomes a medium for disquisitions on death and time. The exclamatory verse of Dyer's *The Ruins of Rome* conveys not only an Addisonian feeling for the evidences of past grandeur but also a landscape-painter's response to visual contrasts; and the first and most impressive volume of Edward Young's *Night Thoughts* employs a less allusive manner to re-affirm, with emotional conviction and rhetorical power, the fact and implications of mortality. A less emphatic but more natural mode of expression is achieved by Robert Blair in a poem of 1743, where the literary echoes are less Miltonic than Shakespearean and the ultimate truths are approached through sympathetic observation and parochial experience:

> Oft, in the lone Church-yard at Night I've seen
> By Glimpse of Moon-shine, chequering thro' the Trees,
> The School-boy with his Satchel in his Hand,
> Whistling aloud to bear his courage up,

[1] *The Excursion.*

And lightly tripping o'er the long flat Stones
(With Nettles skirted, and with Moss o'ergrown)
That tell in homely Phrase who lie below;
Sudden! he starts, and hears, or thinks he hears
The Sound of something purring at his Heels:
Full fast he flies, and dares not look behind him,
Till out of breath he overtakes his Fellows;
Who gather round, and wonder at the Tale
Of horrid *Apparition,* tall and ghastly,
That walks at Dead of Night, or takes his Stand
O'er some new-open'd *Grave;* and strange to tell!
Evanishes at Crowing of the Cock.[1]

These developments in blank verse are paralleled, during the late thirties and early forties, by experiments with other non-lyrical forms of Renaissance origin. The tedious love-elegies of James Hammond, written about 1735 and published in 1743, established the decasyllabic quatrain as the appropriate medium for short poems resembling those of Tibullus and Propertius; and the *Zeitgeist* resolved that such 'elegies' should be quiet and melancholy. The Spenserian stanza was used by William Thompson in 1736 for an epithalamium and a nativity hymn, and by Mark Akenside and William Shenstone in 1737 for whimsical portraits of two contemporary types. Two years later, Gilbert West published a more serious neo-Spenserian work 'on the abuse of travelling'; and in 1742 Shenstone revised and expanded his burlesque, thus creating in *The Schoolmistress* an agreeable poem about childhood and rural life. Through such experiments the imaginative and emotional powers of mid-eighteenth-century poets began to bypass the censoring authority of the Scriblerian intellect.

Writers like Thomson, Young and Shenstone expressed warm admiration for Pope, invoking Spenserian and Miltonic influences not to replace but to enrich the main eighteenth-century traditions of English verse. During the mid-forties, however, one finds in the two sons of an Oxford poetry professor a disposition to set the earlier poets above Dryden and his successors, associating the former with nature and passion and the latter with reason and art. Joseph Warton, who was later to expound this view in *An Essay on the Genius and Writings of Mr. Pope,* defined his basic attitude in a blank-verse poem called *The Enthusiast or The Lover of Nature,* which was published the year Pope died. The following year, when the Highlanders were in Derby and Swift was dying in a Dublin madhouse, Thomas Warton, whose scholarly interest in early literature was later to produce *A History of English Poetry,* provided a fuller definition of the same questionable antithesis:

Thro' Pope's soft song tho' all the Graces breathe,
And happiest art adorn his Attic page;

[1] *The Grave*

Yet does my mind with sweeter transport glow,
As at the root of mossy trunk reclined,
In magic Spenser's wildly-warbled song
I see deserted Una wander wide
Thro' wasteful solitudes, and lurid heaths,
Weary, forlorn; than when the fated fair
Upon the bosom bright of silver Thames
Launches in all the lustre of brocade,
Amid the splendours of the laughing Sun.
The gay description palls upon the sense,
And coldly strikes the mind with feeble bliss.[1]

The most resolute opponent of the Wartonian argument was Samuel Johnson; but while *The Vanity of Human Wishes* is much the greatest poem of the years 1744-59, it is very different from the period's other works in the heroic couplet. More representative of the Popean tradition at this time are Soame Jenyns' lively but shallow imitation of Horace's epistle to Augustus, the coarse and tedious exercises of Paul Whitehead and Richard Owen Cambridge in the mock-heroic manner, and the unreadable epics composed by William Wilkie in the style of Pope's Homer. Interestingly, the most imitated of Pope's original poems was *Eloisa to Abelard;* mid-century specimens of the heroical epistle included James Cawthorn's *Abelard to Eloisa* and William Whitehead's *Anne Boleyn to Henry the Eighth.* While the high-Scriblerian tradition linked with the heroic couplet was thus moribund, the low-Scriblerian tradition linked with the octosyllabic couplet was drowning in sentiment and propriety: the bawdy anecdote is diluted and purified by John Gilbert Cooper in *Ver Vert or the Nunnery Parrot,* and Edward Moore's significantly-titled *Fables for the Female Sex* is less notable for its wit than for its platitudinous moralizing. Only Christopher Smart resists the prevailing atmosphere, emulating Prior in such poems as 'Where's the Poker?' and Gay in the mandrake's rebuke to the country squire:

Proud member of the rambling race,
That vegetate from place to place,
Pursue the leveret at large,
Nor near thy blunderbuss discharge.
Disdainful tho' thou look'st on me,
What art thou, or what can'st thou be?
Nature, that markt thee as a fool,
Gave no materials for the school.
In what consists thy work and fame?
The preservation of the game. –
For what? thou avaritious elf,
But to destroy it all thy-self;

[1] *The Pleasures of Melancholy.*

To lead a life of drink and feast,
T'oppress the poor, and cheat the priest,
Or triumph in a virgin lost,
Is all the manhood thou canst boast. –
Pretty! in nature's various plan,
To see a weed that's like a man,
But 'tis a grievous thing indeed,
To see a man so like a weed.[1]

As apparent heirs to the Parnell-Dyer-Green tradition of meditative poetry, we find a large number of 'odes' by the Wartons and others, in which the style and verse-form of 'L'Allegro' and 'Il Penseroso' are mechanically employed to assert Whig-romantic ideals. There was more vitality in the blank-verse tradition; but even here the creative impetus of the preceding years was not sustained. Thomson and Young continued to enlarge *The Seasons* and *Night Thoughts,* the former by introducing new passages into a completed text and the latter by adding another five Nights to the original four. In new blank-verse poems, however, there was some reversion to the straightforward didacticism of *Cyder* and *The Chace.* Thomson's friend John Armstrong, one of the century's numerous doctor-poets, gave professional advice about air, diet, exercise and the passions in *The Art of Preserving Health;* and Mark Akenside, a butcher's son from Newcastle, expounded an Addisonian aesthetic theory in *The Pleasures of Imagination.* Smart's *The Hop-Garden* followed John Philips both in its mock-heroic style and in its georgic subject-matter; and Robert Dodsley, the most celebrated publisher of the century, contributed a poem of his own entitled *Agriculture.* The most impressive work in this tradition, however, is John Dyer's *The Fleece,* whose four books about sheep-farming, wool, the woollen industry and the wool trade constitute an eloquent statement of that mid-century patriotism which sees Britain's prosperity as the fruit of political freedom and purposeful labour. Dyer's technique is less subtle than that of John Philips, but like Philips he achieves a blend of the heroic and the mock-heroic which effectively conveys his secular enthusiasm:

Wide around
Hillock and valley, farm and village, smile:
And ruddy roofs, and chimney-tops appear,
Of busy Leeds, up-wafting to the clouds
The incense of thanksgiving: all is joy;
And trade and business guide the living scene,
Roll the full cars, adown the winding Aire
Load the slow-sailing barges, pile the pack
On the long tinkling train of slow-pac'd steeds.
As when a sunny day invites abroad
The sedulous ants, they issue from their cells
In bands unnumber'd, eager for their work;

[1] 'The Country Squire and the Mandrake'.

O'er high, o'er low, they lift, they draw, they haste
With warm affection to each other's aid;
Repeat their virtuous efforts, and succeed.
Thus all is here in motion, all is life:
The creaking wain brings copious store of corn:
The grazier's sleeky kine obstruct the roads;
The neat-dress'd housewives, for the festal board
Crown'd with full baskets, in the field-way paths
Come tripping on; th'echoing hills repeat
The stroke of ax and hammer; scaffolds rise,
And growing edifices; heaps of stone,
Beneath the chissel, beauteous shapes assume
Of frize and column. Some, with even line,
New streets are marking in the neighb'ring fields,
And sacred domes of worship. Industry,
Which dignifies the artist, lifts the swain,
And the straw cottage to a palace turns,
Over the work presides.[1]

Quieter effects were being pursued, not unsuccessfully, in the Spenserian stanza and the decasyllabic quatrain. Cambridge's *Archimage* is a rather frivolous Spenserian burlesque; but it was followed in 1748 by *The Castle of Indolence,* which effectively re-creates not only the style but also the allegorical and didactic method of *The Faerie Queene.* The solemn and whimsical elements which Thomson united were separated three years later in West's *Education* and Moses Mendez' *The Squire of Dames;* but the critical work of Thomas Warton promoted a fuller understanding of Spenser's masterpiece, from which later poets were to profit. The quatrain acquired a new melodic sophistication in the elegies of Shenstone, which combine pastoralism and topicality in an intelligently sentimental way; and its associations with Latin elegiac poetry were confirmed by James Grainger's translation of Tibullus. Many elegies written after 1750, however, were modelled on the deservedly famous work in which Gray united the new elegiac tradition with the graveyard tradition of Parnell and Blair: Gray's masterpiece was echoed, for example, by John Gilbert Cooper in a vision-poem called 'The Tomb of Shakespeare'.

The most interesting developments between 1744 and 1759 were in lyrical poetry. The 1745 rebellion and the wars with France were reflected in Jacobite songs like 'Will ye no come back again', Hanoverian songs like 'God save the king', and patriotic songs like David Garrick's 'Hearts of Oak'. In the work of John and Charles Wesley the great age of English hymnody produced its largest achievement; and the pre-Romantic revival of the sonnet was initiated in the forties by Gray and by Richardson's friend Thomas Edwards. A host of minor poets composed pastoral-sentimental love-lyrics; and Shenstone in 'A Pastoral Ballad' realized the potentialities of

[1] *The Fleece,* Book III

this convention with characteristic tact, giving new life at the same time to the anapaestic stanza of 'Colin's Complaint':

> I have found out a gift for my fair;
> I have found where the wood-pigeons breed:
> But let me that plunder forbear,
> She will say 'twas a barbarous deed.
> For he ne'er could be true, she averr'd,
> Who could rob a poor bird of its young:
> And I lov'd her the more, when I heard
> Such tenderness fall from her tongue.[1]

The central lyrical tradition of this period, however, has to be traced through those publications, from Akenside's collection of 1745 to Gray's volume of 1757, which are related in various ways to the concept of the 'ode'. The poems covered by this word include works in octosyllabic couplets like Grainger's 'Solitude', and works in the Cecilia's Day manner like Collins' 'The Passions'; but most can be seen as belonging either to the Pindaric tradition or to the Horatian tradition. In the irregular or false-Pindaric form, the age produced not only major poems like Collins' 'Ode on the Poetical Character' but also the simple yet convincing 'Monody' in which Lord Lyttleton bewailed the death of his wife. In the regular or true-Pindaric form, it produced not only Gray's 'The Bard' and 'The Progress of Poesy' but also Gilbert West's translation of Pindar; and William Mason, with characteristic perversity, employed this form for the choruses of his *Elfrida* and *Caractacus*. The period's Horatian odes in rhyming stanzas include recognized masterpieces like the unfinished poem by Gray which Mason named 'Ode on the Pleasure arising from Vicissitude'; and they also include vigorous political works by Akenside and Mason, and mock-sentimental poems like Shenstone's 'Ode to Indolence'. In the work of the Wartons, too, we can trace the development or revival of an unrhymed lyrical form based on the Alcaic stanza. This form, devised by Milton for his version of Horace's

> Quis multa gracilis te puer in rosa,

is used by Thomas Warton for two more translations from the Latin; and we meet it again in original poems by his brother Joseph, one of which re-states the message of Pomfret's *The Choice:*

> Welcome Content! from roofs of fretted gold,
> From Persian sofas, and the gems of Ind,
> From courts, and camps, and crowds,
> Fled to my cottage mean...
> O let me dwell in life's low valley, blest
> With the dear nymph I love, true, heart-felt joy,
> With chosen friends to turn
> The polish'd Attic page;

---

[1] 'A Pastoral Ballad'.

> Nor seldom, if nor fortune damp my wings,
> Nor dire disease, to soar to Pindus' hill,
> My hours, my soul devote,
> To poesy and love![1]

Like all the Wartons' poems, this is clumsy and uninspired; but its form is that which Collins, in the 'Ode to Evening', made the vehicle for a major visionary statement.

The most conspicuous fact about the poetic history of the sixties and seventies is the clear emergence of two powerful and creative movements which appear, and in some respects are, fundamentally opposed. On the one hand there were men like Macpherson, Smart, Percy, Gray and Chatterton, who sought to explore or invent cultures wholly different from that which the eighteenth century had inherited from the European Renaissance. On the other hand, there was an impressive revival of those intellectual and socially-conscious modes which had been brought to perfection in the age of Dryden, Prior, Swift, Pope and Ramsay. In the years 1760-62, for example, Robert Lloyd and Charles Churchill were catching the public ear with heroic-couplet poems about the contemporary theatre; and William Falconer was making effective use of his nautical experience in *The Shipwreck,* whose narrative framework does not conceal its didactic intent. At the same time, however, James Macpherson was initiating a cultural fashion of European importance with the first of his Ossianic publications; and a better poet, confined to a madhouse because he 'insisted on people praying with him', was composing an extraordinary liturgy based on the Hebrew text of the psalms:

> Let Hushim rejoice with the King's Fisher, who is of royal beauty, tho' plebeian size:
> For in my nature I quested for beauty, but God, God hath sent me to sea for pearls...
> Let Ithream rejoice with the great Owl, who understandeth that which he professes:
> For I pray God for the professors of the University of Cambridge to attend & to amend...
> Let Abiezer, the Anethothite, rejoice with Phrynos who is the scaled frog:
> For I am like a frog in the brambles, but the Lord hath put his whole armour upon me...
> Let Jether, the son of Gideon, rejoice with Ecchetoe which are musical grashoppers:
> For my seed shall worship the Lord JESUS as numerous & musical as the grashoppers of Paradise...
> Let PETER rejoice with the MOONFISH who keeps up the life in the waters by night:

[1] 'Ode to Content'. Pindus was a mountain sacred to the Muses.

> For I pray the Lord JESUS that cured the LUNATICK to be merciful to all my brethren and sisters in these houses.[1]

The contrast between this and *The Rosciad* appears simple and absolute; but Churchill was a radical satirist closer to Burns and Byron than to the Scriblerians, and it is Smart in *Jubilate Agno* who blesses the Lord Jesus 'for the memory of GAY, POPE, and SWIFT'. The distinction between these two impulses is clarified, during the years 1763-5, not only by new works of Lloyd, Churchill, Macpherson and Smart but also by Oliver Goldsmith's *The Traveller* and Thomas Percy's *Reliques of Ancient English Poetry. The Traveller*, whose preface condemned such forms as poetic prose and the Pindaric ode, was welcomed by Johnson as 'a production to which, since the death of Pope, it would not be easy to find an equal'; but Percy's work proved more influential, stimulating an international ballad-revival whose beneficiaries were to include Goethe, Scott and Coleridge. The Prior tradition of anapaestic light verse was revived, in 1766, by a book which seems to have attracted the authors of *Humphry Clinker* and *The Rivals:*

> Of all the gay Places the World can afford,
> By Gentle and Simple for Pastime ador'd,
> Fine Balls, and fine Concerts, fine Buildings, and Springs,
> Fine Walks, and fine Views, and a thousand fine Things,
> Not to mention the sweet Situation and Air,
> What Place, my dear Mother, with Bath can compare?
> Let *Bristol* for Commerce and Dirt be renown'd,
> At *Sal'sbury* Pen Knives and Scissars be ground;
> The Towns of *Devizes,* of *Bradford,* and *Frome,*
> May boast that they better can manage the Loom;
> I believe that they may;– but the World to refine,
> In Manners, in Dress, in Politeness to shine,
> O *Bath!* – let the Art, let the Glory be thine.[2]

Hae tibi erunt artes: this variation on a theme of Virgil is almost contemporary with the adaptations of early Norse and Welsh heroic poetry which Gray published in his volume of 1768. In the next few years the Popean manner was adapted to modern social issues by Goldsmith in *The Deserted Village* and by John Langhorne in *The Country Justice;* and at the same time a number of poets demonstrated, as Smart had done, that the conflicting impulses of the sixties could interact within a single mind. A Bristol adolescent named Thomas Chatterton was inspired by St. Mary Redcliff and Percy's *Reliques* to create a fifteenth-century world and compose poems for its inhabitants; and he was also provoked by his experience of contemporary society to write a vehement Churchillian satire entitled 'Kew Gardens'. The great orientalist Sir William Jones produced translations of Persian, Turkish, Arabic, Sanskrit and Chinese works, confident that he was thus helping to revitalize English literature; but the style of such pieces as 'A Turkish Ode of Mesihi' was dictated by his classical education and his

[1]Christopher Smart,*Jubilate Agno.* [2]Christopher Anstey,*The New Bath Guide*

Johnsonian taste. The Scots poems which Robert Fergusson was publishing at this time in Ruddiman's *Weekly Magazine* revived a tradition whose roots were in the Middle Ages; but Fergusson took that tradition from Gay's friend Allan Ramsay, and wrote within it a poetry of urban life reminiscent of Swift.

Much of the poetry written and published during the sixties and seventies, however, developed naturally from that of the preceding decade. When Byrom died at an advanced age, he left in manuscript a large number of conversational poems whose subjects ranged from textual problems in Horace to the religious doctrines of Jakob Böhme; and these poems, quietly expressive of their author's humane and unpretentious wisdom, were collected and printed in 1773. Thomas Warton collected his poems in 1777, and Johnson on receiving them lamented the continuing passion for archaic forms:

> Wheresoe'er I turn my view,
> All is strange, yet nothing new:
> Endless labour all along,
> Endless labour to be wrong;
> Phrase that Time has flung away;
> Uncouth words in disarray,
> Trick'd in antique ruff and bonnet,
> Ode, and elegy, and sonnet.[1]

The sonnet form, although used by John Langhorne and W.J. Mickle in translations from the Italian, did not become popular until the eighties; but odes and elegies, together with sentimental fables, are prominent among the minor poems of Langhorne, of the strolling actor John Cunningham, and of the Aberdeen professor James Beattie. The Spenserian tradition continues in Mickle's *The Concubine,* later discreetly re-named *Sir Martyn;* and it evades pastiche in Beattie's *The Minstrel,* which offers with few archaic or allegorical trappings a pre-Wordsworthian account of 'the progress of genius' or 'the growth of a poet's mind':

> Meanwhile, whate'er of beautiful, or new,
> Sublime, or dreadful, in earth, sea, or sky,
> By chance, or search, was offered to his view,
> He scanned with curious and romantic eye.
> Whate'er of lore tradition could supply
> From Gothic tale, or song, or fable old,
> Roused him, still keen to listen and to pry,
> At last, though long by penury controlled,
> And solitude, his soul her graces 'gan unfold.[2]

[1] Quoted by Hester Piozzi in *Anecdotes of the Late Samuel Johnson.* [2] *The Minstrel,* Book I.

Contemporary and comparable with this work is the revised version of Akenside's *The Pleasures of Imagination,* in which imaginative development is associated with the child's response to external nature. Other blank-verse poems of these decades are exercises in the georgic tradition, more interesting in socio-historical than in literary terms. Mason in *The English Garden* and Grainger in *The Sugar Cane* give advice on the improvement of a country estate and the management of a West Indian plantation. In the four books of *Edge Hill* Shenstone's friend Richard Jago explores the cultural significance of a West Midland landscape, digressing to consider (among other topics) Lady Godiva and the Oxford Canal. Such works, acknowledging both the reality of social involvement and the attractions of romantic idealism, reflect and maintain a literary taste which is neither revolutionary nor reactionary. The same claim could be made, almost by definition, for poems designed for the singing voice. Song-writing became increasingly fashionable at this time in Scotland, popular and literary traditions being successfully married in such pieces as John Skinner's 'Tullochgorum' and Lady Anne Barnard's 'Auld Robin Gray'. English hymnody continued to flourish, not only in the volumes issued by the Wesleys but also in those which Smart published after his release from confinement; and in 1779 there appeared a collection named *Olney Hymns,* which included some notable contributions from William Cowper.

The great literary monuments of the late seventies and early eighties are prose works in the Augustan tradition: Burke's speeches on the American War, Johnson's lives of the English poets, *The Decline and Fall of the Roman Empire.* The poetic landscape, on the other hand, looked bleaker in 1780 than it had done for two centuries. Johnson, though he composed 'A Short Song of Congratulation' in this year, had published no major work in verse since 1749; and the deaths of the seventies had included those of Chatterton, Akenside, Smart, Gray, Goldsmith, Fergusson and Langhorne. The laureate, William Whitehead, proclaimed Britain's maritime supremacy in his new-year and birthday odes; and, in Lisbon, Mickle was rewarded for his version of Camoens by membership of the Royal Society of Portugal. Beattie, having completed *The Minstrel,* was turning his attention to criticism and philosophy; and Thomas Warton, having collected his verses, was devoting himself to historical scholarship. Charles Wesley and William Jones responded to contemporary events with *Hymns Written in the Time of Tumults* and *An Inquiry into the Legal Mode of Suppressing Riots;* but Mason proceeded doggedly into Book IV of his poem on gardening.

In rural Ayrshire, however, Robert Burns was drawing up the regulations for a debating society called the Tarbolton Bachelors' Club, whose object was 'to relieve the wearied man worn down with the necessary labours of life'; and in London George Crabbe was quietly dissociating himself from Pomfret's still-popular work of 1700:

> What vulgar title thus salutes the eye, –
> The schoolboy's first attempt at poesy?

INTRODUCTION

The long-worn theme of every humbler Muse,
For wits to scorn and nurses to peruse;
The dull description of a scribbler's brain,
And sigh'd-for wealth, for which he sighs in vain;
A glowing chart of fairy-land estate,
Romantic scenes, and visions out of date,
Clear skies, clear streams, soft banks, and sober bowers,
Deer, whimpering brooks, and wind-perfuming flowers?
   Not thus! too long have I in fancy wove
My slender webs of wealth, and peace, and love;
Have dream'd of plenty, in the midst of want,
And sought, by Hope, what Hope can never grant;
Been fool'd by wishes, and still wish'd again,
And loved the flattery, while I knew it vain... [1]

The Horatian ideal looked more plausible to a resident of Olney, where the bolting of a gingerbread-baker's horse was regarded in June 1780 as a notable event; but even William Cowper, as his minor poems show, was disturbed by the more extensive disorders which took place during that month in London. William Blake's involvement in the Gordon Riots was described long afterwards by his Victorian biographer:

> 'That evening, the artist happened to be walking in a route chosen by one of the mobs at large, whose course lay from Justice Hyde's house near Leicester Fields, for the destruction of which less than an hour had sufficed, through Long Acre, past the quiet house of Blake's old master, engraver Basire, in Great Queen Street, Lincoln's Inn Fields, and down Holborn, bound for Newgate. Suddenly he encountered the advancing wave of triumphant blackguardism, and was forced (for from such a great surging mob there is no disentanglement) to go along in the very front rank, and witness the storm and burning of the fortress-like prison, and release of its three hundred inmates.' [2]

Whatever Blake's feelings may have been on this occasion, there can be little doubt that he thought of Newgate as well as the Bastille when he wrote in *America* about the five gates and the fires of Orc.

In the minds of Burns, Crabbe, Cowper and Blake, some of the poetry of the next twenty years was thus being shaped; and on the shores of Windermere, about this time, a schoolboy named William Wordsworth

> Blew mimic hootings to the silent owls,
> That they might answer him.

D.W. LINDSAY

---

[1] 'The Choice'. [2] Alexander Gilchrist, *The Life of William Blake,* Chapter V.

John Pomfret

THE CHOICE

I

IF Heav'n the grateful Liberty wou'd give,
That I might chuse my Method how to live:
And All those Hours propitious Fate shou'd lend,
In blissful Ease and Satisfaction spend:

II

5   Near some fair Town I'd have a private Seat,
Built uniform, not little nor too great.
Better, if on a rising Ground it stood,
Fields on this side, on that a Neighb'ring Wood.
It shou'd within no other Things contain,
10   But what are Useful, Necessary, Plain:
Methinks, 'tis Nauseous, and I'd ne'er endure
The needless Pomp of gawdy Furniture:
A little Garden, grateful to the Eye,
And a cool Rivulet run Murmuring by:
15   On whose delicious Banks a stately Row
Of shady Lymes, or Sycamores, shou'd grow.
At th'end of which a silent Study plac'd,
Shou'd with the noblest Authors there be grac'd.
Horace and *Virgil,* in whose mighty Lines,
20   Immortal Wit, and solid Learning Shines.
Sharp *Juvenal,* and am'rous *Ovid* too,
Who all the turns of Loves soft Passion knew:
He, that with Judgment reads his charming Lines,
In which strong Art, with stronger Nature joyns,
25   Must grant, his Fancy do's the best Excel:
His Thoughts so tender, and exprest so well;
With all those Moderns, Men of steady Sense,

Esteem'd for Learning, and for Eloquence:
In some of These, as Fancy shou'd advise,
30   I'd always take my Morning Exercise.
For sure, no Minutes bring us more Content,
Than those in pleasing useful Studies spent.

III

I'd have a Clear and Competent Estate,
That I might live Genteelly, but not Great.
35   As much as I could moderately spend,
A little more sometimes t'oblige a Friend.
Nor shou'd the Sons of Poverty Repine
Too much at Fortune, they shou'd taste of Mine;
And all that Objects of true Pity were,
40   Shou'd be reliev'd with what my Wants cou'd spare;
For what our Maker has too largely giv'n,
Shou'd be return'd in gratitude to Heav'n.
A frugal Plenty shou'd my Table spread,
With healthful, not luxurious Dishes, fed:
45   Enough to satisfy, and something more
To feed the Stranger, and the Neighb'ring Poor.
Strong Meat indulges Vice, and pampering Food
Creates Diseases, and inflames the Blood.
But what's sufficient to make Nature Strong,
50   And the bright Lamp of Life continue long,
I'd freely take, and as I did possess
The bounteous Author of my Plenty bless.

IV

I'd have a little Cellar, Cool, and Neat,
With Humming Ale, and Virgin Wine Repleat.
55   Wine whets the Wit, improves its Native Force,
And gives a pleasant Flavour to Discourse;
By making all our Spirits Debonair,
Throws off the Lees, the Sedement of Care.
But as the greatest Blessing Heaven lends
60   May be debauch'd, and serve ignoble Ends;
So, but too oft, the Grapes refreshing Juice,
Does many mischievous Effects produce.
My House shou'd no such rude Disorders know,
As from high Drinking consequently flow.
65   Nor wou'd I use what was so kindly giv'n,
To the dishonour of Indulgent Heav'n.

If any Neighbour came he shou'd be free,
Us'd with respect, and not Uneasy be,
In my Retreat, or to himself, or me.

70   What Freedom, Prudence, and Right Reason give,
All Men, may with Impunity receive:
But the least swerving from their Rules too much;
For what's forbidden Us, 'tis Death to touch.
That Life might be more comfortable yet,

75   And all my Joys refin'd, sincere and great,
I'd chuse two Friends, whose Company wou'd be
A great Advance to my Felicity.
Well born, of Humours suited to my own;
Discreet, and Men as well as Books have known.

80   Brave, Gen'rous, Witty, and exactly free
From loose Behaviour, or Formality.
Airy, and Prudent, Merry, but not Light,
Quick in discerning, and in Judging Right;
Secret they shou'd be, faithful to their Trust,

85   In Reasoning Cool, Strong, Temperate and Just.
Obliging, Open, without huffing, Brave;
Brisk in gay Talking, and in sober Grave.
Close in Dispute, but not tenacious, try'd
By solid Reason, and let that decide;

90   Not prone to Lust, Revenge, or envious Hate;
Nor busy Medlers with Intrigues of State.
Strangers to Slander, and sworn Foes to Spight,
Not Quarrelsome, but Stout enough to Fight:
Loyal and Pious, Friends to *Caesar* true,

95   As dying Martyrs to their Maker too.
In their Society I cou'd not miss,
A permanent, sincere, substantial Bliss.

V

Wou'd bounteous Heav'n once more indulge, I'd chuse
(For, who wou'd so much Satisfaction lose,

100   As Witty Nymphs in Conversation give)
Near some obliging Modest-Fair to live;
For there's that sweetness in a Female Mind,
Which in a Man's we cannot hope to find;
That by a secret, but a pow'rful Art,

105   Winds up the Spring of Life, and do's impart
Fresh Vital Heat to the transported Heart.
I'd have her Reason all her Passions sway,

Easy in Company, in private Gay.
Coy to a Fop, to the Deserving free,
110 Still constant to her self, and just to me.
She shou'd a Soul have for great Actions fit,
Prudence, and Wisdom to direct her Wit.
Courage to look bold danger in the Face;
Not Fear, but only to be proud, or base:
115 Quick to advise by an Emergence prest,
To give good Counsel, or to take the best.
I'd have th'Expressions of her Thoughts be such,
She might not seem Reserv'd, nor talk too much;
That shows a want of Judgment and of Sense:
120 More than enough, is but Impertinence.
Her Conduct Regular, her Mirth Refin'd,
Civil to Strangers, to her Neighbours kind.
Averse to Vanity, Revenge, and Pride,
In all the Methods of Deceit untry'd:
125 So faithful to her Friend, and good to all,
No Censure might upon her Actions fall.
Then wou'd e'en Envy be compell'd to say,
She goes the least of Womankind astray.
To this fair Creature I'd sometimes retire,
130 Her Conversation wou'd new Joys inspire,
Give Life an Edge so keen, no surly Care ⎤
Wou'd venture to assault my Soul, or dare ⎬
Near my Retreat to hide one secret Snare. ⎦
But so Divine, so noble a Repast,
135 I'd seldom, and with Moderation taste.
For highest Cordials all their Virtue lose,
By a too frequent, and too bold an use;
And what would cheer the Spirits in distress,
Ruins our Health when taken to Excess.

VI

140 I'd be concern'd in no litigious Jarr,
Belov'd by all, not vainly popular:
Whate'er Assistance I had pow'r to bring
T'oblige my Country, or to serve my King,
Whene'er they call'd, I'd readily afford,
145 My Tongue, my Pen, my Counsel, or my Sword.
Law Suits I'd shun with as much Studious Care,
As I wou'd Dens, where hungry Lyons are;
And rather put up Injuries, than be

150 A Plague to him, who'd be a Plague to me.
I value Quiet, at a Price too great,
To give for my Revenge so dear a Rate:
For what do we by all our Bustle gain,
But counterfeit Delight for real Pain?

VII

If Heav'n a date of many years wou'd give,
155 Thus I'd in Pleasure, Ease, and Plenty live.
And as I near approach the Verge of Life,
Some kind Relation (for I'd have no Wife)
Shou'd take upon him all my Worldly Care,
While I did for a better State prepare.
160 Then I'd not be with any trouble vext.
Nor have the Evening of my Days perplext.
But by a silent, and a peaceful Death,
Without a Sigh, Resign my Aged Breath:
And when committed to the Dust, I'd have
165 Few Tears, but Friendly dropt into my Grave.
Then wou'd my Exit so propitious be,
All Men wou'd wish to live and dye like me.

John Philips

THE SPLENDID SHILLING

HAPPY the Man, who void of Cares and Strife,
In Silken, or in Leathern Purse retains
A *Splendid Shilling:* He nor hears with Pain
New Oysters cry'd, nor sighs for chearful Ale;
5   But with his Friends, when nightly Mists arise,
To *Juniper's, Magpye,* or *Town-Hall* repairs:
Where, mindful of the Nymph, whose wanton Eye
Transfix'd his Soul, and kindled Amorous Flames,
Chloe, or *Phillis;* he each Circling Glass
10   Wisheth her Health, and Joy, and equal Love.
Mean while he smoaks, and laughs at merry Tale,
Or *Pun* ambiguous, or *Conundrum* quaint.
But I, whom griping penury surrounds,
And Hunger, sure Attendant upon Want,
15   With scanty Offals, and small acid Tiff
(Wretched Repast!) my meagre Corps sustain:
Then Solitary walk, or doze at home
In Garret vile, and with a warming puff
Regale chill'd Fingers; or from Tube as black
20   As Winter-Chimney, or well-polish'd Jet,
Exhale *Mundungus,* ill-perfuming Scent:
Not blacker Tube, nor of a shorter Size
Smoaks *Cambro-Briton* (vers'd in Pedigree,
Sprung from *Cadwalader* and *Arthur,* Kings,
25   Full famous in Romantic tale) when he
O'er many a craggy Hill, and barren Cliff,
Upon a Cargo of fam'd *Cestrian* Cheese,
High over-shadowing rides, with a design
To vend his Wares, or at th'*Arvonian* Mart,
30   Or *Maridunum,* or the ancient Town

6

Yclept *Brechinia,* or where *Vaga's* Stream
Encircles *Ariconium,* fruitful Soil,
Whence flow Nectareous Wines, that well may vye
With *Massic, Setin,* or renown'd *Falern.*
35   Thus while my joyless Minutes tedious flow
With Looks demure, and silent Pace, a *Dunn,*
Horrible Monster! hated by Gods and Men,
To my aerial Citadel ascends;
With Vocal Heel thrice thund'ring at my Gates,
40 With hideous Accent thrice he calls; I know
The Voice ill-boding, and the solemn Sound.
What shou'd I do? or whither turn? amaz'd,
Confounded, to the dark Recess I fly
Of Woodhole; strait my bristling Hairs erect
45 Thro' sudden Fear; a chilly Sweat bedews
My shud'ring Limbs, and (wonderful to tell!)
My Tongue forgets her Faculty of Speech;
So horrible he seems! his faded Brow
Entrench'd with many a Frown, and *Conic* Beard,
50 And spreading Band, admir'd by Modern Saints,
Disastrous Acts forebode; in his Right Hand
Long Scrolls of Paper solemnly he waves,
With Characters, and Figures dire inscrib'd
Grievous to mortal Eyes; (ye Gods avert
55 Such Plagues from righteous Men!) behind him stalks
Another Monster, not unlike himself,
Sullen of Aspect, by the Vulgar call'd
A *Catchpole,* whose polluted Hands the Gods
With Force incredible, and Magick Charms
60 Erst have indu'd; if he his ample Palm
Should haply on ill-fated Shoulder lay
Of Debtor, strait his Body, to the Touch
Obsequious, (as whilom Knights were wont)
To some enchanted Castle is convey'd,
65 Where Gates impregnable, and coercive Chains
In Durance strict detain him, 'till in form
Of Mony, *Pallas* sets the Captive free.
      Beware, ye Debtors, when ye walk beware,
Be circumspect; oft with insidious Ken
70 This Caitif eyes your Steps aloof, and oft
Lies perdue in a Nook or gloomy Cave,
Prompt to enchant some inadvertent wretch
With his unhallow'd Touch. So (Poets sing)

Grimalkin to Domestick Vermin sworn
75 An everlasting Foe, with watchful Eye,
Lyes nightly brooding o'er a chinky gap,
Protending her fell Claws, to thoughtless Mice
Sure Ruin. So her disembowell'd Web
Arachne in a Hall, or Kitchin spreads,
80 Obvious to vagrant Flies: She secret stands
Within her woven Cell; the Humming Prey,
Regardless of their Fate, rush on the toils
Inextricable, nor will aught avail
Their Arts, nor Arms, nor Shapes of lovely Hue;
85 The Wasp insidious, and the buzzing Drone,
And Butterfly proud of expanded wings
Distinct with Góld, entangled in her Snares,
Useless Resistance make: With eager strides,
She tow'ring flies to her expected Spoils;
90 Then with envenom'd Jaws the vital Blood
Drinks of reluctant Foes, and to her Cave
Their bulky Carcasses triumphant drags.
    So pass my Days. But when Nocturnal Shades
This World invelop, and th'inclement Air
95 Persuades Men to repel benumming Frosts,
With pleasant Wines, and crackling blaze of Wood;
Me Lonely sitting, nor the glimmering Light
Of Make-Weight Candle, nor the joyous Talk
Of loving Friend delights; distress'd, forlorn,
100 Amidst the horrors of the tedious Night,
Darkling I sigh, and feed with dismal Thoughts
My anxious Mind; or sometimes mournful Verse
Indite, and sing of Groves and Myrtle Shades,
Or desperate Lady near a purling Stream,
105 Or Lover pendent on a Willow-Tree:
Mean while I Labour with eternal Drought,
And restless Wish, and Rave; my parched Throat
Finds no Relief, nor heavy Eyes Repose:
But if a Slumber haply does Invade
110 My weary Limbs, my Fancy's still awake,
Thoughtful of Drink, and Eager in a Dream,
Tipples Imaginary Pots of Ale;
In Vain; awake, I find the settled Thirst
Still gnawing, and the pleasant Phantom curse.
115   Thus do I live from Pleasure quite debarr'd,
Nor taste the Fruits that the Sun's genial Rays

Mature, *John-Apple,* nor the downy *Peach,*
Nor *Walnut* in rough-furrow'd Coat secure,
Nor *Medlar,* Fruit delicious in decay;
120   Afflictions Great! yet Greater still remain:
My *Galligaskins* that have long withstood
The Winter's Fury, and Encroaching Frosts,
By Time subdu'd, (what will not Time subdue!)
An horrid Chasm disclose, with Orifice
125   Wide, Discontinuous; at which the Winds
Eurus and *Auster,* and the dreadful Force
Of *Boreas,* that congeals the *Cronian* Waves,
Tumultuous enter with dire chilling Blasts,
Portending Agues. Thus a well-fraught Ship
130   Long sail'd secure, or thro' th'Aegean Deep,
Or the *Ionian,* 'till Cruising near
The *Lilybean* Shoar, with hideous Crush
On *Scylla,* or *Charybdis* (dang'rous Rocks)
She strikes rebounding, whence the shatter'd Oak,
135   So fierce a Shock unable to withstand,
Admits the Sea; in at the gaping Side
The crouding Waves Gush with impetuous Rage,
Resistless, Overwhelming; Horrors seize
The Mariners, Death in their Eyes appears,
140   They stare, they lave, they pump, they swear, they pray:
(Vain Efforts!) still the battering Waves rush in
Implacable, 'till delug'd by the Foam,
The Ship sinks found'ring in the vast Abyss.

Isaac Watts

THE DAY OF JUDGMENT

AN ODE

ATTEMPTED IN ENGLISH SAPPHICK

WHEN the fierce Northwind with his airy Forces
Rears up the *Baltick* to a foaming Fury;
And the red Lightning with a Storm of Hail comes
    Rushing amain down,

5   How the poor Sailors stand amaz'd and tremble!
While the hoarse Thunder like a bloody Trumpet
Roars a loud Onset to the gaping Waters
    Quick to devour them.

Such shall the Noise be, and the wild Disorder,
10   (If things Eternal may be like these Earthly)
Such the dire Terror when the great Archangel
    Shakes the Creation;

Tears the strong Pillars of the Vault of Heaven,
Breaks up old Marble the Repose of Princes;
15   See the Graves open, and the Bones arising,
    Flames all around 'em.

Hark the shrill Outcries of the guilty Wretches!
Lively bright Horror and amazing Anguish
Stare thro' their Eye-lids, while the living Worm lies
20   Gnawing within them.

Thoughts like old Vultures prey upon their Heartstrings,
And the Smart twinges, when their Eye beholds the
Lofty Judge frowning, and a Flood of Vengeance
    Rolling afore him.

25   Hopeless Immortals! how they scream and shiver
While Devils push them to the Pit wide yawning
Hideous and gloomy, to receive them headlong
    Down to the Centre.

Stop here my Fancy: (all away ye horrid
30   Doleful Ideas) come arise to *Jesus,*
How he sits God-like! and the Saints around him
    Thron'd, yet adoring!

O may I sit there when he comes Triumphant
Dooming the Nations: then ascend to Glory,
35   While our Hosannahs all along the Passage
    Shout the Redeemer.

Ambrose Philips

TO THE EARL OF DORSET

Copenhagen, March 9, 1709

FROM Frozen Climes and Endless Tracks of Snow,
From Streams that Northern Winds forbid to flow;
What Present shall the Muse to *Dorset* bring;
Or how, so near the Pole, attempt to sing?
5   The hoary Winter here conceals from Sight,
All pleasing Objects that to Verse invite.
The Hills and Dales, and the Delightful Woods,
The Flowry Plains, and Silver Streaming Floods,
    By Snow disguis'd, in bright Confusion lye,
10   And with one dazling Waste fatigue the Eye.
     The ruling Cold retards the coming Spring,
No Birds within the Desart Region sing.
The Ships unmov'd the boist'rous Winds defy,
While ratling Chariots o'er the Ocean fly.
15   The vast *Leviathan* wants Room to play,
And spout his Waters in the Face of Day.
The starving Wolves along the main Sea prowl,
And to the Moon in Icy Valleys howl.
For many a shining League the level Main
20   Here spreads it self into a Glassy Plain:
And there the Frozen Billows of enormous Size,
Alpes of green Ice, in wild Disorder rise.
And yet but lately have I seen, e'en here,
The winter in a lovely Dress appear.
25   E'er yet the Clouds let fall the treasur'd Snow,
Or stormy Winds thick hazy Weather blow.
     First, a keen Eastern Breeze at Ev'ning rose;
Then, the descending Rain unsullied froze.

Soon as the silent Shades of Night withdrew,
30   The ruddy Morn disclos'd at once to View
The Face of Nature in a rich Disguise,
And brighten'd ev'ry Object to my Eyes.
For ev'ry Shrub, and ev'ry Blade of Grass,
And ev'ry pointed Thorn, seem'd wrought in Glass.
35   In Pearls and Rubies rich the Hawthorns show,
While thro' the Ice the Crimson Berries glow.
The thick sprung Reeds the slabby Marshes yield,
Seem polish'd Lances in a hostile Field.
The Stag in limpid Currents with Surprize,
40   Sees Chrystal Branches on his Forehead rise.
The spreading Oak, the Beech, and tow'ring Pine,
Glaz'd over, in the freezing Aether shine.
The frighted Birds the ratling Branches shun,
That wave and glitter in the distant Sun.
45   When if a sudden Gust of Wind arise,
The brittle Forest into Atoms flies:
A spangled Shower from every Tree descends,
And the bright Scene in costly Ruin ends.
Or if a Southern Gale the Region warm,
50   And by Degrees unbinds the Wintry Charm,
The Traveller a miry Country sees,
And Journeys sad beneath the dropping Trees.

John Gay

TRIVIA

OR

THE ART OF WALKING THE STREETS OF LONDON

Quo te Moeri pedes? An, quo via ducit, in Urbem? – Virgil.

BOOK I

OF THE IMPLEMENTS FOR WALKING THE STREETS,
AND SIGNS OF THE WEATHER

THROUGH Winter Streets to steer your Course aright,
How to walk clean by Day, and safe by Night,
How Jostling Crouds, with Prudence, to decline,
When to assert the Wall, and when resign,
5   I sing: Thou, *Trivia,* Goddess, aid my Song,
Thro' spacious Streets conduct thy Bard along;
By thee transported, I securely stray
Where winding Alleys lead the doubtful Way,
The silent Court, and op'ning Square explore,
10   And long perplexing Lanes untrod before.
To pave thy Realm, and smooth the broken Ways,
Earth from her Womb a flinty Tribute pays;
For thee, the sturdy Pavior thumps the Ground,
Whilst ev'ry Stroke his lab'ring Lungs resound;
15   For thee, the Scavinger bids Kennels glide
Within their Bounds, and Heaps of Dirt subside.
My youthful Bosom burns with Thirst of Fame,
From the great Theme to build a glorious Name,

14

To tread in Paths to ancient Bards unknown,
20   And bind my Temples with a *Civic* Crown;
But more, my Country's Love demands the Lays,
My Country's be the Profit, mine the Praise.
      When the *Black Youth* at chosen Stands rejoice,
And *clean your Shoes* resounds from ev'ry Voice;
25   When late their miry Sides Stage-Coaches show,
And their stiff Horses thro' the Town move slow;
When all the *Mall* in leafy Ruin lies,
And Damsels first renew their Oyster Cries:
Then let the prudent Walker Shoes provide,
30   Not of the *Spanish* or *Morocco* Hide;
The wooden Heel may raise the Dancer's Bound,
And with the 'scallop'd Top his Step be crown'd:
Let firm, well-hammer'd Soles protect thy Feet
Thro' freezing Snows, and Rains, and soaking Sleet.
35   Should the big Laste extend the Shoe too wide,
Each Stone will wrench th'unwary Step aside:
The sudden Turn may stretch the swelling Vein,
Thy cracking Joint unhinge, or Ankle sprain;
And when too short the modish Shoes are worn,
40   You'll judge the Seasons by your shooting Corn.
      Nor should it prove thy less important Care,
To chuse a proper Coat for Winter's Wear.
Now in thy Trunk thy *Doily* Habit fold,
The silken Drugget ill can fence the Cold;
45   The Frieze's spongy Nap is soak'd with Rain,
And Show'rs soon drench the Camlet's cockled Grain.
True *Witney* Broad-cloath with it's Shag unshorn,
Unpierc'd is in the lasting Tempest worn:
Be this the Horse-man's Fence; for who would wear
50   Amid the Town the Spoils of Russia's Bear?
Within the *Roquelaure's* Clasp thy Hands are pent,
Hands, that stretch'd forth invading Harms prevent.
Let the loop'd *Bavaroy* the Fop embrace,
Or his deep Cloak be spatter'd o'er with Lace.
55   That Garment best the Winter's Rage defends,
Whose shapeless Form in ample Plaits depends;
By various Names in various Counties known,
Yet held in all the true *Surtout* alone:
Be thine of *Kersey* firm, tho' small the Cost,
60   Then brave unwet the Rain, unchill'd the Frost.
      If the strong Cane support thy walking Hand,

Chairmen no longer shall the Wall command;
Ev'n sturdy Car-men shall thy Nod obey,
And rattling Coaches stop to make thee Way:
65 This shall direct thy cautious Tread aright,
Though not one glaring Lamp enliven Night.
Let Beaus their Canes with Amber tipt produce,
Be theirs for empty Show, but thine for Use.
In gilded Chariots while they loll at Ease,
70 And lazily insure a Life's Disease;
While softer Chairs the tawdry Load convey
To Court, to *White*'s, Assemblies, or the Play;
Rosie-complexion'd Health thy Steps attends,
And Exercise thy lasting Youth defends.
75 Imprudent Men Heav'n's choicest Gifts prophane.
Thus some beneath their Arm support the Cane;
The dirty Point oft checks the careless Pace,
And miry Spots thy clean Cravat disgrace:
O! may I never such Misfortune meet,
80 May no such vicious Walkers croud the Street,
May Providence o'er-shade me with her Wings,
While the bold Muse experienc'd Dangers sings.
    Not that I wander from my native Home,
And tempting Perils foreign Cities roam.
85 Let *Paris* be the theme of *Gallia*'s Muse,
Where Slav'ry treads the Street in wooden Shoes;
Nor do I rove in *Belgia*'s frozen Clime,
And teach the clumsy Boor to skate in Rhyme,
Where, if the warmer Clouds in Rain descend,
90 No miry Ways industrious Steps offend,
The rushing Flood from sloping Pavements pours,
And blackens the Canals with dirty Show'rs.
Let others *Naples* smoother Streets rehearse,
And with proud *Roman* Structures grace their Verse,
95 Where frequent Murders wake the Night with Groans,
And Blood in purple Torrents dies the Stones;
Nor shall the Muse through narrow *Venice* stray,
Where *Gondala*'s their painted Oars display.
O happy Streets to rumbling Wheels unknown,
100 No Carts, no Coaches shake the floating Town!
Thus was of old *Britannia*'s City bless'd,
E'er Pride and Luxury her Sons possess'd:
Coaches and Chariots yet unfashion'd lay,
Nor late invented Chairs perplex'd the Way:

105   Then the proud Lady trip'd along the Town,
       And tuck'd up Petticoats secur'd her Gown,
       Her rosie Cheek with distant Visits glow'd,
       And Exercise unartful Charms bestow'd;
       But since in braided Gold her Foot is bound,
110   And a long trailing Manteau sweeps the Ground,
       Her Shoe disdains the Street; the lazy Fair,
       With narrow Step affects a limping Air.
       Now gaudy Pride corrupts the lavish Age,
       And the Streets flame with glaring Equipage;
115   The tricking Gamester insolently rides,
       With *Loves* and *Graces* on his Chariots Sides;
       In sawcy State the griping Broker sits,
       And laughs at Honesty, and trudging Wits:
       For you, O honest Men, these useful Lays
120   The Muse prepares; I seek no other Praise.
           When Sleep is first disturb'd by Morning Cries;
       From sure Prognosticks learn to know the Skies,
       Lest you of Rheums and Coughs at Night complain;
       Surpriz'd in dreary Fogs, or driving Rain
125   When suffocating Mists obscure the Morn,
       Let thy worst Wig, long us'd to Storms, be worn;
       This knows the powder'd Footman, and with Care,
       Beneath his flapping Hat, secures his Hair.
       Be thou, for ev'ry Season, justly drest,
130   Nor brave the piercing Frost with open Breast;
       And when the bursting Clouds a Deluge pour,
       Let thy Surtout defend the drenching Show'r.
           The changing Weather certain Signs reveal.
       E'er Winter sheds her Snow, or Frosts congeal,
135   You'll see the Coals in brighter Flame aspire,
       And Sulphur tinge with blue the rising Fire:
       Your tender Shins the scorching Heat decline,
       And at the Dearth of Coals the Poor repine;
       Before her Kitchin Hearth, the nodding Dame
140   In Flannel Mantle wrapt, enjoys the Flame;
       Hov'ring, upon her feeble Knees she bends,
       And all around the grateful Warmth ascends.
          Nor do less certain Signs the Town advise,
       Of milder Weather, and serener Skies.
145   The Ladies gayly dress'd, the *Mall* adorn
       With various Dyes, and paint the sunny Morn;
       The wanton Fawns with frisking Pleasure range,

And chirping Sparrows greet the welcome Change:
Not that their Minds with greater Skill are fraught,
150   Endu'd by Instinct, or by Reason taught,
The Seasons operate on every Breast;
'Tis hence that Fawns are brisk, and Ladies drest.
When on his Box the nodding Coachman snores,
And dreams of fancy'd Fares; when Tavern Doors
155   The Chairmen idly croud; then ne'er refuse
To trust thy busy Steps in thinner Shoes.

But when the swinging Signs your Ears offend
With creaking Noise, then rainy Floods impend;
Soon shall the Kennels swell with rapid Streams,
160   And rush in muddy Torrents to the *Thames*.
The Bookseller, whose Shop's an open Square,
Foresees the Tempest, and with early Care
Of Learning strips the Rails; the rowing Crew
To tempt a Fare, cloath all their Tilts in Blue:
165   On Hosier's Poles depending Stockings ty'd,
Flag with the slacken'd Gale, from side to side;
Church-Monuments foretell the changing Air;
Then *Niobe* dissolves into a Tear,
And sweats with secret Grief; you'll hear the Sounds
170   Of whistling Winds, e'er Kennels break their Bounds;
Ungrateful Odours Common-shores diffuse,
And dropping Vaults distil unwholesome Dews,
E'er the Tiles rattle with the smoaking Show'r,
And Spouts on heedless Men their Torrents pour.
175   All Superstition from thy Breast repel.
Let cred'lous Boys, and prattling Nurses tell,
How, if the Festival of *Paul* be clear,
Plenty from lib'ral Horn shall strow the Year;
When the dark Skies dissolve in Snows or Rain,
180   The lab'ring Hind shall yoke the Steer in vain;
But if the threatning Winds in Tempests roar,
Then War shall bathe her wasteful Sword in Gore.
How, if on *Swithin*'s Feast the Welkin lours,
And ev'ry Penthouse streams with hasty Show'rs,
185   Twice twenty Days shall Clouds their Fleeces drain,
And wash the Pavement with incessant Rain.
Let not such vulgar Tales debase thy Mind;
Nor *Paul* nor *Swithin* rule the Clouds and Wind.

If you the Precepts of the Muse despise,
190   And slight the faithful Warning of the Skies,

Others you'll see, when all the Town's afloat,
Wrapt in th'Embraces of a Kersey coat,
Or double-button'd Freize; their guarded Feet
Defie the muddy Dangers of the Street,
195 While you, with Hat unloop'd, the Fury dread
Of Spouts high-streaming, and with cautious Tread
Shun ev'ry dashing Pool; or idly stop,
To seek the kind Protection of a Shop.
But Bus'ness summons; Now with hasty Scud
200 You jostle for the Wall; the spatter'd Mud
Hides all thy Hose behind; in vain you scow'r,
Thy Wig alas! uncurl'd, admits the Show'r.
So fierce *Alecto*'s snaky Tresses fell,
When *Orpheus* charm'd the rig'rous Pow'rs of Hell,
205 Or thus hung *Glaucus*' Beard, with briny Dew
Clotted and strait, when first his am'rous View
Surpris'd the bathing Fair; the frighted Maid
Now stands a Rock, transform'd by *Circe*'s Aid.
    Good Huswives all the Winter's Rage despise,
210 Defended by the Riding-hood's Disguise:
Or underneath th'*Umbrella*'s oily Shed,
Safe thro' the Wet on clinking Pattens tread.
Let *Persian* Dames th'*Umbrella*'s Ribs display,
To guard their Beauties from the sunny Ray;
215 Or sweating Slaves support the shady Load,
When Eastern Monarchs shew their State abroad;
Britain in Winter only knows its Aid,
To guard from chilly Show'rs the walking Maid.
But, O! forget not, Muse, the *Patten*'s Praise,
220 That female Implement shall grace thy Lays;
Say from what Art Divine th'Invention came,
And from its Origine deduce the Name.
    Where *Lincoln* wide extends her fenny Soil,
A goodly Yeoman liv'd grown white with Toil;
225 One only Daughter blest his nuptial Bed,
Who from her infant Hand the Poultry fed:
Martha (her careful Mother's Name) she bore,
But now her careful Mother was no more.
Whilst on her Father's Knee the Damsel play'd
230 *Patty* he fondly call'd the smiling Maid;
As Years increas'd, her ruddy Beauty grew,
And *Patty*'s Fame o'er all the Village flew.
    Soon as the blushing Morning warms the Skies,

And in the doubtful Day the Woodcock flies,
235 Her cleanly Pail the pretty Houswife bears,
And singing, to the distant Field repairs:
And when the Plains with ev'ning Dews are spread,
The milky Burthen smoaks upon her Head,
Deep, thro' a miry Lane she pick'd her Way,
240 Above her Ankle rose the chalky Clay.
    Vulcan, by chance the bloomy Maiden spies,
With Innocence and Beauty in her Eyes,
He saw, he lov'd; for yet he ne'er had known
Sweet Innocence and Beauty meet in One.
245 Ah *Mulciber!* recall thy nuptial Vows,
Think on the Graces of thy *Paphian* Spouse,
Think how her Eyes dart inexhausted Charms,
And canst thou leave her Bed for *Patty*'s Arms?
    The *Lemnian* Pow'r forsakes the Realms above,
250 His Bosom glowing with terrestrial Love:
Far in the Lane, a lonely Hut he found,
No Tenant ventur'd on th'unwholesome Ground.
Here smoaks his Forge, he bares his sinewy Arm,
And early Strokes the sounding Anvil warm;
255 Around his Shop the steely Sparkles flew,
As for the Steed he shap'd the bending Shoe.
    When blue-ey'd *Patty* near his Window came,
His Anvil rests, his Forge forgets to flame.
To hear his soothing Tales, she feigns Delays;
260 What Woman can resist the Force of Praise?
    At first she coyly ev'ry Kiss withstood,
And all her Cheek was flush'd with modest Blood:
With headless Nails he now surrounds her Shoes,
To save her Steps from Rains and piercing Dews;
265 She lik'd his soothing Tales, his Presents wore,
And granted Kisses, but would grant no more.
Yet Winter chill'd her Feet, with Cold she pines,
And on her Cheek the fading Rose declines;
No more her humid Eyes their Lustre boast,
270 And in hoarse Sounds her melting Voice is lost.
    This *Vulcan* saw, and in his heav'nly Thought,
A new Machine Mechanick Fancy wrought,
Above the Mire her shelter'd Steps to raise,
And bear her safely through the Wintry Ways.
275 Strait the new Engine on his Anvil glows,
And the pale Virgin on the Patten rose.

No more her Lungs are shook with dropping Rheums,
And on her Cheek reviving Beauty blooms.
The God obtain'd his Suit, though Flatt'ry fail,
280   Presents with Female Virtue must prevail.
The Patten now supports each frugal Dame,
Which from the blue-ey'd *Patty* takes the Name.

BOOK II

OF WALKING THE STREETS BY DAY

Thus far the Muse has trac'd in useful Lays,
The proper Implements for Wintry Ways:
Has taught the Walker, with judicious Eyes,
To read the various Warnings of the Skies.
5   Now venture, Muse, from Home to range the Town,
And for the publick Safety risque thy own.
    For Ease and for Dispatch, the Morning's best:
No Tides of Passengers the Street molest.
You'll see a draggled Damsel, here and there,
10   From *Billingsgate* her fishy Traffick bear;
On Doors the sallow Milk-maid chalks her Gains;
Ah! how unlike the Milk-maid of the Plains!
Before proud Gates attending Asses bray,
Or arrogate with solemn Pace the way;
15   These grave Physicians with their milky Chear
The Love-sick Maid, and dwindling Beau repair;
Here Rows of Drummers stand in martial File,
And with their Vellom-Thunder shake the Pile,
To greet the new-made Bride. Are Sounds like these
20   The proper Prelude to a State of Peace?
Now Industry awakes her busy Sons,
Full charg'd with News the breathless Hawker runs,
Shops open, Coaches roll, Carts shake the Ground,
And all the Streets with passing Cries resound.
25   If cloath'd in Black, you tread the busy Town.
Or if distinguish'd by the rev'rend Gown,
Three Trades avoid; oft' in the mingling Press,
The *Barber*'s Apron soils the sable Dress;
Shun the *Perfumer*'s Touch with cautious Eye,
30   Nor let the *Baker*'s Step advance too nigh:
Ye Walkers too that youthful Colours wear,
Three sullying Trades avoid with equal Care;

21

The little *Chimney-sweeper* skulks along,
And marks with sooty Stains the heedless Throng;
35   When *Small-coal* murmurs in the hoarser Throat,
From smutty Dangers guard thy threaten'd Coat:
The *Dust-man*'s Cart offends thy Cloaths and Eyes,
When through the Street a Cloud of Ashes flies;
But whether Black, or lighter Dyes are worn,
40   The *Chandler*'s Basket, on his Shoulder born,
With Tallow spots thy Coat; resign the Way,
To shun the surly *Butcher*'s greasy Tray,
Butchers, whose Hands are dy'd with Blood's foul Stain,
And always foremost in the Hangman's Train.
45   Let due Civilities be strictly paid.
The Wall surrender to the hooded Maid;
Nor let thy sturdy Elbow's hasty Rage
Jostle the feeble Steps of trembling Age:
And when the Porter bends beneath his Load,
50   And pants for Breath; clear thou the crouded Road.
But above all, the groaping Blind direct,
And from the pressing Throng the Lame protect.
You'll sometimes meet a Fop, of nicest Tread,
Whose mantling Peruke veils his empty Head,
55   At ev'ry Step he dreads the Wall to lose,
And risques, to save a Coach, his red-heel'd Shoes;
Him, like the *Miller,* pass with Caution by,
Lest from his Shoulder Clouds of Powder fly.
But when the Bully, with assuming Pace,
60   Cocks his broad Hat, edg'd round with tarnish'd Lace,
Yield not the Way; defie his strutting Pride,
And thrust him to the muddy Kennel's side;
He never turns again, nor dares oppose,
But mutters coward Curses as he goes.
65   If drawn by Bus'ness to a Street unknown,
Let the sworn Porter point thee through the Town;
Be sure observe the Signs, for Signs remain,
Like faithful Land-marks to the walking Train.
Seek not from Prentices to learn the Way,
70   Those fabling Boys will turn thy Steps astray;
Ask the grave Tradesman to direct thee right,
He ne'er deceives, but when he profits by't.
      Where fam'd Saint *Giles*'s ancient Limits spread,
An inrail'd Column rears its lofty Head,
75   Here to sev'n Streets, sev'n Dials count the Day,

And from each other catch the circling Ray.
Here oft the Peasant, with enquiring Face,
Bewilder'd, trudges on from Place to Place;
He dwells on ev'ry Sign, with stupid Gaze,
80 Enters the narrow Alley's doubtful Maze,
Trys ev'ry winding Court and Street in vain,
And doubles o'er his weary Steps again.
Thus hardy *Theseus*, with intrepid Feet,
Travers'd the dang'rous Labyrinth of *Crete;*
85 But still the wandring Passes forc'd his Stay,
Till *Ariadne's* Clue unwinds the Way.
But do not thou, like that bold Chief, confide
Thy ventrous Footsteps to a female Guide;
She'll lead thee, with delusive Smiles along,
90 Dive in thy Fob, and drop thee in the Throng.
When waggish Boys the stunted Beesom ply,
To rid the slabby Pavement; pass not by
E'er thou hast held their Hands; some heedless Flirt
Will over-spread thy Calves with spatt'ring Dirt.
95 Where Porters Hogsheads roll from Carts aslope,
Or Brewers down steep Cellars stretch the Rope,
Where counted Billets are by Carmen tost;
Stay thy rash Steps, and walk without the Post.
Where elevated o'er the gaping Croud,
100 Clasp'd in the Board the perjur'd Head is bow'd,
Betimes retreat; here, thick as Hailstones pour,
Turnips, and half-hatch'd Eggs, (a mingled Show'r)
Among the Rabble rain: Some random Throw
May with the trickling Yolk thy Cheek o'erflow.
105 Though Expedition bids, yet never stray
Where no rang'd Posts defend the rugged Way.
Here laden Carts with thundring Waggons meet,
Wheels clash with Wheels, and bar the narrow Street;
The lashing Whip resounds, the Horses strain,
110 And Blood in Anguish bursts the swelling Vein.
O barb'rous Men, your cruel Breasts asswage,
Why vent ye on the gen'rous Steed your Rage?
Does not his Service earn your daily Bread?
Your Wives, your Children by his Labours fed!
115 If, as the *Samian* taught, the Soul revives,
And shifting Seats, in other Bodies lives;
Severe shall be the brutal Coachman's Change,
Doom'd, in a *Hackney* Horse, the Town to range:

23

Carmen, transform'd, the groaning Load shall draw,
120 Whom other Tyrants, with the Lash, shall awe.
  Who would of *Watling-street* the Dangers share,
When the broad Pavement of *Cheap-side* is near?
Or who that rugged Street would traverse o'er,
That stretches, O *Fleet-ditch,* from thy black Shore
125 To the *Tow'r*s moated Walls? Here Streams ascend
That, in mix'd Fumes, the wrinkled Nose offend.
Where Chandlers Cauldrons boil; where fishy Prey
Hides the wet Stall, long absent from the Sea;
And where the Cleaver chops the Heifer's Spoil,
130 And where huge Hogsheads sweat with trainy Oil,
Thy breathing Nostril hold; but how shall I
Pass, where in Piles *Cornavian* Cheeses lye;
Cheese, that the Table's closing Rites denies,
And bids me with th'unwilling Chaplain rise.
135   O bear me to the Paths of fair *Pell-mell,*
Safe are thy Pavements, grateful is thy Smell!
At distance, rolls along the gilded Coach,
Nor sturdy Carmen on thy Walks encroach;
No Lets would bar thy Ways, were Chairs deny'd.
140 The soft Supports of Laziness and Pride;
Shops breathe Perfumes, thro' Sashes Ribbons glow,
The mutual Arms of Ladies, and the Beau.
Yet still ev'n Here, when Rains the Passage hide,
Oft' the loose Stone spirts up a muddy Tide
145 Beneath thy careless Foot; and from on high,
Where Masons mount the Ladder, Fragments fly;
Mortar, and crumbled Lime in Show'rs descend,
And o'er thy Head destructive Tiles impend.
  But sometimes let me leave the noisie Roads,
150 And silent wander in the close Abodes
Where Wheels ne'er shake the Ground; there pensive stray,
In studious Thought, the long uncrouded Way.
Here I remark each Walker's diff'rent Face,
And in their Look their various Bus'ness trace.
155 The Broker here his spacious Beaver wears,
Upon his Brow sit Jealousies and Cares;
Bent on some Mortgage to avoid Reproach
He seeks bye Streets, and saves th'expensive Coach.
Soft, at low Doors, old Letchers tap their Cane,
160 For fair Recluse, that travels *Drury-lane;*
Here roams uncomb'd, the lavish Rake, to shun

His *Fleet-street* Draper's everlasting Dun.
    Careful Observers, studious of the Town,
Shun the Misfortunes that disgrace the Clown.
165 Untempted, they contemn the Jugler's Feats,
Pass by the *Meuse,* nor try the Thimble's Cheats.
When Drays bound high, they never cross behind,
Where bubbling Yest is blown by Gusts of Wind:
And when up *Ludgate-hill* huge Carts move slow,
170 Far from the straining Steeds, securely go,
Whose dashing Hoofs, behind them, fling the Mire,
And mark, with muddy Blots, the gazing 'Squire.
The *Parthian* thus his Jav'lin backward throws,
And as he flies, infests pursuing Foes.
175   The thoughtless Wits shall frequent Forfeits pay,
Who 'gainst the Centry's Box discharge their Tea.
Do thou some Court, or secret Corner seek,
Nor flush with Shame the passing Virgin's cheek.
    Yet let me not descend to trivial Song,
180 Nor vulgar Circumstance my Verse prolong;
Why should I teach the Maid when Torrents pour,
Her Head to shelter from the sudden Show'r?
Nature will best her ready Hand inform,
With her spread Petticoat to fence the Storm.
185 Does not each Walker know the warning Sign,
When Wisps of Straw depend upon the Twine
Cross the close Street; that then the Pavior's Art
Renews the Ways, deny'd to Coach and Cart?
Who knows not, that the Coachman lashing by,
190 Oft', with his flourish, cuts the heedless Eye;
And when he takes his Stand, to wait a Fare,
His Horses Foreheads shun the Winter's Air?
Nor will I roam, when Summer's sultry Rays
Parch the dry Ground, and spread with Dust the Ways;
195 With whirling Gusts, the rapid Atoms rise,
Smoak o'er the Pavement, and involve the Skies.
    Winter my Theme confines; whose nitry Wind
Shall crust the slabby Mire, and Kennels bind;
She bids the Snow descend in flaky Sheets,
200 And in her hoary Mantle cloath the Streets.
Let not the Virgin tread these slipp'ry Roads,
The gath'ring Fleece the hollow Patten loads;
But if thy Footsteps slide with clotted Frost,
Strike off the breaking Balls against the Post.

205 On silent Wheel the passing Coaches roll;
 Oft' look behind and ward the threatning Pole.
 In harden'd Orbs the School-boy moulds the Snow,
 To mark the Coachman with a dextrous Throw.
 Why do ye, Boys, the Kennel's Surface spread,
210 To tempt with faithless Pass the Matron's Tread?
 How can ye Laugh, to see the Damsel spurn,
 Sink in your Frauds, and her green Stocking mourn?
 At *White*'s the harness'd Chairman idly stands,
 And swings, around his Waste, his tingling Hands:
215 The Sempstress speeds to *'Change* with red-tipt Nose;
 The *Belgian* Stove beneath her Footstool glows;
 In half-whipt Muslin Needles useless lie,
 And Shuttle-cocks across the Counter fly.
 These Sports warm harmless; why then will ye prove,
220 Deluded Maids, the dang'rous Flame of Love?
  Where *Covent-garden*'s famous Temple stands,
 That boasts the Work of *Jones'* immortal Hands;
 Columns, with plain Magnificence, appear,
 And graceful Porches lead along the Square:
225 Here oft' my Course I bend, when lo! from far
 I spy the Furies of the Foot-ball War:
 The 'Prentice quits his Shop, to join the Crew
 Encreasing Crouds the flying Game pursue.
 Thus, as you roll the Ball o'er snowy Ground,
230 The gath'ring Globe augments with ev'ry Round;
 But whither shall I run? the Throng draws nigh,
 The Ball now Skims the Street, now soars on high;
 The dext'rous Glazier strong returns the Bound,
 And gingling Sashes on the Pent-house sound.
235 O roving Muse, recal that wond'rous Year,
 When Winter reign'd in bleak *Britannia*'s Air;
 When hoary *Thames,* with frosted Oziers crown'd,
 Was three long Moons in icy Fetters bound,
 The Waterman, forlorn along the Shore,
240 Pensive reclines upon his useless Oar,
 Sees harness'd Steeds desert the stony Town,
 And wander Roads unstable, not their own:
 Wheels o'er the harden'd Waters smoothly glide,
 And rase with whiten'd Tracks the slipp'ry Tide.
245 Here the fat Cook piles high the blazing Fire,
 And scarce the Spit can turn the Steer entire.
 Booths sudden hide the *Thames,* long Streets appear,

And num'rous Games proclaim the crouded Fair.
So when a Gen'ral bids the martial Train
250 Spread their Encampment o'er the spatious Plain;
Thick-rising Tents a Canvas City build,
And the loud Dice resound thro' all the Field.
'Twas here the Matron found a doleful Fate:
In Elegiac Lay the Woe relate,
255 Soft, as the Breath of distant Flutes, at Hours
When silent Ev'ning closes up the Flow'rs;
Lulling, as falling Water's hollow noise;
Indulging Grief, like *Philomela's* Voice.
    Doll ev'ry Day had walk'd these treach'rous Roads;
260 Her Neck grew warpt beneath autumnal Loads
Of various Fruit; she now a Basket bore,
That Head, alas! shall Basket bear no more.
Each Booth she frequent past, in quest of Gain,
And Boys with Pleasure heard her shrilling Strain.
265 Ah *Doll!* all Mortals must resign their Breath,
And Industry it self submit to Death!
The cracking Crystal yields, she sinks, she dyes,
Her Head, chopt off, from her lost Shoulders flies;
Pippins she cry'd, but Death her Voice confounds,
270 And Pip-Pip-Pip along the Ice resounds.
So when the *Thracian* Furies *Orpheus* tore,
And left his bleeding Trunk deform'd with Gore,
His sever'd Head floats down the silver Tide,
His yet warm Tongue for his lost Consort cry'd;
275 *Eurydice,* with quiv'ring Voice, he mourn'd,
And *Heber's* Banks *Eurydice* return'd.
    But now the western Gale the Flood unbinds,
And black'ning Clouds roll on with warmer Winds.
The wooden Town its frail Foundation leaves,
280 And *Thames'* full Urn rolls down his plenteous Waves;
From ev'ry Penthouse streams the fleeting Snow,
And with dissolving Frost the Pavements flow.
    Experienc'd Men, inur'd to City Ways,
Need not the *Calendar* to count their Days.
285 When through the Town, with slow and solemn Air,
Led by the Nostril, walks the muzled Bear;
Behind him moves majestically dull,
The Pride of *Hockley-hole*, the surly Bull;
Learn hence the Periods of the Week to name,
290 *Mondays* and *Thursdays* are the Days of Game.

When fishy Stalls with double Store are laid;
The golden-belly'd Carp, the broad-finn'd Maid,
Red-speckled Trouts, the Salmon's silver Joul,
The jointed Lobster, and unscaly Soale,
295   And luscious 'Scallops, to allure the Tastes
Of rigid Zealots to delicious Fasts;
Wednesdays and *Fridays* you'll observe from hence,
Days, when our Sires were doom'd to Abstinence.
When dirty Waters from Balconies drop,
300   And dextrous Damsels twirle the sprinkling Mop,
And cleanse the spatter'd Sash, and scrub the Stairs;
Know *Saturday's* conclusive Morn appears.
Successive Crys the Season's Change declare,
And mark the Monthly Progress of the Year.
305   Hark, how the Streets with treble Voices ring,
To sell the bounteous Product of the Spring!
Sweet-smelling Flow'rs, and Elders early Bud,
With Nettle's tender Shoots, to cleanse the Blood:
And when *June's* Thunder cools the sultry Skies,
310   Ev'n *Sundays* are prophan'd by Mackrell Cries.
Wallnuts the Fruit'rer's Hand, in Autumn, stain,
Blue Plumbs and juicy Pears augment his Gain;
Next Oranges the longing Boys entice,
To trust their Copper-Fortunes to the Dice.
315   When Rosemary, and Bays, the Poet's Crown,
Are bawl'd, in frequent Cries, through all the Town,
Then judge the Festival of *Christmas* near,
Christmas, the joyous Period of the Year.
Now with bright Holly all your Temples strow,
320   With Laurel green, and sacred Misletoe.
Now, Heav'n-born *Charity,* thy Blessings shed;
Bid meagre Want uprear her sickly Head:
Bid shiv'ring Limbs be warm; let Plenty's Bowle,
In humble Roofs, make glad the needy Soul.
325   See, see, the Heav'n-born Maid her Blessings shed;
Lo! meagre Want uprears her sickly Head;
Cloath'd are the Naked, and the Needy glad,
While selfish Avarice alone is sad.
Proud Coaches pass, regardless of the Moan
330   Of Infant Orphans, and the Widow's Groan;
While Charity still moves the Walker's Mind,
His lib'ral Purse relieves the Lame and Blind.
Judiciously thy Half-pence are bestow'd,

28

Where the laborious Beggar sweeps the Road.
335 Whate'er you give, give ever at Demand,
Nor let Old-Age long stretch his palsy'd Hand.
Those who give late, are importun'd each Day,
And still are teaz'd, because they still delay.
If e'er the Miser durst his Farthings spare,
340 He thinly spreads them through the publick Square,
Where, all beside the Rail, rang'd Beggars lie,
And from each other catch the doleful Cry;
With Heav'n, for Two-pence, cheaply wipes his Score,
Lifts up his Eyes, and hasts to beggar more.
345 Where the brass Knocker, wrapt in Flannel Band,
Forbids the Thunder of the Footman's Hand;
Th'Upholder, rueful Harbinger of Death
Waits, with Impatience, for the dying Breath;
As Vultures, o'er a Camp, with hov'ring Flight,
350 Snuff up the future Carnage of the Fight.
Here canst thou pass, unmindful of a Pray'r,
That Heav'n in Mercy may thy Brother spare?
Come, Fortescue, sincere, experienc'd Friend,
Thy Briefs, thy Deeds, and ev'n thy Fees suspend;
355 Come, let us leave the *Temple*'s silent Walls,
Me Bus'ness to my distant Lodging calls:
Through the long *Strand* together let us stray:
With thee conversing, I forget the Way.
Behold that narrow Street, which steep descends,
360 Whose Building to the slimy Shore extends;
Here *Arundel*'s fam'd Structure rear'd its Frame,
The Street alone retains an empty Name:
Where *Titian*'s glowing Paint the Canvas warm'd,
And *Raphael*'s fair Design, with Judgment, charm'd,
365 Now hangs the Bell-man's Song, and pasted here
The colour'd Prints of *Overton* appear.
Where Statues breath'd, the Work of *Phidias*' Hands,
A wooden Pump, or lonely Watch-house stands.
There *Essex* stately Pile adorn'd the Shore,
370 There *Cecil*'s, *Bedford*'s, *Viller*'s, now no more.
Yet *Burlington*'s fair Palace still remains;
Beauty within, without Proportion reigns.
Beneath his Eye declining Art revives,
The Wall with animated Picture lives;
375 There Hendel strikes the Strings, the melting Strain
Transports the Soul, and thrills through ev'ry Vein;

GAY

There oft' I enter (but with cleaner Shoes)
For *Burlington's* belov'd by ev'ry Muse.
　　O ye associate Walkers, O my Friends,
380　Upon your State what Happiness attends!
What, though no Coach to frequent Visit rolls,
Nor for your Shilling Chairmen sling their Poles;
Yet still your Nerves rheumatic Pains defye,
Nor lazy Jaundice dulls your Saffron Eye;
385　No wasting Cough discharges Sounds of Death,
Nor wheezing Asthma heaves in vain for Breath;
Nor from your restless Couch is heard the Groan
Of burning Gout, or sedentary Stone.
Let others in the jolting Coach confide,
390　Or in the leaky Boat the *Thames* divide;
Or, box'd within the Chair, contemn the Street,
And trust their Safety to another's Feet,
Still let me walk; for oft' the sudden Gale
Ruffles the Tide, and shifts the dang'rous Sail,
395　Then shall the Passenger, too late, deplore
The whelming Billow, and the faithless Oar;
The drunken Chairman in the Kennel spurns,
The Glasses shatters, and his Charge o'erturns.
Who can recount the Coach's various Harms,
400　The Legs disjointed, and the broken Arms?
　　I've seen a Beau, in some ill-fated Hour,
When o'er the Stones choak'd Kennels swell the Show'r,
In gilded Chariot loll; he with Disdain,
Views spatter'd Passengers, all drench'd in Rain;
405　With Mud fill'd high, the rumbling Cart draws near,
Now rule thy prancing Steeds, lac'd Charioteer!
The *Dustman* lashes on with spiteful Rage,
His pond'rous Spokes thy painted Wheel engage,
Crush'd is thy Pride, down falls the shrieking Beau,
410　The slabby Pavement crystal Fragments strow,
Black Floods of Mire th'embroider'd Coat disgrace,
And Mud enwraps the Honours of his Face.
So when dread *Jove,* the Son of Phoebus hurl'd,
Scarr'd with dark Thunder, to the nether World;
415　The headstrong Coursers tore the silver Reins,
And the Sun's beamy Ruin gilds the Plains.
　　If the pale Walker pants with weak'ning Ills,
His sickly Hand is stor'd with friendly Bills:
From hence, he learns the seventh-born Doctor's Fame,

420   From hence, he learns the cheapest Tailor's Name.
        Shall the large Mutton smoak upon your Boards?
    Such, *Newgate's* copious Market best affords.
    Would'st thou with mighty Beef augment thy Meal?
    Seek *Leaden-hall; St. James's* sends thee Veal.
425   *Thames-street* gives Cheeses; *Covent-garden* Fruits;
    Moor-fields old Books; and *Monmouth-street* old Suits.
    Hence may'st thou well supply the Wants of Life,
    Support thy Family, and cloath thy Wife.
        Volumes, on shelter'd Stalls, expanded lye,
430   And various Science lures the learned Eye;
    The bending Shelves with pond'rous Scholiasts groan,
    And deep Divines to modern Shops unknown:
    Here, like the Bee, that on industrious Wing
    Collects the various Odours of the Spring,
435   Walkers, at leisure, Learning's Flow'rs may spoil,
    Nor watch the Wasting of the Midnight Oil,
    May Morals snatch from *Plutarch's* tatter'd Page,
    A mildew'd *Bacon,* or *Stagyra's* Sage.
    Here saunt'ring 'Prentices o'er *Otway* weep,
440   O'er *Congreve* smile, or over *Dennis* sleep;
    Pleas'd Sempstresses the *Lock's* fam'd *Rape* unfold,
    And *Squirts* read *Garth,* 'till *Apozems* grow cold.
        O *Lintot,* let my Labours obvious lie,
    Rang'd on thy Stall, for ev'ry curious Eye;
445   So shall the Poor these Precepts *gratis* know,
    And to my Verse their future Safeties owe.
        What Walker shall his mean Ambition fix
    On the false Lustre of a Coach and Six?
    Let the vain Virgin, lur'd by glaring Show,
450   Sigh for the Liv'rys of th'embroider'd Beau.
        See, yon' bright Chariot on its Harness swing,
    With *Flanders* Mares, and on an arched Spring;
    That Wretch, to gain an Equipage and Place,
    Betray'd his Sister to a lewd Embrace.
455   This Coach, that with the blazon'd 'Scutcheon glows,
    Vain of his unknown Race, the Coxcomb shows.
    Here the brib'd Lawyer, sunk in Velvet, sleeps;
    The starving Orphan, as he passes, weeps;
    There flames a Fool, begirt with tinsilled Slaves.
460   Who wastes the Wealth of a whole Race of Knaves.
    That other, with a clustring Train behind,
    Owes his new Honours to a sordid Mind.

This next in Court Fidelity excells,
The Publick rifles, and his Country sells.
465 May the proud Chariot never be my Fate,
If purchas'd at so mean, so dear a Rate;
O rather give me sweet Content on Foot,
Wrapt in my Vertue, and a good *Surtout!*

BOOK III

OF WALKING THE STREETS BY NIGHT

O *Trivia,* Goddess, leave these low Abodes,
And traverse o'er the wide Ethereal Roads,
Celestial Queen, put on thy Robes of Light,
Now *Cynthia* nam'd, fair Regent of the Night.
5 At Sight of thee, the Villain sheaths his Sword,
Nor scales the Wall, to steal the wealthy Hoard.
Oh! may thy Silver Lamp from Heav'n's high Bow'r
Direct my Footsteps in the Midnight Hour.
    When Night first bids the twinkling Stars appear,
10 Or with her cloudy Vest inwraps the Air,
Then swarms the busie Street; with Caution tread,
Where the Shop-Windows falling threat thy Head;
Now Lab'rers home return, and join their Strength
To bear the tott'ring Plank, or Ladder's Length;
15 Still fix thy Eyes intent upon the Throng,
And as the Passes open, wind along.
    Where the fair Columns of Saint *Clement* stand,
Whose straiten'd Bounds encroach upon the *Strand;*
Where the low Penthouse bows the Walker's Head,
20 And the rough Pavement wounds the yielding Tread;
Where not a Post protects the narrow Space,
And strung in Twines, Combs dangle in thy Face;
Summon at once thy Courage, rouze thy Care,
Stand firm, look back, be resolute, beware.
25 Forth issuing from steep Lanes, the *Collier's* Steeds
Drag the black Load; another Cart succeeds,
Team follows Team, Crouds heap'd on Crouds appear,
And wait impatient, 'till the Road grow clear.
    Now all the Pavement sounds with trampling Feet,
30 And the mixt Hurry barricades the Street.
Entangled here, the Waggon's lengthen'd Team
Cracks the tough Harness; Here a pond'rous Beam

Lies over-turn'd athwart; For Slaughter fed,
Here lowing Bullocks raise their horned Head.
35 Now Oaths grow loud, with Coaches Coaches jar,
And the smart Blow provokes the sturdy War;
From the high Box they whirl the Thong around,
And with the twining Lash their Shins resound:
Their Rage ferments, more dang'rous Wounds they try,
40 And the Blood gushes down their painful Eye.
And now on Foot the frowning Warriors light,
And with their pond'rous Fists renew the Fight;
Blow answers Blow, their Cheeks are smear'd with Blood,
'Till down they fall, and grappling roll in Mud.
45 So when two Boars, in wild *Ytene* bred,
Or on *Westphalia's* fatt'ning Chest-nuts fed,
Gnash their sharp Tusks, and rous'd with equal Fire,
Dispute the Reign of some luxurious Mire;
In the black Flood they wallow o'er and o'er,
50 'Till their arm'd Jaws distill with Foam and Gore.
    Where the Mob gathers, swiftly shoot along,
Nor idly mingle in the noisy Throng.
Lur'd by the silver Hilt, amid the Swarm,
The subtil Artist will thy Side disarm.
55 Nor is thy Flaxen Wigg with Safety worn;
High on the Shoulder, in the Basket born,
Lurks the sly Boy; whose Hand to Rapine bred,
Plucks off the curling Honours of the Head.
Here dives the skulking Thief, with practis'd Slight,
60 And unfelt Fingers make thy Pocket light.
Where's now thy Watch, with all its Trinkets, flown?
And thy late Snuff-box is no more thy own.
But lo! his bolder Thefts some Tradesman spies,
Swift from his Prey the scudding Lurcher flies;
65 Dext'rous he 'scapes the Coach, with nimble Bounds,
Whilst ev'ry honest Tongue *Stop Thief* resounds.
So speeds the wily Fox, alarm'd by Fear,
Who lately filch'd the Turkey's callow Care;
Hounds following Hounds grow louder as he flies,
70 And injur'd Tenants joyn the Hunter's Cries.
Breathless he stumbling falls: Ill-fated Boy!
Why did not honest Work thy Youth employ?
Seiz'd by rough Hands, he's dragg'd amid the Rout,
And stretch'd beneath the Pump's incessant Spout:
75 Or plung'd in miry Ponds, he gasping lies,

33

Mud choaks his Mouth, and plaisters o'er his Eyes.
    Let not the Ballad-Singer's shrilling Strain
Amid the Swarm thy list'ning Ear detain:
Guard well thy Pocket; for these *Syrens* stand
80 To aid the Labours of the diving Hand;
Confed'rate in the Cheat, they draw the Throng,
And *Cambrick* Handkerchiefs reward the Song.
But soon as Coach or Cart drives rattling on,
The Rabble part, in Shoals they backward run.
85 So *Jove's* loud Bolts the mingled War divide,
And *Greece* and *Troy* retreats on either side.
    If the rude Throng pour on with furious Pace,
And hap to break thee from a Friend's Embrace,
Stop short; nor struggle thro' the Croud in vain,
90 But watch with careful Eye the passing Train.
Yet I (perhaps too fond) if chance the Tide
Tumultuous, bears my Partner from my Side,
Impatient venture back; despising Harm,
I force my Passage where the thickest swarm.
95 Thus his lost Bride the Trojan sought in vain
Through Night, and Arms, and Flames, and Hills of Slain.
Thus *Nisus* wander'd o'er the pathless Grove,
To find the brave Companion of his Love,
The pathless Grove in vain he wanders o'er:
100 *Euryalus,* alas! is now no more.
That Walker, who regardless of his Pace,
Turns oft' to pore upon the Damsel's Face,
From Side to Side by thrusting Elbows tost,
Shall strike his aking Breast against the Post;
105 Or Water, dash'd from fishy Stalls, shall stain
His hapless Coat with Spirts of scaly Rain.
But if unwarily he chance to stray,
Where twirling Turnstiles intercept the Way,
The thwarting Passenger shall force them round,
110 And beat the Wretch half breathless to the Ground.
    Let constant Vigilance thy Footsteps guide,
And wary Circumspection guard thy Side;
Then shalt thou walk unharm'd the dang'rous Night,
Nor need th'officious Link-Boy's smoaky Light.
115 Thou never wilt attempt to cross the Road,
Where Alehouse Benches rest the Porter's Load,
Grievous to heedless Shins; No Barrow's Wheel,
That bruises oft' the Truant Schoolboy's Heel,

Behind thee rolling, with insidious Pace,
120   Shall mark thy Stocking with a miry Trace.
Let not thy vent'rous Steps approach too nigh,
Where gaping wide, low steepy Cellars lie;
Should thy Shoe wrench aside, down, down you fall,
And overturn the scolding Huckster's Stall,
125   The scolding Huckster shall not o'er thee moan,
But Pence exact for Nuts and Pears o'erthrown.
     Though you through cleanlier Allies wind by Day,
To shun the Hurries of the publick Way,
Yet ne'er to those dark Paths by Night retire;
130   Mind only Safety, and contemn the Mire.
Then no impervious Courts thy Haste detain,
Nor sneering Ale-Wives bid thee turn again.
     Where *Lincoln's-Inn,* wide Space, is rail'd around,
Cross not with vent'rous Step; there oft' is found
135   The lurking Thief, who while the Day-light shone,
Made the Walls eccho with his begging Tone:
That Crutch which late Compassion mov'd, shall wound
Thy bleeding Head, and fell thee to the Ground.
Though thou art tempted by the Link-man's call,
140   Yet trust him not along the lonely Wall;
In the Mid-way he'll quench the flaming Brand,
And share the Booty with the pilf'ring Band.
Still keep the publick Streets, where oily Rays
Shot from the Crystal Lamp, o'erspread the Ways.
145   Happy *Augusta!* Law-defended Town!
Here no dark Lanthorns shade the Villain's Frown;
No *Spanish* Jealousies thy Lanes infest,
Nor *Roman* Vengeance stabs th'unwary Breast;
Here *Tyranny* ne'er lifts her purple Hand,
150   But Liberty and Justice guard the Land;
No *Bravos* here profess the bloody Trade,
Nor is the Church the Murd'rer's Refuge made.
     Let not the Chairman, with assuming Stride,
Press near the Wall, and rudely thrust thy Side:
155   The Laws have set him Bounds; his servile Feet
Should ne'er encroach where Posts defend the Street.
Yet who the Footman's Arrogance can quell,
Whose Flambeau gilds the Sashes of *Pell-Mell,*
When in long Rank a Train of Torches flame,
160   To light the Midnight Visits of the Dame?
Others, perhaps, by happier Guidance led,

May where the Chairman rests, with Safety tread;
Whene'er I pass, their Poles unseen below,
Make my Knee tremble with the jarring Blow.
165　　　If Wheels bar up the Road, where Streets are crost,
With gentle Words the Coachman's Ear accost:
He ne'er the Threat, or harsh Command obeys,
But with Contempt the spatter'd Shoe surveys.
Now man with utmost Fortitude thy Soul,
170　　To cross the Way where Carts and Coaches roll;
Yet do not in thy hardy Skill confide,
Nor rashly risque the Kennel's spacious Stride;
Stay till afar the distant Wheel you hear,
Like dying Thunder in the breaking Air;
175　　Thy Foot will slide upon the miry Stone,
And passing Coaches crush thy tortur'd Bone,
Or Wheels enclose the Road; on either Hand
Pent round with Perils, in the midst you stand,
And call for Aid in vain; the Coachman swears,
180　　And Carmen drive, unmindful of thy Prayers.
Where wilt thou turn? ah! whither wilt thou fly?
On ev'ry side the pressing Spokes are nigh.
So Sailors, while *Charybdis'* Gulphs they shun,
Amaz'd, on *Scylla'*s craggy Dangers run.
185　　　Be sure observe where brown *Ostrea* stands,
Who boasts her shelly Ware from *Wallfleet* Sands;
There may'st thou pass, with safe unmiry Feet,
Where the rais'd Pavement leads athwart the Street.
If where *Fleet-Ditch* with muddy Current flows,
190　　You chance to roam; where Oyster-Tubs in Rows
Are rang'd beside the Posts; there stay thy Haste,
And with the sav'ry Fish indulge thy Taste:
The Damsel's Knife the gaping Shell commands,
While the salt Liquor streams between her Hands.
195　　　The Man had sure a Palate cover'd o'er
With Brass or Steel, that on the rocky Shore
First broke the oozy Oyster's pearly Coat,
And risqu'd the living Morsel down his Throat.
What will not Lux'ry taste? Earth, Sea, and Air
200　　Are daily ransack'd for the Bill of Fare.
Blood stuff'd in Skins is *British* Christian's Food,
And *France* robs Marshes of the croaking Brood;
Spungy *Morells* in strong *Ragousts* are found,
And in the *Soupe* the slimy Snail is drown'd.

205   When from high Spouts the dashing Torrents fall,
Ever be watchful to maintain the Wall;
For should'st thou quit thy Ground, the rushing Throng
Will with impetuous Fury drive along;
All press to gain those Honours thou hast lost,
210 And rudely shove thee far without the Post.
Then to retrieve the Shed you strive in vain,
Draggled all o'er, and soak'd in Floods of Rain.
Yet rather bear the Show'r, and Toils of Mud,
Than in the doubtful Quarrel risque thy Blood.
215 O think on *Œdipus'* detested State,
And by his Woes be warn'd to shun thy Fate.
      Where three Roads join'd, he met his Sire unknown;
(Unhappy Sire, but more unhappy Son!)
Each claim'd the Way, their Swords the Strife decide,
220 The hoary Monarch fell, he groan'd and dy'd!
Hence sprung the fatal Plague that thinn'd thy Reign,
Thy cursed Incest! and thy Children slain!
Hence wert thou doom'd in endless Night to stray
Through *Theban* Streets, and cheerless groap thy Way.
225   Contemplate, Mortal, on thy fleeting Years;
See, with black Train the Funeral Pomp appears!
Whether some Heir attends in sable State,
And mourns with outward Grief a Parent's Fate;
Or the fair Virgin, nipt in Beauty's Bloom,
230 A Croud of Lovers follow to her Tomb.
Why is the Herse with 'Scutcheons blazon'd round,
And with the nodding Plume of Ostrich crown'd?
No: The Dead know it not, nor Profit gain;
It only serves to prove the Living vain.
235 How short is Life! how frail is human Trust!
Is all this Pomp for laying Dust to Dust?
      Where the nail'd Hoop defends the painted Stall,
Brush not thy sweeping Skirt too near the Wall;
Thy heedless Sleeve will drink the colour'd Oil,
240 And Spot indelible thy Pocket soil.
Has not wise Nature strung the Legs and Feet
With firmest Nerves, design'd to walk the Street?
Has she not given us Hands, to groap aright,
Amidst the frequent Dangers of the Night?
245 And think'st thou not the double Nostril meant,
To warn from oily Woes by previous Scent?
      Who can the various City Frauds recite,

With all the petty Rapines of the Night?
Who now the *Guinea-Dropper's* Bait regards,
250   Trick'd by the Sharper's Dice, or Juggler's Cards?
Why should I warn thee ne'er to join the Fray,
Where the Sham-Quarrel interrupts the Way?
Lives there in these our Days so soft a Clown,
Brav'd by the Bully's Oaths, or threat'ning Frown?
255   I need not strict enjoyn the Pocket's Care,
When from the crouded *Play* thou lead'st the Fair;
Who has not here, or Watch, or Snuff-Box lost,
Or Handkerchiefs that *India's* Shuttle boast?
    O! may thy Virtue guard thee through the Roads
260   Of *Drury's* mazy Courts, and dark Abodes,
The Harlots' guileful Paths, who nightly stand,
Where *Katherine-street* descends into the *Strand*.
Say, vagrant Muse, their Wiles and subtil Arts,
To lure the Stranger's unsuspecting Hearts;
265   So shall our Youth on healthful Sinews tread,
And City Cheeks grow warm with rural Red.
    'Tis She who nightly strowls with saunt'ring Pace,
No stubborn Stays her yielding Shape embrace;
Beneath the Lamp her tawdry Ribbons glare,
270   The new-scower'd Manteau, and the slattern Air;
High-draggled Petticoats her Travels show,
And hollow Cheeks with artful Blushes glow;
With flatt'ring Sounds she sooths the cred'lous Ear,
My noble Captain! Charmer! Love! my Dear!
275   In Riding-hood near Tavern-Doors she plies,
Or muffled Pinners hide her livid Eyes.
With empty Bandbox she delights to range,
And feigns a distant Errand from the *Change;*
Nay, she will oft' the Quaker's Hood prophane,
280   And trudge demure the Rounds of *Drury-Lane.*
She darts from Sarsnet Ambush wily Leers,
Twitches thy Sleeve, or with familiar Airs
Her Fan will pat thy Cheek; these Snares disdain,
Nor gaze behind thee, when she turns again.
285   I knew a Yeoman, who for thirst of Gain,
To the great City drove from *Devon's* Plain
His num'rous lowing Herd; his Herds he sold,
And his deep leathern Pocket bagg'd with Gold;
Drawn by a fraudful Nymph, he gaz'd, he sigh'd;
290   Unmindful of his Home, and distant Bride,

She leads the willing Victim to his Doom,
Through winding Alleys to her Cobweb Room,
Thence thro' the Street he reels from Post to Post,
Valiant with Wine, nor knows his Treasure lost.
295   The vagrant Wretch th'assembled Watchmen spies,
He waves his Hanger, and their Poles defies;
Deep in the *Round-house* pent, all Night he snores,
And the next Morn in vain his Fate deplores.
    Ah hapless Swain, unus'd to Pains and Ills!
300   Canst thou forego Roast-Beef for nauseous Pills?
How wilt thou lift to Heav'n thy Eyes and Hands,
When the long Scroll the Surgeon's Fees demands!
Or else (ye Gods avert that worse Disgrace)
Thy ruin'd Nose falls level with thy Face,
305   Then shall thy Wife thy loathsome Kiss disdain,
And wholesome Neighbours from thy Mug refrain.
    Yet there are Watchmen, who with friendly Light
Will teach thy reeling Steps to tread aright;
For *Sixpence* will support thy helpless Arm,
310   And Home conduct thee, safe from nightly Harm;
But if they shake their Lanthorns, from afar
To call their Breth'ren to confed'rate War,
When Rakes resist their Pow'r; if hapless you
Should chance to wander with the scow'ring Crew;
315   Though Fortune yield thee Captive, ne'er despair,
But seek the Constable's consid'rate Ear;
He will reverse the Watchman's harsh Decree,
Moved by the Rhet'rick of a Silver Fee.
Thus would you gain some fav'rite Courtier's Word;
320   Fee not the petty Clarks, but bribe my Lord.
Now is the Time that Rakes their Revells keep;
Kindlers of Riot, Enemies of Sleep.
His scatter'd Pence the flying *Nicker* flings,
And with the Copper Show'r the Casement rings.
325   Who has not heard the *Scowrer's* Midnight Fame?
Who has not trembled at the *Mohock's* Name?
Was there a Watchman took his hourly Rounds,
Safe from their Blows, or new-invented Wounds?
I pass their desp'rate Deeds, and Mischiefs done
330   Where from *Snow-hill* black steepy Torrents run;
How Matrons, hoop'd within the Hogshead's Womb,
Were tumbled furious thence, the rolling Tomb
O'er the Stones thunders, bounds from Side to Side.

So *Regulus* to save his Country dy'd.
335   Where a dim Gleam the paly Lanthorn throws
O'er the mid Pavement; heapy Rubbish grows,
Or arched Vaults their gaping Jaws extend,
Or the dark Caves to Common-Shores descend.
Oft' by the Winds extinct, the Signal lies,
340 Or smother'd in the glimm'ring Socket dies,
E'er Night has half roll'd round her Ebon Throne;
In the wide Gulph the shatter'd Coach o'erthrown,
Sinks with the snorting Steeds; the Reins are broke,
And from the crackling Axle flies the Spoke.
345 So when fam'd *Eddystone*'s far-shooting Ray,
That led the Sailor through the stormy Way,
Was from its rocky Roots by Billows torn,
And the high Turret in the Whirlewind born,
Fleets bulg'd their Sides against the craggy Land,
350 And pitchy Ruines blacken'd all the Strand.
    Who then through Night would hire the harness'd Steed,
And who would choose the rattling Wheel for Speed?
    But hark! Distress with screaming Voice draws nigh'r,
And wakes the slumb'ring Street with Cries of Fire.
355 At first a glowing Red enwraps the Skies,
And born by Winds the scatt'ring Sparks arise;
From Beam to Beam, the fierce Contagion spreads;
The spiry Flames now lift aloft their Heads,
Through the burst Sash a blazing Deluge pours,
360 And splitting Tiles descend in rattling Show'rs.
Now with thick Crouds th'enlighten'd Pavement swarms,
The Fire-man sweats beneath his crooked Arms,
A leathern Casque his vent'rous Head defends,
Boldly he climbs where thickest Smoak ascends;
365 Mov'd by the Mother's streaming Eyes and Pray'rs,
The helpless Infant through the Flame he bears,
With no less Virtue, than through hostile Fire
The *Dardan* Hero bore his aged Sire.
See forceful Engines spout their levell'd Streams,
370 To quench the Blaze that runs along the Beams;
The grappling Hook plucks Rafters from the Walls,
And Heaps on Heaps the smoaky Ruine falls.
Blown by strong Winds the fiery Tempest roars,
Bears down new Walls, and pours along the Floors;
375 The Heav'ns are all a-blaze, the Face of Night
Is cover'd with a sanguine dreadful Light:

'Twas such a Light involv'd thy Tow'rs, O *Rome,*
The dire Presage of mighty *Caesar's* Doom,
When the Sun veil'd in Rust his mourning Head,
380   And frightful Prodigies the Skies o'erspread.
Hark! the Drum thunders! far, ye Crouds, retire:
Behold! the ready Match is tipt with Fire,
The nitrous Store is laid, the smutty Train
With running Blaze awakes the barrell'd Grain;
385   Flames sudden wrap the Walls; with sullen Sound
The shatter'd Pile sinks on the smoaky Ground.
So when the Years shall have revolv'd the Date,
Th'inevitable Hour of *Naples'* Fate,
Her sap'd Foundations shall with Thunders shake,
390   And heave and toss upon the sulph'rous Lake;
Earth's Womb at once the fiery Flood shall rend,
And in th'Abyss her plunging Tow'rs descend.
      Consider, Reader, what Fatigues I've known,
The Toils, the Perils of the wintry Town;
395   What Riots seen, what bustling Crouds I bor'd,
How oft' I cross'd where Carts and Coaches roar'd;
Yet shall I bless my Labours, if Mankind
Their future Safety from my Dangers find.
Thus the bold Traveller, inur'd to Toil,
400   Whose Steps have printed *Asia's* desert Soil,
The barb'rous *Arabs* haunt; or shiv'ring crost
Dark *Greenland's* Mountains of eternal Frost;
Whom Providence, in Length of Years, restores
To the wish'd Harbour of his native Shores;
405   Sets forth his Journals to the publick View,
To caution, by his Woes, the wandring Crew.
      And now compleat my gen'rous Labours lye,
Finish'd, and ripe for Immortality.
Death shall entomb in Dust this mould'ring Frame,
410   But never reach th'eternal Part, my Fame.
When *Ward* and *Gildon,* mighty Names, are dead;
Or but at *Chelsea* under Custards read;
When Criticks crazy Bandboxes repair,
And Tragedies, turn'd Rockets, bounce in Air:
415   High-rais'd on *Fleetstreet* Posts, consign'd to Fame,
This Work shall shine, and Walkers bless my Name.

Thomas Parnell

A NIGHT-PIECE ON DEATH

BY the blue Tapers trembling Light,
No more I waste the wakeful Night,
Intent with endless view to pore
The Schoolmen and the Sages o'er:
5   Their Books from Wisdom widely stray,
Or point at best the longest Way.
I'll seek a readier Path, and go
Where Wisdom's surely taught *below*.
    How deep yon Azure dies the Sky!
10   Where Orbs of Gold unnumber'd lye,
While thro' their Ranks in silver pride
The nether Crescent seems to glide.
The slumb'ring Breeze forgets to breathe,
The Lake is smooth and clear beneath,
15   Where once again the spangled Show
Descends to meet our Eyes below.
The Grounds which on the right aspire,
In dimness from the View retire:
The Left presents a Place of Graves,
20   Whose Wall the silent Water laves.
That Steeple guides thy doubtful sight
Among the livid gleams of Night.
There pass with melancholy State,
By all the solemn Heaps of Fate,
25   And think, as softly-sad you tread
Above the venerable Dead,
Time was, like thee they Life possest,
And Time shall be, that thou shalt Rest.
    Those Graves, with bending Osier bound,
30   That nameless heave the crumbled Ground,

Quick to the glancing Thought disclose
Where *Toil* and *Poverty* repose.
    The flat smooth Stones that bear a Name,
The Chissels slender help to Fame,
35   (Which e'er our Sett of Friends decay
Their frequent Steps may wear away)
A *middle Race* of Mortals own,
Men, half ambitious, all unknown.
    The Marble Tombs that rise on high,
40   Whose Dead in vaulted Arches lye,
Whose Pillars swell with sculptur'd Stones,
Arms, Angels, Epitaphs and Bones,
These (all the poor Remains of State)
Adorn the *Rich*, or praise the *Great*;
45   Who while on Earth in Fame they live,
Are sensless of the Fame they give.
    Ha! while I gaze, pale *Cynthia* fades,
The bursting Earth unveils the Shades!
All slow, and wan, and wrap'd with Shrouds,
50   They rise in visionary Crouds,
And all with sober Accent cry,
Think, Mortal, what it is to dye.
    Now from yon black and fun'ral Yew,
That bathes the Charnel House with Dew,
55   Methinks I hear a *Voice* begin;
(Ye Ravens, cease your croaking Din,
Ye tolling Clocks, no Time resound
O'er the long Lake and midnight Ground)
It sends a Peal of hollow Groans,
60   Thus speaking from among the Bones.
    When Men my Scythe and Darts supply,
How great a *King* of *Fears* am I!
They view me like the last of Things:
They make, and then they dread, my Stings.
65   Fools! if you less provok'd your Fears,
No more my Spectre-Form appears.
Death's but a Path that must be trod,
If Man wou'd ever pass to God:
A Port of Calms, a State of Ease
70   From the rough Rage of swelling Seas.
    Why then thy flowing sable Stoles,
Deep pendent Cypress, mourning Poles,
Loose Scarfs to fall athwart thy Weeds,

Long Palls, drawn Herses, cover'd Steeds,
75   And Plumes of black, that as they tread,
Nod o'er the 'Scutcheons of the Dead?
     Nor can the parted Body know,
Nor wants the Soul, these Forms of Woe:
As Men who long in Prison dwell,
80   With Lamps that glimmer round the Cell,
When e'er their suffering Years are run,
Spring forth to greet the glitt'ring Sun:
Such Joy, tho' far transcending Sense,
Have pious Souls at parting hence.
85   On Earth, and in the Body plac't,
A few, and evil Years, they wast:
But when their Chains are cast aside,
See the glad Scene unfolding wide,
Clap the glad Wing and tow'r away,
90   And mingle with the Blaze of Day.

Matthew Prior

ALMA: OR, THE PROGRESS OF THE MIND

IN THREE CANTOS

Πάντα γέλως, καὶ πάντα κόνις, καὶ πάντα τὸ μηδεν·
Πάντα γὰρ ἐξ ἀλόγων ἐστὶ τα γιγνόμενα

Incert. ap. Stobaeum.

THE FIRST CANTO

MATTHEW met RICHARD; when or where
From Story is not mighty clear:
Of many knotty Points They spoke;
And *Pro* and *Con* by turns They took.
5   Ratts half the Manuscript have eat:
Dire Hunger! which We still regret:
O! may they ne'er again digest
The Horrors of so sad a Feast.
Yet less our Grief, if what remains,
10   Dear JACOB, by thy Care and Pains
Shall be to future Times convey'd.
It thus begins:
**** Here MATTHEW said:
   ALMA in Verse; in Prose, the MIND,
15   By ARISTOTLE's Pen defin'd,
Throughout the Body squat or tall,
Is, *bonâ fide*, All in All,
And yet, slap dash, is All again
In every Sinew, Nerve, and Vein.
20   Runs here and there, like HAMLET's Ghost;
While every where She rules the roast.

This *System*, RICHARD, We are told,
The Men of OXFORD firmly hold.
The CAMBRIDGE Wits, You know, deny
25 With *Ipse dixit* to comply.
They say (for in good truth They speak
With small Respect of that old GREEK)
That, putting all his Words together,
'Tis Three blew Beans in One blew Bladder.
30 ALMA, They strenuously maintain,
Sits Cock-horse on Her Throne, the Brain;
And from that Seat of Thought dispenses
Her Sov'reign Pleasure to the Senses.
Two *Optic* Nerves, They say, She tyes,
35 Like Spectacles, a-cross the Eyes;
By which the Spirits bring her Word,
Whene'er the Balls are fix'd, or stirr'd;
How quick at Park and Play they strike;
The Duke they court; the Toast they like;
40 And at ST. JAMES's turn their Grace
From former Friends, now out of Place.
  Without these Aids, to be more serious,
Her Pow'r, They hold, had been precarious:
The Eyes might have conspir'd her Ruin;
45 And She not known, what They were doing.
Foolish it had been, and unkind,
That They shou'd see, and She be blind.
  Wise Nature likewise, They suppose,
Has drawn two Conduits down our Nose:
50 Cou'd ALMA else with Judgment tell,
When *Cabbage* stinks, or *Roses* smell?
Or who wou'd ask for her Opinion
Between an *Oyster*, and an *Onion*?
For from most Bodies, DICK, You know,
55 Some little Bits ask Leave to flow;
And, as thro' these Canals They roll,
Bring up a Sample of the Whole.
Like Footmen running before Coaches,
To tell the Inn, what Lord approaches.
60 By Nerves about our Palate plac'd,
She likewise judges of the Taste.
Else (dismal Thought!) our Warlike Men
Might drink thick *Port* for fine *Champagne*;
And our ill-judging Wives and Daughters

65   Mistake Small-beer for *Citron*-Waters.
            Hence too, that She might better hear,
        She sets a Drum at either Ear;
        And Loud or Gentle, Harsh or Sweet,
        Are but th'*Alarums* which They beat.

70   Last, to enjoy her Sense of Feeling
        (A thing She much delights to deal in)
        A thousand little Nerves She sends
        Quite to our Toes, and Fingers Ends;
        And These in Gratitude again

75   Return their Spirits to the Brain;
        In which their Figure being printed
        (As just before, I think, I hinted)
        ALMA inform'd can try the Case,
        As She had been upon the Place.

80   Thus, while the Judge gives diff'rent Journeys
        To Country Counsel, and Attornies;
        He on the Bench in quiet sits,
        Deciding, as They bring the Writs.
        The POPE thus prays and sleeps at ROME,

85   And very seldom stirs from Home:
        Yet sending forth his Holy Spies,
        And having heard what They advise,
        He rules the Church's blest Dominions;
        And sets Men's Faith by His opinions.

90   The Scholars of the STAGYRITE,
        Who for the Old Opinion fight,
        Would make their Modern Friends confess,
        The diff'rence but from More to Less.
        The MIND, say They, while You sustain

95   To hold her Station in the Brain;
        You grant, at least, She is extended:
        Ergo the whole Dispute is ended.
        For, 'till To-morrow shou'd You plead
        From Form and Structure of the Head;

100   The MIND as visibly is seen
        Extended thro' the whole *Machine*.
        Why shou'd all Honor then be ta'en
        From Lower Parts to load the Brain;
        When other Limbs we plainly see,

105   Each in his way, as brisk as He?
        For Music, grant the Head receives it;
        It is the Artist's Hand that gives it.

And tho' the Scull may wear the Laurel;
The Soldier's Arm sustains the Quarrel.
110   Besides, the Nostrils, Ears, and Eyes
Are not his Parts, but his Allies.
Ev'n what You hear the Tongue proclaim,
Comes *ab Origine* from them.
What could the Head perform Alone,
115   If all Their friendly Aids were gone?
A foolish figure He must make;
Do nothing else, but sleep and ake.
    Nor matters it, that You can show,
How to the Head the Spirits go.
120   Those Spirits started from some Goal,
Before they thro' the Veins cou'd roll.
Now We shou'd hold Them much to blame,
If They went back, before They came.
    If therefore, as We must suppose,
125   They came from Fingers, and from Toes;
Or Toes, or Fingers, in this Case,
Of *Num-scull's* Self shou'd take the Place.
Disputing fair, You grant thus much,
That all Sensation is but Touch.
130   Dip but your Toes into cold Water;
Their Correspondent Teeth will chatter:
And strike the Bottom of your Feet;
You set your Head into a Heat.
The Bully beat, and happy Lover
135   Confess, that Feeling lies all over.
    Note here, LUCRETIUS dares to teach
(As all our Youth may learn from CREECH)
That Eyes were made, but cou'd not view;
Nor Hands embrace, nor Feet pursue:
140   But heedless Nature did produce
The Members first, and then the Use.
What Each must act, was yet unknown,
'Till All is mov'd by Chance alone.
    A Man first builds a Country Seat;
145   Then finds the Walls not good to eat.
Another plants, and wond'ring sees
Nor Books, nor Medals on his Trees.
Yet Poet and Philosopher
Was He, who durst such Whims aver.
150   Blest, for his Sake, be human Reason,

That came at all, tho' late, in Season.
    But no Man sure e'er left his House
And saddl'd *Ball*, with Thoughts so wild,
To bring a Midwife to his Spouse,
155 Before He knew She was with Child.
And no Man ever reapt his Corn,
Or from the Oven drew his Bread,
E'er Hinds and Bakers yet were born,
That taught him both to Sow, and Knead.
160 Before They're ask'd, can Maids refuse?
Can — Pray, says DICK, hold in your Muse.
While You *Pindaric* Truths rehearse;
She hobbles in Alternate Verse.
Verse? MAT. reply'd: is that my Care?
165 Go on, quoth RICHARD, soft and fair.
    This looks, friend DICK, as Nature had
But exercis'd the *Salesman's* Trade:
As if She haply had sat down,
And cut out Cloaths for all the Town;
170 Then sent them out to *Monmouth*-Street,
To try, what Persons they wou'd fit.
But ev'ry Free and Licens'd Taylor
Would in this *Thesis* find a Failure.
Should Whims like these his Head perplex,
175 How could he work for either Sex?
His Cloaths, as Atomes might prevail,
Might fit a Pismire, or a Whale.
No, no: He views with studious Pleasure
Your Shape, before He takes your Measure.
180 For real KATE He made the Boddice,
And not for an *Ideal* Goddess.
No Error near his Shop-board lurk'd:
He knew the Folks for whom He work'd.
Still to Their Size He aim'd his Skill:
185 Else, pr'ythee, who wou'd pay his Bill?
    Next, DICK, if Chance her self shou'd vary;
Observe, how Matters would miscarry:
Across your Eyes, Friend, place your Shoes;
Your Spectacles upon your Toes:
190 Then You and MEMMIUS shall agree,
How nicely Men would walk, or see.
    But Wisdom, peevish and cross-gain'd,
Must be oppos'd, to be sustain'd.

And still your Knowledge will increase,
195 As You make other People's less.
In Arms and Science 'tis the same:
Our Rival's Hurts create our Fame.
At Faubert's if Disputes arise
Among the Champions for the Prize;
200 To prove, who gave the fairer Butt,
JOHN shows the Chalk on ROBERT's Coat.
So, for the Honor of your Book,
It tells, where other Folks mistook:
And, as their Notions You confound,
205 Those You invent get farther Ground.
    The Commentators on old ARI-
STOTLE ('tis urg'd) in Judgment vary:
They to their own Conceits have brought
The Image of his general Thought.
210 Just as the Melancholic Eye
Sees Fleets and Armies in the Sky;
And to the poor Apprentice Ear
The Bells sound *Whittington* Lord May'r.
The Conj'rer thus explains his *Scheme*
215 Thus Spirits walk, and Prophets dream:
NORTH BRITONS thus have *Second Sight*;
And GERMANS free from Gunshot fight.
    THEODORET, and ORIGEN,
And fifty other Learned Men
220 Attest, that if their Comments find
The Traces of their Master's Mind;
ALMA can ne'er decay nor dye:
This flatly t'other Sect deny,
SIMPLICIUS, THEOPHRAST, DURAND;
225 Great Names, but Hard in Verse to stand.
They wonder Men should have mistook
The *Tenets* of their Master's Book;
And hold, that ALMA yields her Breath,
O'ercome by Age, and seiz'd by Death.
230 Now which were Wise? and which were Fools?
Poor ALMA sits between two Stools:
The more She reads, the more perplext;
The Comment ruining the Text;
Now fears, now hopes her doubtful Fate:
235 But, RICHARD, let her look to That —
Whilst We our own Affairs pursue.

These diff'rent *Systems*, Old or New,
A Man with half an Eye may see,
Were only form'd to disagree.
240 Now to bring Things to fair Conclusion,
And save much Christian Ink's Effusion;
Let me propose an Healing *Scheme*,
And sail along the Middle Stream:
For, DICK, if We could reconcile
245   Old ARISTOTLE with GASSENDUS;
How many would admire our Toil;
   And yet how few would comprehend us?
   Here, RICHARD, let my *Scheme* Commence.
Oh! may my Words be lost in Sense;
250 While pleas'd THALIA deigns to write
The Slips and Bounds of ALMA'S Flight.
   My simple *System* shall suppose,
That ALMA enters at the Toes;
That then She mounts by just Degrees
255 Up to the Ancles, Legs, and Knees:
Next, as the Sap of Life does rise,
She lends her Vigor to the Thighs:
And, all these under-Regions past,
She nestles somewhere near the Waste:
260 Gives Pain or Pleasure, Grief or Laughter;
As We shall show at large hereafter.
Mature, if not improv'd, by Time
Up to the Heart She loves to climb:
From thence, compell'd by Craft and Age,
265 She makes the Head her latest Stage.
   From the Feet upward to the Head;
Pithy, and short, says DICK: proceed.
   DICK, this is not an idle Notion:
Observe the Progress of the Motion.
270 First I demonstratively prove,
That Feet were only made to move;
And Legs desire to come and go:
For they have nothing else to do.
   Hence, long before the Child can crawl,
275 He learns to kick, and wince, and sprawl:
To hinder which, your Midwife knows
To bind Those Parts extremely close;
Lest ALMA newly enter'd in,
And stunn'd at her own Christ'ning's Din,

280 Fearful of future Grief and Pain,
Should silently sneak out again.
Full piteous seems young ALMA's Case:
As in a luckless Gamester's Place,
She would not play, yet must not pass.

285 Again as She grows something stronger,
And Master's Feet are swath'd no longer,
If in the Night too oft He kicks,
Or shows his *Loco-motive* Tricks;
These first Assaults fat KATE repays Him,

290 When half asleep She overlays Him.
Now mark, Dear RICHARD, from the Age
That Children tread this Worldly Stage,
Broom-staff or Poaker they bestride,
And round the Parlor love to ride;

295 'Till thoughtful Father's pious Care
Provides his Brood, next *Smithfield* Fair,
With Supplemental Hobby-Horses:
And happy be their Infant Courses!
Hence for some Years they ne'er stand still:

300 Their Legs, You see, direct their Will.
From opening Morn 'till setting Sun,
A-round the Fields and Woods They run:
They frisk, and dance, and leap, and play;
Nor heed, what FRIEND or SNAPE can say.

305 To Her next Stage as ALMA flies,
And likes, as I have said, the Thighs:
With *Sympathetic* Pow'r She warms,
Their good Allies and Friends, the Arms.
While BETTY dances on the Green;

310 And SUSAN is at Stool-ball seen:
While JOHN for Nine-pins does declare;
And ROGER loves to pitch the Bar;
Both Legs and Arms spontaneous move:
Which was the Thing I meant to prove.

315 Another Motion now She makes:
O need I name the Seat She takes?
His Thought quite chang'd the Stripling finds;
The Sport and Race no more He minds:
Neglected *Tray* and *Pointer* lye;

320 And Covies unmolested fly.
Sudden the jocund Plain He leaves;
And for the Nymph in Secret grieves.

In dying Accents He complains
Of cruel Fires, and raging Pains.
325 The Nymph too longs to be alone;
Leaves all the Swains; and sighs for One.
The Nymph is warm'd with young Desire;
And feels, and dies to quench His Fire.
They meet each Evening in the Grove:
330 Their Parley but augments their Love.
So to the Priest their Case They tell:
He ties the Knot; and all goes well.

But, O my MUSE, just Distance keep:
Thou art a Maid, and must not peep.
335 In nine Months Time the Boddice loose,
And Petticoats too short, disclose,
That at This Age the active Mind
About the Waste lies most confin'd;
And that young Life, and quick'ning Sense
340 Spring from His Influence darted thence.
So from the Middle of the World
The SUN's prolifick Rays are hurl'd:
'Tis from That Seat He darts those Beams,
Which quicken Earth with genial Flames.
345 DICK, who thus long had passive sat,
Here stroak'd his Chin, and cock'd his Hat;
Then slapp'd his Hand upon the Board;
And thus the Youth put in his Word.
Love's Advocates, sweet Sir, would find Him
350 A higher Place, than You assign'd Him.
Love's Advocates, DICK, who are those? —
The Poets, You may well suppose.
I'm sorry, Sir, You have discarded
The Men, with whom 'till now you herded.
355 *Prose-Men* alone, for private Ends,
I thought, forsook their ancient Friends.
In cor stillavit, crys LUCRETIUS;
If He may be allow'd to teach Us.
The self-same Thing soft OVID says
360 (A proper Judge in such a Case.)
HORACE his Phrase is *torret Jecur;*
And happy was that curious Speaker.
Here VIRGIL too has plac'd this Passion:
What signifies too long Quotation?
365 In *Ode* and *Epic* plain the Case is,

That Love holds One of these Two Places.
　　DICK, without Passion or Reflection,
I'll strait demolish this Objection.
　　First Poets, all the World agrees,
370　Write half to profit, half to please.
Matter and Figure They produce;
For Garnish This, and That for Use;
And, in the Structure of their Feasts,
They seek to feed, and please their Guests:
375　But One may balk this good Intent,
And take Things otherwise than meant.
Thus, if You Dine with my Lord May'r,
Roast-Beef, and Ven'son is your Fare;
Thence You proceed to Swan, and Bustard,
380　And persevere in Tart, and Custard:
But *Tulip-leaves,* and *Limon-peel*
Help only to adorn the Meal;
And painted Flags, superb and neat,
Proclaim You welcome to the Treat.
385　The Man of Sense his Meat devours;
But only smells the Peel, and Flow'rs:
And He must be an idle Dreamer,
Who leaves the Pie, and gnaws the Streamer.
　　That CUPID goes with Bow and Arrows,
390　And VENUS keeps her Coach and Sparrows,
Is all but Emblem, to acquaint One,
The Son is sharp, the Mother wanton.
Such Images have sometimes shown
A *Mystic* Sense, but oft'ner None.
395　For who conceives, what Bards devise,
That Heav'n is plac'd in CELIA's Eyes?
Or where's the Sense, direct or moral,
That Teeth are Pearl, or Lips are Coral?
　　Your HORACE owns, He various writ,
400　As wild, or sober Maggots bit:
And, where too much the Poet ranted,
The Sage Philosopher recanted.
His grave *Epistles* may disprove
The wanton *Odes* He made to LOVE.
405　　LUCRETIUS keeps a mighty Pother
With CUPID, and his fancy'd Mother:
Calls her great Queen of Earth and Air;
Declares, that Winds and Seas obey Her;

54

And, while Her Honor he rehearses,
410 Implores Her to inspire his Verses.
　　Yet, free from this Poetic Madness;
Next Page, He says in sober Sadness,
That She and all her fellow-Gods
Sit idling in their high Abodes,
415 Regardless of this World below,
Our Health or Hanging, Weal or Woe;
Nor once disturb their Heav'nly Spirits
With SCAPIN's Cheats, or CAESAR's Merits.
　　Nor e'er can LATIN Poets prove,
420 Where lies the real Seat of Love.
Jecur they burn, and *Cor* they pierce,
As either best supplies their Verse:
And, if Folks ask the Reason for't,
Say, one was long, and t'other short.
425 Thus, I presume, the BRITISH Muse,
May take the Freedom Strangers use.
In Prose our Property is greater:
Why should it then be less in Metre?
If CUPID throws a single Dart;
430 We make him wound the Lover's *Heart:*
　　But let your Friends in Verse suppose,
'Tis sure, He must transfix the *Liver:*
For Rhime with Reason may dispense;
And Sound has Right to govern Sense.
435 But let your Friends in Verse suppose,
What ne'er shall be allow'd in Prose:
Anatomists can make it clear,
The *Liver* minds his own Affair:
Kindly supplies our publick Uses;
440 And parts, and strains the Vital Juices:
Still lays some useful Bile aside,
To tinge the Chyle's insipid Tide:
Else We should want both Gibe and Satyr;
And all be burst with pure Good-nature.
445 Now Gall is bitter with a Witness;
And Love is all Delight and Sweetness.
My *Logic* then has lost it's Aim,
If Sweet and Bitter be the same:
And He, methinks, is no great Scholar,
450 Who can mistake Desire for Choler.
　　The like may of the *Heart* be said:

55

Courage and Terror there are bred.
All those, whose *Hearts* are loose and low,
Start, if they hear but the *Tattoo*:
455   And mighty Physical their Fear is:
For, soon as Noise of Combat near is,
Their Heart, descending to their Breeches,
Must give their Stomach cruel Twitches.
But Heroes who o'ercome or dye,
460   Have their Hearts hung extremely high;
The Strings of which, in Battel's Heat,
Against their very *Corslets* beat;
Keep Time with their own Trumpet's Measure;
And yield 'em most excessive Pleasure.
465   Now if 'tis chiefly in the Heart,
That Courage does it self exert;
'Twill be prodigious hard to prove,
That This is eke the Throne of Love.
Would Nature make One Place the Seat
470   Of fond Desire, and fell Debate?
Must People only take Delight in
Those Hours, when They are tir'd with Fighting?
And has no Man, but who has kill'd
A Father, right to get a Child?
475   These Notions then I think but idle:
And Love shall still possess the Middle.
This Truth more plainly to discover,
Suppose your Hero were a Lover.
Tho' He before had Gall and Rage,
480   Which Death, or Conquest must asswage;
He grows dispirited and low:
He hates the Fight, and shuns the Foe.
In scornful Sloth ACHILLES slept;
And for his Wench, like TALL-BOY, wept:
485   Nor would return to War and Slaughter;
'Till They brought back the Parson's Daughter.
ANTONIUS fled from ACTIUM's Coast,
AUGUSTUS pressing, ASIA lost:
His Sails by CUPID's Hand unfurl'd,
490   To keep the Fair, he gave the World.
EDWARD our Fourth, rever'd and crown'd,
Vig'rous in Youth, in Arms renown'd;
While ENGLAND's Voice, and WARWICK's Care
Design'd him GALLIA's Beauteous Heir;

495   Chang'd Peace and Pow'r for Rage and Wars,
        Only to dry One Widow's Tears.
            FRANCE's fourth HENRY we may see,
        A Servant to the fair D'ESTREE;
        When quitting COUTRAS prosp'rous Field,
500   And Fortune taught at length to yield,
        He from his Guards and Mid-night Tent,
        Disguis'd o'er Hills and Vallies went,
        To wanton with the sprightly Dame;
        And in his Pleasure lost his Fame.
505   Bold is the Critic, who dares prove,
          These Heroes were no Friends to Love;
        And bolder He, who dares aver,
        That they were Enemies to War.
        Yet, when their Thought should, now or never,
510   Have rais'd their *Heart*, or fir'd their *Liver*;
        Fond ALMA to those Parts was gone,
        Which LOVE more justly calls his own.
           Examples I could cite You more;
        But be contented with these Four:
515   For when One's Proofs are aptly chosen;
        Four are as valid as four Dozen.
        One came from GREECE, and one from ROME;
        The other Two grew nearer Home.
        For some in Antient Books delight:
520   Others prefer what Moderns write:
        Now I should be extremely loath,
        Not to be thought expert in Both.

THE SECOND CANTO

        But shall we take the MUSE abroad,
        To drop her idly on the Road?
        And leave our Subject in the middle;
        As BUTLER did his Bear and Fiddle?
5   Yet He, consummate Master, knew
        When to recede, and where pursue:
        His noble Negligences teach,
        What Others Toils despair to reach.
        He, perfect Dancer, climbs the Rope,
10   And balances your Fear and Hope:
        If after some distinguish'd Leap,
        He drops his Pole, and seems to slip;

Straight gath'ring all his active Strength,
He rises higher half his Length.
15 With Wonder You approve his Slight;
And owe your Pleasure to your Fright.
But, like poor ANDREW, I advance,
False *Mimic* of my Master's Dance:
A-round the Cord a while I sprawl;
20 And thence, tho' low, in earnest fall.
    My Preface tells You, I digress'd:
He's half absolv'd who has confess'd.
    I like, quoth DICK, your *Simile:*
And in Return, take Two from Me.
25 As Masters in the *Clare-obscure,*
With various Light your Eyes allure:
A flaming Yellow here They spread;
Draw off in Blew, or charge in Red:
Yet from these Colors odly mix'd,
30 Your Sight upon the Whole is fix'd.
Or as, again, your Courtly Dames,
(Whose Cloaths returning Birth-Day claims,)
By Arts improve the Stuffs they vary;
And Things are best, as most contrary.
35 The Gown with stiff Embroid'ry shining,
Looks charming with a slighter Lining:
The Out-, if INDIAN Figures stain;
The In-side must be rich and plain.
So You, great Authors, have thought fit,
40 To make Digression temper Wit:
When Arguments too fiercely glare;
You calm 'em with a milder Air:
To break their Points, You turn their Force;
And *Furbelow* the plain Discourse.
45 RICHARD, quoth MAT, these Words of Thine,
Speak something sly, and something fine:
But I shall e'en resume by *Theme;*
However Thou may'st praise, or blame.
    As People marry now, and settle;
50 Fierce Love abates his usual Mettle:
Worldly Desires, and Household Cares
Disturb the Godhead's soft Affairs:
So now, as Health or Temper changes,
In larger Compass ALMA ranges,
55 This Day below, the next above;

As light, or solid Whimsies move.
So Merchant has his House in Town,
And Country-Seat near BANSTED Down:
From One he dates his Foreign Letters,
60   Sends out his Goods, and duns his Debtors:
In t'other, at his Hours of Leisure,
He smokes his Pipe, and takes his Pleasure.
    And now your Matrimonial CUPID,
Lash'd on by Time, grows tir'd and stupid.
65   For Story and Experience tell Us,
That Man grows cold, and Woman jealous.
Both would their little Ends secure:
He sighs for Freedom, She for Pow'r.
His Wishes tend abroad to roam;
70   And Her's, to domineer at Home.
Thus Passion flags by slow Degrees;
And ruffl'd more, delighted less,
The busy Mind does seldom go
To those once charming Seats below:
75   But, in the Breast incamp'd, prepares
For well-bred Feints, and future Wars.
The Man suspects his Lady's crying
(When he last Autumn lay a-dying)
Was but to gain him to appoint Her
80   By Codicil a larger Jointure.
The Woman finds it all a Trick,
That He could swoon, when She was sick;
And knows, that in That Grief he reckon'd
On black-ey'd SUSAN for his Second.
85   Thus having strove some tedious Years
With feign'd Desires, and real Fears;
And tir'd with Answers, and Replies,
Of JOHN affirms, and MARTHA lies;
Leaving this endless Altercation,
90   The Mind affects a higher Station.
    POLTIS, that gen'rous King of THRACE,
I think, was in this very Case.
All ASIA now was by the Ears:
And Gods beat up for Voluntiers
95   To GREECE, and TROY; while POLTIS sat
In Quiet, governing his State.
And whence, said the Pacific King,
Does all this Noise, and Discord spring?

Why, PARIS took ATRIDES' Wife —
100   With Ease I could compose this Strife:
The injur'd Hero should not lose,
Nor the young Lover want a Spouse:
But HELEN chang'd her first Condition,
Without her Husband's just Permission.
105   What from the Dame can PARIS hope?
She may as well from Him elope.
Again, how can her old Good-man
With Honor take Her back again?
From hence I logically gather,
110   The Woman cannot live with Either,
Now I have Two right honest Wives,
For whose Possession No Man strives:
One to ATRIDES I will send;
And t'other to my TROJAN Friend.
115   Each Prince shall thus with Honor have,
What Both so warmly seem to crave:
The Wrath of Gods and Man shall cease;
And POLTIS live and die in Peace.
     DICK, if this Story pleaseth Thee,
120   Pray thank DAN POPE, who told it Me.
     Howe'er swift ALMA's Flight may vary;
(Take this by way of *Corollary*:)
Some Limbs She finds the very same,
In Place, and Dignity, and Name:
125   These dwell at such convenient Distance,
That each may give his Friend Assistance.
Thus He who runs or dances, begs
The equal Vigor of Two Legs:
So much to both does ALMA trust,
130   She ne'er regards, which goes the first.
TEAGUE would make neither of them stay,
When with Himself he ran away.
The Man who struggles in the Fight,
Fatigues left Arm, as well as right:
135   For whilst one Hand exalts the Blow,
And on the Earth extends the Foe;
T'other would take it wond'rous ill,
If in your Pocket He lay still.
And when you shoot, and shut one Eye,
140   You cannot think, He would deny
To lend the t'other friendly Aid,

Or wink, as Coward, and affraid.
No, Sir; whilst He withdraws his Flame,
His Comrade takes the surer Aim.
145 One Moment if his Beams recede;
As soon as e'er the Bird is dead,
Opening again, He lays his Claim,
To half the Profit, half the Fame,
And helps to Pocket up the Game.
150 'Tis thus, One Tradesman slips away,
To give his Part'ner fairer Play.
    Some Limbs again in Bulk or Stature
Unlike, and not a-kin by Nature,
In Concert act, like modern Friends;
155 Because one serves the t'other's Ends.
The Arm thus waits upon the Heart,
So quick to take the Bully's Part,
That one, tho' warm, decides more slow,
Than t'other executes the Blow.
160 A Stander-by may chance to have it,
E'er HACK himself perceives, He gave it.
    The am'rous Eyes thus always go
A-stroling for their Friends below:
For long before the 'Squire and Dame
165 Have *tête à tête* reliev'd their Flame;
E'er Visits yet are brought about,
The Eye by Sympathy looks out;
Knows FLORIMEL, and longs to meet Her;
And, if He sees, is sure to greet Her,
170 Tho' at Sash-Window, on the Stairs,
At Court, nay (Authors say) at Pray'rs.—
    The Funeral of some valiant Knight
May give this Thing it's proper Light.
View his Two Gantlets: these declare,
175 That Both his Hands were us'd to War.
And from his Two gilt Spurs 'tis learn'd,
His Feet were equally concern'd.
But have You not with Thought beheld
The Sword hang dangling o'er the Shield?
180 Which shows the Breast, That Plate was us'd to,
Had an Ally right Arm to trust to.
And by the Peep-holes in his Crest,
Is it not virtually confest,
That there his Eye took distant Aim,

185   And glanc'd Respect to that bright Dame,
        In whose Delight his Hope was center'd,
        And for whose Glove his Life he ventur'd?
            Objections to my general *System*
        May 'rise, perhaps, and I have mist them:
190   But I can call to my Assistance
        Proximity (mark that!) and Distance:
        Can prove, that all Things, on Occasion,
        Love Union, and desire Adhesion;
        That ALMA merely is a Scale;
195   And Motives, like the Weights, prevail.
        If neither Side turn down or up,
        With Loss or Gain, with Fear or Hope;
        The Balance always would hang ev'n,
        Like MAH'MET's Tomb, 'twixt Earth and Heav'n.
200   This RICHARD, is a curious Case:
        Suppose your Eyes sent equal Rays
        Upon two distant Pots of Ale,
        Not knowing, which was Mild or Stale:
        In this sad State your doubtful Choice
205   Would never have the casting Voice:
        Which Best, or Worst, You could not think;
        And die You must, for want of Drink:
        Unless some Chance inclines your Sight,
        Setting one Pot in fairer Light;
210   Then You prefer or A, or B,
        As Lines and Angles best agree:
        Your Sense resolv'd impells your Will;
        She guides your Hand, — So drink your Fill.
            Have you not seen a Baker's Maid
215   Between two equal Panniers sway'd?
        Her Tallies useless lie, and idle,
        If plac'd exactly in the Middle:
        But forc'd from this unactive State,
        By virtue of some casual Weight;
220   On either Side You hear 'em clatter,
        And judge of right and left-hand Matter.
            Now, RICHARD, this coercive Force,
        Without your Choice, must take it's Course.
        Great Kings to Wars are pointed forth,
225   Like loaded Needles to the North.
        And Thou and I, by Pow'r unseen,
        Are barely Passive, and suck'd in

To HENAULT's Vaults, or CELIA's Chamber,
As Straw and Paper are by Amber.
230 If we sit down to play or set
(Suppose at *Ombre* or *Basset*)
Let People call us Cheats, or Fools;
Our Cards and We are equal Tools.
We sure in vain the Cards condemn:
235 Our selves both cut and shuffl'd them.
In vain on Fortune's Aid rely:
She only is a Stander-by.
Poor Men! poor Papers! We and They
Do some impulsive Force obey;
240 And are but play'd with: — Do not play.
But Space and Matter we should blame:
They palm'd the Trick that lost the Game.
     Thus to save further Contradiction,
Against what You may think but Fiction;
245 I for Attraction, DICK, declare:
Deny it those bold Men that dare.
As well your Motion, as your Thought
Is all by hidden Impulse wrought:
Ev'n saying, that You Think or Walk,
250 How like a Country 'Squire you talk?
     Mark then: — Where Fancy or Desire
Collects the Beams of Vital Fire;
Into that Limb fair ALMA slides,
And there, *pro tempore*, resides.
255 She dwells in NICHOLINI's Tongue,
When PYRRHUS chants the Heav'nly Song.
When PEDRO does the Lute command,
She guides the cunning Artist's Hand.
Thro' MACER's Gullet she runs down,
260 When the vile Glutton dines alone.
And void of Modesty and Thought,
She follows BIBO's endless Draught.
Thro' the soft Sex again She ranges;
As Youth, Caprice, or Fashion changes.
265 Fair ALMA careless and serene,
In FANNY's sprightly Eyes is seen;
While they diffuse their Infant Beams,
Themselves not conscious of their Flames.
Again fair ALMA sits confest,
270 On FLORIMEL's experter Breast;

When She the rising Sigh constrains,
And by concealing speaks her Pains.
In CYNTHIA's Neck fair ALMA glows;
When the vain Thing her Jewels shows:
275   When JENNY's Stays are newly lac'd,
Fair ALMA plays about her Waste;
And when the swelling Hoop sustains
The rich Brocard, fair ALMA deigns
Into that lower Space to enter,
280   Of the large Round, Her self the Center.
    Again: That Single Limb or Feature
(Such is the cogent Force of Nature)
Which most did ALMA's Passion move,
In the first Object of her Love,
285   For ever will be found confest,
And printed on the am'rous Breast.
    O ABELARD, ill-fated Youth,
Thy Tale will justify this Truth:
But well I weet, thy cruel Wrong
290   Adorns a nobler Poet's Song.
Dan POPE for thy Misfortune griev'd,
With kind Concern, and Skill has weav'd
A silken Web; and ne'er shall fade
It's Colors: gently has He laid
295   The Mantle o'er thy sad Distress:
And VENUS shall the Texture bless.
He o'er the weeping Nun has drawn,
Such artful Folds of Sacred Lawn,
That LOVE with equal Grief and Pride,
300   Shall see the Crime, He strives to hide:
And softly drawing back the Veil,
The God shall to his Vot'ries tell
Each conscious Tear, each blushing Grace,
That deck'd Dear ELOISA's Face.
305   Happy the Poet, blest the Lays,
Which BUCKINGHAM has deign'd to praise.
    Next, DICK, as Youth and Habit sways,
A hundred Gambols ALMA plays.
If, whilst a Boy, JACK run from Schole,
310   Fond of his Hunting-horn, and Pole;
Tho' Gout and Age his Speed detain,
Old JOHN halloo's his Hounds again.
By his Fire-side he starts the Hare;

And turns Her in his Wicker-Chair:
315 His Feet, however lame, You find,
Have got the better of his Mind.
    If while the Mind was in her Leg,
The Dance affected nimble PEG;
Old MADGE, bewitch'd at Sixty one,
320 Calls for *Green Sleeves*, and *Jumping Joan*.
In public Mask, or private Ball,
From *Lincoln's Inn*, to *Goldsmith's Hall*,
All Christmas long away She trudges;
Trips it with Prentices and Judges:
325 In vain her Children urge her Stay;
And Age or Palsey bar the Way.
But if those Images prevail,
Which whilom did affect the Tail;
She still reviews the ancient Scene;
330 Forgets the forty Years between:
Awkwardly gay, and odly merry,
Her Scarf pale Pink, her Head-Knot Cherry;
O'er heated with *Ideal* Rage,
She cheats her Son, to wed her Page.
335   If ALMA, whilst the Man was young,
Slip'd up too soon into his Tongue:
Pleas'd with his own fantastic Skill,
He lets that Weapon ne'er lie still.
On any Point if You dispute;
340 Depend upon it, He'll confute:
Change Sides; and You increase your Pain;
For He'll confute You back again.
For One may speak with TULLY's Tongue;
Yet all the while be in the wrong.
345 And 'tis remarkable, that They
Talk most, who have the least to say.
Your dainty Speakers have the Curse,
To plead bad Causes down to worse:
As Dames, who Native Beauty want,
350 Still uglier look, the more They paint.
    Again: If in the Female Sex
ALMA should on this Member fix;
(A cruel and a desp'rate Case,
From which Heav'n shield my lovely Lass!)
355 For evermore all Care is vain,
That would bring ALMA down again.

As in habitual Gout, or Stone,
The only Thing that can be done,
Is to correct your Drink and Diet,
360   And keep the inward Foe in Quiet:
So, if for any Sins of Our's,
Or our Forefathers, Higher Pow'rs,
Severe tho' just, afflict our Life
With that Prime Ill, a talking Wife;
365   'Till Death shall bring the kind Relief,
We must be Patient, or be Deaf,
     You know, a certain Lady, DICK,
Who saw Me, when I last was sick:
She kindly talk'd, at least three Hours,
370   Of *Plastic* Forms, and *Mental* Pow'rs:
Describ'd our pre-existing Station,
Before this vile Terrene Creation:
And lest I should be weary'd, Madam,
To cut Things short, came down to ADAM;
375   From whence, as fast as She was able,
She drowns the World, and builds up BABEL;
Thro' SYRIA, PERSIA, GREECE She goes;
And takes the ROMANS in the Close.
     But We'll descant on gen'ral Nature:
380   This is a *System*, not a Satyr.
     Turn We this Globe; and let Us see,
How diff'rent Nations disagree,
In what We wear, or eat and drink;
Nay, DICK, perhaps in what We think.
385   In Water as You smell and tast
The Soyls, thro' which it rose and past:
In ALMA's Manners You may read
The Place, where She was born and bred.
     One People from their swadling Bands
390   Releas'd their Infants Feet and Hands:
Here ALMA to these Limbs was brought;
And SPARTA's Offspring kick'd and fought.
     Another taught their Babes to talk,
E'er they could yet in Goe-carts walk:
395   There ALMA settl'd in the Tongue;
And Orators from ATHENS sprung.
     Observe but in these Neighb'ring Lands,
The diff'rent Use of Mouths and Hands:
As Men repos'd their various Hopes,

400   In Battles These, and Those in Tropes.
        In BRITAIN's Isles, as HEYLYN notes,
      The Ladies trip in Petticoats;
      Which, for the Honour of their Nation,
      They quit but on some great Occasion.
405   Men there in Breeches clad You view:
      They claim that Garment, as their due.
      In TURKEY the Reverse appears;
      Long Coats the haughty Husband wears,
      And greets His Wife with angry Speeches;
410   If She be seen without her Breeches.
        In our Fantastic *Climes* the Fair
      With cleanly Powder dry their Hair:
      And round their lovely Breast and Head
      Fresh Flow'rs their mingl'd Odors shed.
415   Your nicer HOTTENTOTES think meet
      With Guts and Tripe to deck their Feet:
      With down-cast Looks on TOTTA's Legs,
      The ogling Youth most humbly begs,
      She would not from his Hopes remove
420   At once his Breakfast, and his Love:
      And if the skittish Nymph should fly;
      He in a double Sense must die.
        We simple *Toasters* take Delight
      To see our Women's Teeth look white.
425   And ev'ry saucy ill-bred Fellow
      Sneers at a Mouth profoundly yellow.
      In CHINA none hold Women sweet,
      Except their Snags are black as Jett.
      King CHIHU put Nine Queens to Death,
430   Convict on Statute, *Iv'ry Teeth.*.
        At TONQUIN if a Prince should die;
      (As Jesuits write, who never lye)
      The Wife, and Counsellor, and Priest,
      Who serv'd Him most, and lov'd Him best;
435   Prepare, and light his Fun'ral Fire,
      And chearful on the Pile expire.
      In EUROPE 'twould be hard to find
      In each Degree One half so kind.
        Now turn We to the farthest East,
440   And there observe the Gentry Drest.
      Prince GIOLO, and his Royal Sisters,
      Scarr'd with ten thousand comely Blisters;

The Marks remaining on the Skin,
To tell the Quality within.
445 Distinguish'd Slashes deck the Great:
As each excells in Birth, or State;
His Oylet-holes are more, and ampler:
The King's own Body was a Samplar.
Happy the Climate, where the *Beau*
450 Wears the same Suit for Use, and Show:
And at a small Expence your Wife,
If once well pink'd, is cloth'd for Life.
    Westward again the INDIAN Fair,
Is nicely smear'd with Fat of Bear.
455 Before You see, You smell your Toast,
And sweetest She, who stinks the most.
The finest Sparks and cleanest *Beaux*
Drip from the Shoulders to the Toes.
How sleek their Skins! their Joints how easy!
460 There Slovens only are not greasy.
    I mention'd diff'rent Ways of Breeding:
Begin We in our Children's Reading.
To Master JOHN the ENGLISH Maid
A Horn-book gives of Ginger-bread:
465 And that the Child may learn the better,
As He can name, He eats the Letter:
Proceeding thus with vast Delight,
He spells, and gnaws, from Left to Right.
But shew a HEBREW's hopeful Son,
470 Where We suppose the Book begun;
The Child would thank You for your Kindness,
And read quite backward from our *Finis:*
Devour He Learning ne'er so fast;
Great A would be reserv'd the last.
475   An equal Instance of this Matter,
Is in the Manners of a Daughter.
In EUROPE, if a harmless Maid,
By Nature and by Love betray'd,
Should e'er a Wife become a Nurse;
480 Her Friends would look on Her the Worse.
In CHINA, DAMPIER's Travels tell Ye;
(Look in his Index for PAGELLI:)
Soon as the BRITISH Ships unmoore,
And jolly Long-boat rows to Shore;
485 Down come the Nobles of the Land:

Each brings his Daughter in his Hand,
Beseeching the Imperious Tar
To make Her but One Hour his Care.
The tender Mother stands affrighted,
490 Lest her dear Daughter should be slighted:
And poor Miss YAYA dreads the Shame
Of going back the Maid She came.
    Observe how Custom, DICK, compells
The Lady that in EUROPE dwells:
495 After her Tea She slips away;
And what to do, One need not say.
Now see how great POMONQUE's Queen
Behav'd Herself amongst the Men:
Pleas'd with her Punch, the Gallant Soul
500 First drank, then water'd in the Bowl;
And sprinkl'd in the Captain's Face
The Marks of Her Peculiar Grace —
    To close this Point, We need not roam
For Instances so far from Home.
505 What parts gay FRANCE from sober SPAIN?
A little rising Rocky Chain.
Of Men born South or North o'th' Hill,
Those seldom move; These ne'er stand still.
DICK, You love Maps, and may perceive
510 ROME not far distant from GENEVE.
If the good POPE remains at Home,
He's the First Prince in CHRISTENDOME.
Choose then, good POPE, at Home to stay;
Nor Westward curious take Thy Way.
515 Thy Way unhappy should's Thou take
From TIBER'S Bank to LEMAN-Lake;
Thou art an Aged Priest no more,
But a Young flaring Painted Whore:
Thy Sex is lost: Thy Town is gone,
520 No longer ROME, but BABYLON.
That some few Leagues should make this Change,
To Men unlearn'd seems mighty strange.
    But need We, Friend, insist on This?
Since in the very CANTONS SWISS,
525 All your philosophers agree
And prove it plain, that One may be
A Heretic, or True Believer,
On this, or t'other Side a River.

Here with an artful Smile, quoth DICK,
530   Your Proofs come mighty full, and thick —
      The Bard on this extensive Chapter,
Wound up into Poetic Rapture,
Continu'd: RICHARD, cast your Eye
By Night upon a Winter-Sky:
535   Cast it by Day-light on the Strand,
Which compasses fair ALBION's Land:
If You can count the Stars that glow
Above, or Sands that lie below;
Into those Common-places look,
540   Which from great Authors I have took;
And count the Proofs I have collected,
To have my Writings well protected.
These I lay by for Time of Need;
And Thou may'st at thy Leisure read.
545   For standing every Critic's Rage,
I safely will to future Age
My *System*, as a Gift, bequeath,
Victorious over Spight, and Death.

THE THIRD CANTO

RICHARD, who now was half a-sleep,
Rous'd; nor would longer Silence keep:
And Sense like this, in vocal Breath
Broke from his twofold Hedge of Teeth.
5   Now if this Phrase too harsh be thought;
POPE, tell the World, 'tis not my Fault.
Old HOMER taught us thus to speak;
If 'tis not Sense; at least 'tis GREEK.
      As Folks, quoth RICHARD, prone to Leasing,
10   Say Things at first because they're pleasing;
Then prove what they have once asserted,
Nor care to have their Lie deserted;
'Till their own Dreams at Length deceive 'em;
And oft repeating, they believe 'em.
15   Or as again those am'rous Blades,
Who trifle with their Mother's maids;
Tho' at the first their wild Desire,
Was but to quench a present Fire;
Yet if the object of their Love
20   Chance by LUCINA's Aid to prove;

They seldom let the Bantling roar
In Basket, at a Neighbour's Door:
But by the flatt'ring Glass of Nature,
Viewing themselves in *Cake-bread's* Feature;
25   With serious Thought and Care support,
What only was begun in Sport.
    Just so with You, my Friend, it fares,
Who deal in Philosophic Wares:
Atoms You cut; and Forms You measure,
30   To gratifie your private Pleasure;
'Till airy Seeds of casual Wit
Do some fantastic Birth beget:
And pleas'd to find your *System* mended,
Beyond what You at first intended,
35   The happy Whimsey You pursue;
'Till You at length believe it true.
Caught by your own delusive Art,
You fancy first, and then assert.
    Quoth MATTHEW: Friend, as far as I
40   Thro' Art or Nature cast my Eye,
This *Axiom* clearly I discern,
That One must Teach, and t'Other Learn.
No Fool PYTHAGORAS was thought:
While He his weighty Doctrines taught;
45   He made his list'ning Scholars stand,
Their Mouth still cover'd with their Hand:
Else, may be, some odd-thinking Youth,
Less Friend to Doctrine than to Truth,
Might have refus'd to let his Ears
50   Attend the Musick of the Spheres;
Deny'd all *transmigrating* Scenes,
And introduc'd the Use of Beans.
From great LUCRETIUS take His Void;
And all the World is quite destroy'd.
55   Deny DES-CART His subtil Matter;
You leave Him neither Fire, nor Water.
How odly would Sir ISAAC look,
If You, in Answer to his Book,
Say in the Front of your Discourse,
60   That Things have no *Elastic* Force?
How could our *Chymic* Friends go on,
To find the *Philosophic* Stone;
If You more pow'rful Reasons bring,

PRIOR

To prove, that there is no such Thing?
65   Your Chiefs in Sciences and Arts,
Have great Contempt of ALMA's Parts.
They find, She giddy is, or dull;
She doubts, if Things are void, or full:
And who should be presum'd to tell,
What She Her self should see, or feel?
70   She doubts, if two and two make four;
Tho' She has told them ten times o'er.
It can't — it may be — and it must:
To which of these must ALMA trust?
Nay, further yet They make Her go,
75   In doubting, if She doubts, or no.
Can *Syllogysm* set Things right?
No: *Majors* soon with *Minors* fight:
Or, Both in friendly Consort join'd;
The *Consequence* limps false behind.
80   So to some Cunning-Man She goes,
And asks of Him, how much She knows.
With Patience grave He hears Her speak;
And from his short Notes, gives Her back
What from her Tale He comprehended:
85   Thus the Dispute is wisely ended.
    From the Account the Loser brings,
The Conj'ror knows, who stole the Things.
    'Squire (interrupted DICK) since when
Were You amongst these Cunning-Men?
90   Dear DICK, quoth MAT, let not Thy Force
Of Eloquence spoil my Discourse.
I tell Thee, this is ALMA's Case,
Still asking, what some Wise-man says,
Who does his Mind in Words reveal,
95   Which All must grant; tho' Few can spell.
You tell Your Doctor, that Y'are ill:
And what does He, but write a Bill,
Of which You need not read one Letter?
The worse the Scrawl, the Dose the better.
100   For if You knew but what You take;
Tho' You recover, He must break.
    Ideas, Forms, and *Intellects*,
Have furnish'd out three diff'rent Sects.
Substance, or *Accident* divides
105   All EUROPE into adverse Sides.

72

Now, as engag'd in Arms or Laws,
You must have Friends to back your Cause:
In *Philosophic* Matters so
Your Judgment must with others go.
110   For as in Senates, so in Scholes,
Majority of Voices rules.
      Poor ALMA, like a lonely Deer,
O'er Hills and Dales does doubtful err:
With panting Haste, and quick Surprise,
115   From ev'ry Leaf that stirs, She flies;
'Till mingl'd with the neighb'ring Herd,
She slights what erst She singly hear'd:
And now, exempt from Doubt and Dread,
She dares pursue; if They dare lead:
120   As Their Example still prevails;
She tempts the Stream, or leaps the Pales.
      He then, quoth DICK, who by Your Rule
Thinks for Himself, becomes a Fool.
As Party-Man who leaves the rest,
125   Is call'd but *Whimsical* at Best.
Now, by Your Favour, Master MAT,
Like RALPHO, here I smell a Rat.
I must be listed in Your Sect;
Who, tho' They teach not, can protect.
130   Right, RICHARD, MAT. in Triumph cri'd;
So put off all Mistrust and Pride.
And while My Principles I beg;
Pray answer only with Your Leg.
Believe what friendly I advise:
135   Be first secure; and then be wise.
The Man within the Coach that sits,
And to another's Skill submits,
Is safer much (whate'er arrives)
And warmer too, than Hee that drives.
140   So, DICK *Adept,* tuck back Thy Hair;
And I will pour into Thy Ear
Remarks, which None did e'er disclose,
In smooth-pac'd Verse, or hobling Prose.
Attend, Dear DICK; but don't reply:
145   And Thou may'st prove as Wise as I.
      When ALMA now in diff'rent Ages,
Has finish'd Her ascending Stages;
Into the Head at length She gets,

And There in Public Grandeur sits,
150 To judge of Things, and censure Wits.
 Here, RICHARD, how could I explain,
The various Lab'rinths of the Brain?
Surprise My Readers, whilst I tell 'em
Of *Cerebrum*, and *Cerebellum?*
155 How could I play the Commentator
On *Dura*, and on *Pia Mater?*
Where Hot and Cold, and Dry and Wet,
Strive each the t'other's Place to get;
And with incessant Toil and Strife,
160 Would keep Possession during Life.
I could demonstrate every Pore,
Where Mem'ry lays up all her Store;
And to an Inch compute the Station,
'Twixt Judgment, and Imagination.
165 O Friend! I could display much Learning,
At least to Men of small Discerning.
The Brain contains ten thousand Cells:
In each some active Fancy dwells;
Which always is at Work, and framing
170 The several Follies I was naming.
As in a Hive's vimineous Dome,
Ten thousand Bees enjoy their Home;
Each does her studious Action vary,
To go and come, to fetch and carry:
175 Each still renews her little Labor;
Nor justles her assiduous Neighbour:
Each — whilst this *Thesis* I maintain;
I fancy, DICK, I know thy Brain.
O with the mighty *Theme* affected,
180 Could I but see thy Head dissected!
 My Head, quoth DICK, to serve your Whim?
Spare That, and take some other Limb.
Sir, in your nice Affairs of *System*,
Wise Men propose; but Fools assist 'em.
185 Says MATTHEW: RICHARD, keep thy Head,
And hold thy Peace; and I'll proceed.
 Proceed? quoth DICK: Sir, I aver,
You have already gone too far.
When People once are in the Wrong;
190 Each Line they add, is much too long.
Who fastest walks, but walks astray,

Is only furthest from his Way.
Bless your Conceits! must I believe,
Howe'er absurd, what You conceive;
195 And, for your Friendship, live and dye
A Papist in Philosophy?
I say, whatever You maintain
Of ALMA in the Heart, or Brain;
The plainest Man alive may tell Ye,
200 Her Seat of Empire is the Belly:
From hence She sends out those Supplies,
Which make Us either stout, or wise:
The Strength of ev'ry other Member,
Is founded on your Belly-Timber:
205 The Qualms or Raptures of your Blood
Rise in Proportion to your Food:
And if you would improve your Thought;
You must be fed, as well as taught.
Your Stomach makes your Fabric roll;
210 Just as the Biass rules the Bowl.
That great ACHILLES might imploy
The Strength, design'd to ruin TROY;
He Din'd on Lion's Marrow, spread
On Toasts of Ammunition-Bread:
215 But by His Mother sent away,
Amongst the THRACIAN Girls to play,
Effeminate He sat, and quiet:
Strange Product of a Cheese-cake Diet!
Now give my Argument fair Play;
220 And take the Thing the t'other Way:
The Youngster, who at Nine and Three
Drinks with his Sisters Milk and Tea,
From Break-fast reads, 'till twelve a Clock,
BURNET and HEYLYN, HOBBES and LOCK:
225 He pays due Visits after Noon
To Cousin ALICE, and Uncle JOHN:
At Ten from Coffee-House or Play
Returning, finishes the Day.
But give him Port, and potent Sack;
230 From *Milk-sop* He starts up *Mohack:*
Holds that the Happy know no Hours;
So thro' the Street at Midnight scow'rs:
Breaks Watch-men's Heads, and Chairmen's Glasses;
And thence proceeds to nicking Sashes:

235 Till by some tougher Hand o'ercome,
  And first knock'd down, and then led Home;
  He damns the Foot-man, strikes the Maid,
  And decently reels up to Bed.
   Observe the various Operations
240 Of Food, and Drink in several Nations.
  Was ever TARTAR fierce or cruel,
  Upon the Strength of Water-Gruel?
  But who shall stand His Rage and Force;
  If first he rides, then eats his Horse?
245 Sallads, and Eggs, and lighter Fare
  Tune the ITALIAN Spark's Guitar.
  And, if I take *Dan* CONGREVE right;
  Pudding and Beef makes BRITONS fight.
  TOKAY and COFFEE cause this Work,
250 Between the GERMAN and the TURK:
  And Both, as They Provisions want,
  Chicane, avoid, retire, and faint.
   Hunger and Thirst, or Guns and Swords,
  Give the same Death in diff'rent Words.
255 To push this Argument no further;
  To starve a Man, in Law, is Murther.
   As in a WATCHE's fine Machine,
  Tho' many artful Springs are seen;
  The added Movements, which declare
260 How full the Moon, how old the Year,
  Derive their secondary Pow'r
  From that, which simply points the Hour.
  For, tho' these Gim-cracks were away;
  (QUARE would not swear; but QUARE would say)
265 However more reduc'd and plain,
  The Watch would still a Watch remain:
  But if the *Horal* Orbite ceases;
  The whole stands still, or breaks to pieces;
  Is now no longer what it was;
270 And You may e'en go sell the Case.
  So if unprejudic'd you scan
  The Goings of this Clock-work, Man;
  You find a hundred Movements made
  By fine Devices in his Head:
275 But 'tis the Stomach's solid Stroke,
  That tells his Being, what's a Clock.
  If You take off his *Rhet'ric-Trigger;*

He talks no more in Mood and Figure:
Or clog his *Mathematic*-Wheel;
280   His Buildings fall; his Ship stands still.
Or lastly, break his *Politic*-Weight;
His Voice no longer rules the State.
Yet if these finer Whims were gone;
Your Clock, tho' plain, would still go on:
285   But spoil the Engine of Digestion;
And You entirely change the Question.
ALMA's Affairs no Pow'r can mend;
The Jest, alas! is at an End:
Soon ceases all this worldly Bustle;
290   And you consign the Corps to RUSSEL.
    Now make your ALMA come or go,
From Leg to Hand, from Top to Toe;
Your *System*, without My Addition,
Is in a very sad Condition.
295   So HARLEQUIN extoll'd his Horse,
Fit for the War, or Road, or Course;
His Mouth was soft; his Eye was good;
His Foot was sure as ever trod:
One Fault he had, a Fault indeed;
300   And what was that? The Horse was Dead.
    DICK, from these Instances and Fetches,
Thou mak'st of Horses, Clocks, and Watches,
Quoth MAT, to Me thou seem'st to mean,
That ALMA is a mere *Machine;*
305   That telling others what's a Clock,
She knows not what Her self has struck;
But leaves to Standers-by the Tryal,
Of what is mark'd upon her Dial.
    Here hold a Blow, good Friend, quoth DICK,
310   And rais'd his Voice exceeding quick:
Fight fair, Sir: what I never meant
Don't You infer. In Argument,
Similies are like Songs in Love:
They much describe; they nothing prove.
315   MAT, who was here a little gravel'd,
Tost up his Nose, and would have cavil'd:
But calling HERMES to his Aid,
Half pleas'd, half angry, thus He said:
    Where mind ('tis for the Author's Fame)
320   That MATTHEW call'd, and HERMES came.

In Danger Heroes, and in Doubt
Poets find Gods to help 'em out.
   Friend RICHARD, I begin to see,
That You and I shall scarce agree.
325   Observe how odly you behave:
The more I grant, the more You crave.
But, Comrade, as I said just now,
I should affirm, and You allow.
We *System*-makers can sustain
330   The *Thesis*, which, You grant, was plain;
And with Remarks and Comments teaze Ye;
In case the Thing before was easy.
But in a Point obscure and dark,
We fight as LEIBNITS did with CLARK;
335   And when no Reason we can show,
Why Matters This or That Way go;
The shortest Way the Thing We try,
And what We know not, We deny:
True to our own o'erbearing Pride,
340   And false to all the World beside.
   That old Philospher grew cross,
Who could not tell what Motion was:
Because He walk'd against his Will;
He fac'd Men down, that He stood still.
345   And He who reading on the Heart,
(When all his *Quodlibets* of Art
Could not expound it's Pulse and Heat)
Swore, He had never felt it beat.
CHRYSIPPUS, foil'd by EPICURUS,
350   Makes bold (JOVE bless Him!) to assure Us,
That all things, which our Mind can view,
May be at once both false, and true.
And MALBRANCH has an odd Conceit,
As ever enter'd FRENCHMAN's Pate:
355   Says He, so little can our Mind
Of Matter, or of Spirit find,
That We by Guess, at least, may gather
Something, which may be Both, or Neither.
Faith, DICK, I must confess, 'tis true
360   (But this is only *Entre Nous*)
That many knotty Points there are,
Which All discuss, but Few can clear:
As Nature slily had thought fit,

For some by-Ends, to cross-bite Wit.
365 Circles to square, and Cubes to double,
Would give a Man excessive Trouble:
The Longitude uncertain roams,
In spight of WHISTON and his Bombs.
What *System*, DICK, has right averr'd
370 The Cause, why Woman has no Beard;
Or why, as Years our Frame attack,
Our Hair grows white, our Teeth grow black?
In Points like These We must agree,
Our Barber knows as much as We.
375 Yet still unable to explain,
We must persist the best We can;
With Care our *Systems* still renew,
And prove Things likely, tho' not true.
      I could, Thou see'st, in quaint Dispute,
380 By dint of *Logic* strike Thee mute;
With learned Skill, now push, now parry,
From *Darii* to *Bocardo* vary,
And never yield, or what is worst,
Never conclude the Point discours'd.
385 Yet, that you *hic & nunc* may know,
How much You to my Candor owe;
I'll from the Disputant descend,
To show Thee, I assume the Friend:
I'll take Thy Notion for my own —
390 (So most Philosophers have done)
It makes my *System* more complete:
DICK, can it have a Nobler Fate?
Take what Thou wilt, said DICK, Dear Friend;
But bring thy Matters to an End.
395   I find, quoth MAT, Reproof is vain:
Who first offend will first complain.
Thou wishest, I should make to Shoar;
Yet still put'st in Thy thwarting Oar.
What I have told Thee fifty times
400 In Prose, receive for once in Rhimes:
A huge fat Man in Countrey-Fair,
Or City-Church, (no matter where)
Labor'd and push'd amidst the Croud,
Still bauling out extremely loud;
405 Lord save Us! why do People press?
Another marking his Distress,

Friendly reply'd; Plump Gentleman,
Get out as fast as e'er You can:
Or cease to push, or to exclaim:
410 You make the very Croud You blame.
  Says DICK, your Moral does not need
The least Return; So e'en proceed:
Your Tale, howe'er apply'd, was short:
So far, at least, I thank You for't.
415   MAT took his Thanks, and in a Tone
More Magisterial, thus went on.
  Now ALMA settles in the Head;
As has before been sung, or said:
And here begins this Farce of Life;
420 Enter Revenge, Ambition, Strife:
Behold on both Sides Men advance,
To form in Earnest BAYS's Dance.
L'AVARE not using Half his Store,
Still grumbles, that He has no more;
425 Strikes not the present Tun, for fear
The Vintage should be bad next Year:
And eats To-day with inward Sorrow,
And Dread of fancy'd Want To-morrow.
Abroad if the *Sour-tout* You wear,
430 Repells the Rigor of the Air;
Would You be warmer, if at Home
You had the Fabric, and the Loom?
And if two Boots keep out the Weather;
What need You have two Hides of Leather?
435 Could PEDRO, think You, make no Tryal
Of a *Sonata* on his Viol,
Unless he had the total Gut,
Whence every String at first was cut?
  When RARUS shows You his Carton;
440 He always tells You, with a Groan,
Where two of that same Hand were torn,
Long before You, or He were born.
  Poor VENTO's Mind so much is crost,
For Part of His PETRONIUS lost;
445 That He can never take the Pains
To understand what yet remains.
  What Toil did honest CURIO take?
What strict Enquiries did He make,
To get one Medal wanting yet,

450 And perfect all his ROMAN Sett?
'Tis found: and O his happy Lot!
'Tis bought, lock'd up, and lies forgot:
Of These no more You hear Him speak:
He now begins upon the GREEK.
455 These rang'd and show'd, shall in their Turns
Remain obscure, as in their Urns.
My Copper-Lamps at any Rate,
For being True Antique, I bought;
Yet wisely melted down my Plate,
460 On Modern Models to be wrought:
And Trifles I alike pursue;
Because They're Old; because They're New.
     DICK, I have seen You with Delight,
For GEORGY make a Paper-Kite.
465 And simple Odes too many show Ye,
My servile Complaisance to CLOE.
Parents and Lovers are decreed
By Nature Fools — That's brave indeed!
Quoth DICK: such Truths are worth receiving:
470 Yet still DICK look'd, as not believing.
     Now, ALMA, to Divines and Prose
I leave Thy Frauds, and Crimes, and Woes:
Nor think To-night of Thy Ill-Nature,
But of Thy Follies, Idle Creature,
475 The turns of Thy uncertain Wing,
And not the Malice of Thy Sting:
Thy Pride of being great and wise,
I do but mention, to despise.
I view with Anger and Disdain,
480 How little gives Thee Joy, or Pain:
A Print, a *Bronze,* a Flow'r, a Root,
A Shell, a Butter-fly can do't.
Ev'n a Romance, a Tune, a Rhime
Help Thee to pass the tedious Time,
485 Which else would on thy Hand remain:
Tho' flown, it ne'er looks back again.
And Cards are dealt, and Chess-boards brought,
To ease the Pain of Coward-Thought.
Happy Result of Human Wit!
490 That ALMA may Her self forget.
     DICK, thus We act; and thus We are,
Or toss'd by Hope, or sunk by Care.

81

With endless Pain This Man pursues
What, if he gain'd, He could not use:
495   And T'other fondly Hopes to see
What never was, nor e'er shall be.
We err by Use, go wrong by Rules;
In Gesture grave, in Action Fools:
We join Hypocrisie to Pride,
500   Doubling the Faults, We strive to hide.
Or grant, that with extreme Surprize,
We find our selves at Sixty wise;
And twenty pretty Things are known,
Of which we can't accomplish One;
505   Whilst, as my *System* says, the Mind
Is to these upper Rooms confin'd:
Should I, my Friend, at large repeat
Her borrow'd Sense, her fond Conceit;
The Bede-roll of her Vicious Tricks;
510   My Poem would be too prolix.
For could I my Remarks sustain,
Like SOCRATES, or MILES MONTAIGNE;
Who in these Times would read my Books,
But TOM O' STILES, or JOHN O' NOKES?
515   As BRENTFORD Kings discrete and wise,
After long Thought and grave Advice,
Into LARDELLA's Coffin peeping,
Saw nought to cause their Mirth or Weeping:
So ALMA now to Joy or Grief
520   Superior, finds her late Relief:
Weary'd of being High, or Great,
And nodding in her Chair of State;
Stun'd and worn out with endless Chat,
Of WILL did this, and NAN said that;
525   She finds, poor Thing, some little Crack,
Which Nature, forc'd by Time, must make;
Thro' which She wings her destin'd Way:
Upward She soars; and down drops Clay:
While some surviving Friend supplies
530   *Hic jacet*, and a hundred Lies.
      O RICHARD, 'till that Day appears,
Which must decide our Hopes and Fears:
Would FORTUNE calm her present Rage,
And give us Play-things for our Age:
535   Would CLOTHO wash her Hands in Milk,

And twist our Thread with Gold and Silk:
Would She in Friendship, Peace, and Plenty,
Spin out our Years to four times Twenty:
And should We both in this Condition,
540   Have conquer'd Love, and worse Ambition;
(Else those two Passions, by the way,
May chance to show us scurvy Play:)
Then RICHARD, then should We sit down,
Far from the Tumult of this Town:
545   I fond of my well-chosen Seat,
My Pictures, Medals, Books compleat:
Or should We mix our friendly Talk,
O'er-shaded in that Fav'rite Walk,
Which Thy own Hand had whilom planted,
550   Both pleas'd with all we thought We wanted:
Yet then, ev'n then one cross Reflection
Would spoil Thy Grove, and My Collection:
Thy Son and his, e'er that, may die;
And Time some uncouth Heir supply;
555   Who shall for nothing else be known,
But spoiling All, that Thou hast done.
Who set the Twigs, shall He remember,
That is in Hast to sell the Timber?
And what shall of thy woods remain,
560   Except the Box that threw the Main?
     Nay may not Time and Death remove
The near Relations, whom I love?
And my COZ TOM, or his COZ MARY
(Who hold the Plough, or skim the Dairy)
565   My Fav'rite Books and Pictures sell
To SMART, or DOILEY by the Ell?
Kindly throw in a little Figure,
And set their Price upon the bigger?
Those who could never read their Grammar;
570   When my dear Volumes touch the Hammer;
May think Books best, as richest bound.
My Copper Medals by the Pound
May be with learned Justice weigh'd:
To turn the Ballance, OTHO's Head
575   May be thrown in; And for the Mettle,
The Coin may mend a Tinker's Kettle —
     Tir'd with these Thoughts — Less tir'd than I,
Quoth DICK, with Your Philosophy —

That People live and dye, I knew
580 An hour ago, as well as You.
And if Fate spins Us longer Years,
Or is in haste to take the Shears;
I know, We must Both Fortunes try,
And bear our Evils, wet or dry.
585 Yet let the Goddess smile, or frown;
Bread We shall eat, or white, or brown:
And in a Cottage, or a Court,
Drink fine *Champaigne,* or muddl'd *Port.*
What need of Books these Truths to tell,
590 Which Folks perceive, who cannot spell?
And must We spectacles apply,
To view, what hurts our naked Eye?
        Sir, if it be Your Wisdom's Aim,
To make Me merrier than I am;
595 I'll be all Night at Your Devotion —
Come on, Friend; broach the pleasing Notion:
But if you would depress my Thought;
Your *System* is not worth a Groat —
        For PLATO's Fancies what care I?
600 I hope You would not have me die,
Like simple CATO in the Play,
For any Thing that He can say?
E'en let Him of *Ideas* speak
        To Heathens in his Native GREEK.
605 If to be sad is to be wise;
I do most heartily despise
Whatever SOCRATES has said,
Or TULLY writ, or WANLEY read.
        Dear DRIFT, to set our Matters right,
610 Remove these Papers from my Sight;
Burn MAT's DES-CART', and ARISTOTLE:
Here, JONATHAN, Your Master's Bottle.

Allan Ramsay

LUCKY SPENCE'S LAST ADVICE

THREE Times the Carline grain'd and rifted,
Then frae the Cod her Pow she lifted,
In bawdy Policy well gifted,
    When she now faun,
5   *That Death na langer wad be shifted,*
    She thus began:

My loving Lasses, I maun leave ye,
But dinna wi' ye'r Greeting grieve me,
Nor wi' your Draunts and Droning deave me,
10   But bring's a Gill;
For Faith, my Bairns, ye may believe me,
    'Tis 'gainst my Will.

O black Ey'd *Bess* and mim Mou'd *Meg*,
O'er good to work or yet to beg;
15 Lay Sunkots up for a sair Leg,
       For whan ye fail,
Ye'r Face will not be worth a Feg,
    Nor yet ye'r Tail.

Whan e'er ye meet a Fool that's fow,
20 That ye're a Maiden gar him trow,
Seem nice, but stick to him like Glew;
       And whan set down,
Drive at the Jango till he spew,
    Syn he'll sleep soun.

25 Whan he's asleep, then dive and catch
His ready Cash, his Rings or Watch;
And gin he likes to light his Match
       At your Spunk-box,
Ne'er stand to let the fumbling Wretch
30   E'en take the Pox.

Cleek a' ye can be Hook or Crook,
Ryp ilky Poutch frae Nook to Nook;
Be sure to truff his Pocket-book,
      Saxty Pounds *Scots*
35   Is nae deaf Nits: In little Bouk
      Lie great Bank-Notes.

To get a Mends of whinging Fools,
That's frighted for Repenting-Stools.
Wha often, whan their Metal cools,
40   Turn sweer to pay,
Gar the Kirk-Boxie hale the Dools
      Anither Day.

But dawt Red Coats, and let them scoup,
Free for the Fou of cutty Stoup;
45   To gee them up, ye need na hope
      E'er to do well:
They'll rive ye'r Brats and kick your Doup,
      And play the Deel.

There's ae sair Cross attends the Craft,
50   That curst Correction-house, where aft
Vild Hangy's Taz ye'r Riggings saft
      Makes black and blae,
Enough to pit a Body daft;
      But what'll ye say.

55   Nane gathers Gear withoutten Care,
Ilk Pleasure has of Pain a Skare;
Suppose then they should tirl ye bare,
      And gar ye sike,
E'en learn to thole; 'tis very fair
60   Ye're Nibour like.

Forby, my Looves, count upo' Losses,
Ye'r Milk-white Teeth and Cheeks like Roses,
Whan Jet-black Hair and Brigs of Noses,
      Faw doun wi' Dads
65   To keep your Hearts up 'neath sic Crosses,
      Set up for Bawds.

Wi' well crish'd Loofs I hae been canty,
Whan e'er the Lads wad fain ha'e faun t'ye;
To try the auld Game *Taunty Raunty*,
70   Like Coosers keen,
They took Advice of me Your Aunty,
        If ye were clean.

Then up I took my Siller Ca'
And whistle'd benn whiles ane, whiles twa;
75 Roun'd in his Lug, That there was a
        Poor Country *Kate*,
As halesom as the Well of *Spaw*,
        But unka blate.

Sae whan e'er Company came in,
80 And were upo' a merry Pin,
I slade away wi' little Din,
        And muckle Mense,
Lest Conscience Judge, it was a' ane
        To Lucky *Spence*.

85 My Bennison come on good Doers,
Who spend their Cash on Bawds and Whores;
May they ne'er want the Wale of Cures
        For a sair Snout:
Foul fa' the Quacks wha that Fire smoors,
90   And puts nae out.

My Malison light ilka Day
On them that drink, and dinna pay,
But tak a Snack and rin away;
        May't be their Hap
95 Never to want a Gonorrhoea,
        Or rotten Clap.

Lass gi'e us in anither Gill,
A Mutchken, Jo, let's tak our Fill;
Let Death syne registrate his Bill
100   Whan I want Sense,
I'll slip away with better Will,
        Quo' Lucky *Spence*.

John Dyer

GRONGAR HILL

SILENT Nymph, with curious Eye!
Who, the purple Ev'ning, lye
On the Mountain's lonely Van,
Beyond the Noise of busy Man,
5   Painting fair the form of Things,
While the yellow Linnet sings;
Or the tuneful Nightingale
Charms the Forest with her Tale;
Come with all thy various Hues,
10 Come, and aid thy Sister Muse;
Now while *Phoebus* riding high
Gives Lustre to the Land and Sky!
Grongar Hill invites my Song,
Draw the Landskip bright and strong;
15 *Grongar,* in whose Mossie Cells
Sweetly-musing Quiet dwells:
Grongar, in whose silent Shade,
For the modest Muses made,
So oft I have, the Even still,
20 At the Fountain of a Rill,
Sate upon a flow'ry Bed,
With my Hand beneath my Head;
And stray'd my Eyes o'er *Towy*'s Flood,
Over Mead, and over Wood,
25 From House to House, from Hill to Hill,
'Till Contemplation had her fill.
　　About his chequer'd Sides I wind,
And leave his Brooks and Meads behind,
And Groves, and Grottoes where I lay,
30 And Vistoes shooting Beams of Day:

Wider and wider spreads the Vale;
As Circles on a smooth Canal:
The Mountains round, unhappy Fate,
Sooner of later, of all Height!
35 Withdraw their Summits from the Skies,
And lessen as the others rise:
Still the Prospect wider spreads,
Adds a thousand Woods and Meads,
Still it widens, widens still,
40 And sinks the newly-risen Hill,
    Now, I gain the Mountain's Brow,
What a Landskip lies below!
No Clouds, no Vapours intervene,
But the gay, the open Scene
45 Does the Face of Nature show,
In all the Hues of Heaven's Bow!
And, swelling to embrace the Light,
Spreads around beyond the Sight.
    Old Castles on the Cliffs arise,
50 Proudly tow'ring in the Skies!
Rushing from the Woods, the Spires
Seem from hence ascending Fires!
Half his Beams *Apollo* sheds,
On the yellow Mountain-Heads!
55 Gilds the Fleeces of the Flocks;
And glitters on the broken Rocks!
    Below me Trees unnumber'd rise,
Beautiful in various Dies:
The gloomy Pine, the Poplar blue,
60 The yellow Beech, the sable Yew,
The slender Firr, that taper grows,
The sturdy Oak with broad-spread Boughs.
And beyond the purple Grove,
Haunt of *Phillis,* Queen of Love!
65 Gawdy as the op'ning Dawn,
Lies a long and level Lawn,
On which a dark Hill, steep and high,
Holds and charms the wand'ring Eye!
Deep are his Feet in *Towy's* Flood,
70 His Sides are cloath'd with waving Wood,
And antient Towers crown his Brow,
That cast an awful Look below;
Whose ragged Walls the Ivy creeps,

And with her Arms from falling keeps.
75 So both a Safety from the Wind
On mutual Dependance find.
 'Tis now the Raven's bleak Abode;
'Tis now th' Apartment of the Toad;
And there the Fox securely feeds; ⎫
80 And there the pois'nous Adder breeds, ⎬
Conceal'd in Ruins, Moss and Weeds: ⎭
While, ever and anon, there falls,
Huge heaps of hoary moulder'd Walls.
Yet Time has seen, that lifts the low,
85 And level lays the lofty Brow,
Has seen this broken Pile compleat, ⎫
Big with the Vanity of State; ⎬
But transient is the Smile of Fate! ⎭
A little Rule, a little Sway,
90 A Sun-beam in a Winter's Day
Is all the Proud and Mighty have,
Between the Cradle and the Grave.
 And see the Rivers how they run,
Thro' Woods and Meads, in Shade and Sun,
95 Sometimes swift, and sometimes slow,
Wave succeeding Wave they go
A various Journey to the Deep,
Like human Life to endless Sleep!
Thus is Nature's Vesture wrought,
100 To instruct our wand'ring Thought;
Thus she dresses green and gay,
To disperse our Cares away.
 Ever charming, ever new,
When will the Landskip tire the View!
105 The Fountain's Fall, the River's Flow,
The woody Vallies, warm and low;
The windy Summit, wild and high,
Roughly rushing on the Sky!
The pleasent Seat, the ruin'd Tow'r,
110 The naked Rock, the shady Bow'r;
The Town and Village, Dome and Farm, ⎫
Each give each a double Charm, ⎬
As Pearls upon an *Aethiop*'s Arm. ⎭
 See on the Mountain's southern side, ⎫
115 Where the Prospect opens wide, ⎬
Where the Ev'ning gilds the Tide; ⎭

How close and small the Hedges lie!
What streaks of Meadows cross the Eye!
A Step methinks may pass the Stream,
120 So little distant Dangers seem;
So we mistake the Future's face,
Ey'd thro' Hope's deluding Glass;
As yon Summits soft and fair,
Clad in colours of the Air,
125 Which, to those who journey near,
Barren, and brown, and rough appear.
Still we tread tir'd the same coarse Way.
The Present's still a cloudy Day.
    O may I with my self agree,
130 And never covet what I see:
Content me with an humble Shade,
My Passions tam'd, my Wishes laid;
For while our Wishes wildly roll,
We banish Quiet from the Soul:
135 'Tis thus the Busy beat the Air;
And Misers gather Wealth and Care.
    Now, ev'n now, my Joy runs high,
As on the Mountain-turf I lie;
While the wanton *Zephir* sings,
140 And in the Vale perfumes his Wings;
While the Waters murmur deep;
While the Shepherd charms his Sheep;
While the Birds unbounded fly, ⎫
And with Musick fill the Sky. ⎬
145 Now, ev'n now, my Joy runs high.⎭
    Be full, ye Courts, be great who will;
Search for Peace, with all your Skill:
Open wide the lofty Door,
Seek her on the marble Floor,
150 In vain ye search, she is not there;
In vain ye search the Domes of Care!
Grass and Flowers Quiet treads,
On the Meads, and Mountain-heads,
Along with Pleasure, close ally'd,
155 Ever by each other's Side: ⎫
And often, by the murm'ring Rill, ⎬
Hears the Thrush, while all is still, ⎬
Within the Groves of *Grongar Hill.* ⎭

Richard Savage

THE BASTARD

A POEM INSCRIB'D WITH ALL DUE REVERENCE TO MRS BRET, ONCE COUNTESS OF MACCLESFIELD

Decet haec dare Dona Novercam. Ov. Met.

IN gayer hours, when high my fancy ran,
The muse, exulting, thus her lay began.
    Blest be the *Bastard*'s birth! thro' wond'rous ways,
He shines eccentric like a Comet's blaze.
5   No sickly fruit of faint compliance he;
He! stampt in nature's mint of extasy!
He lives to build, not boast, a gen'rous race:
No tenth transmitter of a foolish face.
His daring hope, no sire's example bounds;
10   His first-born lights, no prejudice confounds.
He, kindling from within, requires no flame;
He glories in a *Bastard*'s glowing name.
    Born to himself, by no possession led,
In freedom foster'd, and by fortune fed;
15   Nor Guides, nor Rules, his sov'reign choice controul,
His body independant, as his soul,
Loos'd to the world's wide range — enjoyn'd no aim;
Prescrib'd no duty, and assign'd no Name:
Nature's unbounded son, he stands alone,
20   His heart unbias'd, and his mind his own.
    O *Mother*, yet *no* Mother! — 'tis to you,
My thanks for such distinguish'd claims are due.
You, unenslav'd to nature's narrow laws,
Warm championess for *freedom*'s sacred cause,
25   From all the dry devoirs of blood and line,
From ties maternal, moral and divine,

Discharg'd my grasping soul; push'd me from shore,
And launch'd me into life without an oar.
   What had I lost, if conjugally kind,
30   By nature hating, yet by vows confin'd,
Untaught the matrimonial bounds to slight,
And coldly conscious of a husband's right,
You had *faint-drawn* me with a *form* alone,
A lawful lump of life by force your own!
35   Then, while your backward will retrench'd desire,
And unconcurring spirits lent no fire,
I had been born your dull, domestic heir;
Load of your life, and motive of your care;
Perhaps been poorly rich, and meanly great;
40   The slave of pomp, a cypher in the state;
Lordly neglectful of a worth unknown,
And slumb'ring in a *seat,* by *chance* my own.
   Far other blessings wait the *Bastard's* lot;
Conceiv'd in rapture, and with fire begot!
45   Strong, as necessity, he starts away,
Climbs against wrongs, & brightens into day.
   Thus unprophetic, lately misinspir'd,
I sung; gay, flatt'ring hope my fancy fir'd;
Inly secure, thro' conscious scorn of ill;
50   Nor taught by wisdom how to ballance will,
Rashly deceiv'd, I saw no *pits* to shun;
But thought to *purpose,* and to *act* were *one;*
Heedless what pointed cares pervert his way,
Whom caution arms not, and whom woes betray;
55   But now expos'd and shrinking from distress,
I fly to shelter, while the tempests press;
My muse to grief resigns the varying tone,
The raptures languish, and the numbers groan.
   O memory! — thou soul of joy and pain!
60   Thou actor of our passions o'er again!
Why dost thou aggravate the wretch's woe?
Why add continuous smart to ev'ry blow?
Few are my joys; alas! how soon forgot!
On that *kind* quarter thou invad'st me not,
65   While sharp & numberless my sorrows fall
Yet thou repeat'st and multiply'st 'em all.
   Is chance a guilt? that my disastrous heart,
For mischief never meant must ever smart?
Can self-defence be sin? — Ah, plead no more!

70   What tho' no purpos'd malice stain'd thee o'er?
Had heav'n befriended thy unhappy side,
Thou had'st not been provok'd — Or *thou* had'st died.
    Far be the guilt of home-shed blood from all,
On whom unsought, embroiling dangers fall!
75   Still the pale *dead* revives and lives to me,
To me! thro' *Pity*'s eye condemn'd to see.
Remembrance veils his rage, but swells his fate;
Griev'd I forgive, and am grown cool too late,
Young and unthoughtful then; who knows one day,
80   What rip'ning virtues might have made their way!
He might have liv'd till folly died in shame,
Till kindling wisdom felt a thirst for fame.
He might perhaps his country's friend have prov'd,
Been gen'rous, happy, candid and belov'd.
85   He might have sav'd some worth, now doom'd to fall,
And I, perchance, in him have *murder'd* all.
    O fate of late Repentance! always vain:
Thy remedies but lull undying pain.
Where shall my hope find rest? — No mother's care
90   Shielded my infant innocence with prayer:
No father's guardian hand my youth maintain'd,
Call'd forth my virtues, and from vice restrain'd.
Is it not time to snatch some pow'rful arm,
First to advance, then screen from future harm?
95   Am I return'd from death, to live in pain?
Or would *imperial pity* save in vain?
Distrust it not! — What blame can *mercy* find,
Which gives at once a life, and rears a mind?
    Mother, miscall'd, farewell — Of soul severe,
100   This sad reflection yet may force one tear:
All I was wretched by to You I ow'd,
Alone from strangers ev'ry comfort flow'd.
    Lost to the life *you* gave, *your* son no more,
And now *adopted*, who was *doom'd* before,
105   *New-born* I may a nobler mother claim;
But dare not whisper her immortal *name;*
Supreamly lovely, and serenely great!
Majestic *mother* of a kneeling *state!*
Queen of a people's hearts, who ne'er before
110   Agreed — yet now with one consent *adore!*
One contest yet remains in this desire,
Who most shall give applause, where all admire.

Edward Young

ON LIFE, DEATH, AND IMMORTALITY

HUMBLY INSCRIBED TO THE
RIGHT HON. ARTHUR ONSLOW, ESQ.
SPEAKER OF THE HOUSE OF COMMONS

TIR'D nature's sweet restorer, balmy *Sleep*!
He, like the world, his ready visit pays
Where Fortune smiles; the wretched he forsakes:
Swift on his downy pinion flies from Woe,
5   And lights on lids unsully'd with a Tear.
     From short (as usual) and disturb'd Repose,
I wake: How happy they who wake no more!
Yet that were vain, if Dreams infest the Grave.
I wake, emerging from a sea of Dreams
10   Tumultuous; where my wreck'd, desponding thought
From wave to wave of *fancy'd* Misery,
At random drove, her helm of Reason lost.
Tho' now restor'd, 'tis only Change of Pain,
(A bitter change!) severer for severe.
15   The *Day* too short for my distress! and *Night*,
Even in the *Zenith* of her dark Domain,
Is Sunshine, to the colour of my Fate.
     Night, sable Goddess! from her *Ebon* throne,
In rayless Majesty, now stretches forth
20   Her leaden Scepter o'er a slumb'ring world.
Silence, how dead? and Darkness, how profound?
Nor Eye, nor list'ning Ear an Object finds;
Creation sleeps. 'Tis, as the gen'ral Pulse
Of Life stood still, and Nature made a Pause;
25   An aweful Pause! prophetic of her End.

95

And let her prophecy be soon fulfill'd;
Fate! drop the Curtain; I can lose no more.
 Silence, and *Darkness!* solemn Sisters! Twins
From antient *Night*, who nurse the tender Thought
30 To *Reason*, and on *Reason* build *Resolve*,
(That column of true Majesty in Man)
Assist me: I will thank you in the Grave;
The grave, your Kingdom: *There* this frame shall fall
A victim sacred to your dreary shrine.
35 But what are Ye? THOU, who didst put to flight
Primaeval *Silence*, when the Morning-Stars
Exulting, shouted o'er the rising Ball;
O THOU! whose Word from solid *Darkness* struck
That spark, the Sun; strike Wisdom from my soul;
40 My soul which flies to thee, her Trust, her Treasure:
As misers to their Gold, while others rest.
 Thro' this Opaque of *Nature*, and of Soul,
This double Night, transmit one pitying ray,
To lighten, and to chear. O lead my Mind,
45 (A Mind that fain would wander from its Woe,)
Lead it thro' various scenes of *Life*, and *Death*,
And from each scene, the noblest Truths inspire.
Nor less inspire my *Conduct*, than my *Song;*
Teach my best Reason, Reason; my best Will
50 Teach Rectitude; and fix my firm Resolve
Wisdom to wed, and pay her long Arrear.
Nor let the Vial of thy Vengeance, pour'd
On this devoted head, be pour'd in vain.
 The Bell strikes *One*. We take no note of Time,
55 But from its Loss. To give it then a Tongue,
Is wise in man. As if an Angel spoke,
I feel the solemn Sound. If heard aright,
It is the *Knell* of my departed Hours;
Where are they? With the Years beyond the Flood.
60 It is the *Signal* that demands Dispatch;
How much is to be done? my Hopes and Fears
Start up alarm'd, and o'er life's narrow Verge
Look down — on what? a fathomless Abyss;
A dread Eternity! how surely *mine!*
65 And can Eternity belong to me,
Poor Pensioner on the bounties of an Hour?
 How poor? how rich? how abject? how august?
How complicate? how wonderful is man?

How passing wonder HE, who made him such?
70 Who centred in our make such strange Extremes?
From different Natures marvelously mixt,
Connection exquisite of distant Worlds!
Distinguisht *Link* in Being's endless Chain!
Midway from *Nothing* to the *Deity!*
75 A Beam etherial sully'd, and absorpt!
Tho' sully'd, and dishonour'd, still Divine!
Dim Miniature of Greatness absolute!
An Heir of Glory! a frail Child of Dust!
Helpless Immortal! Insect *infinite!*
80 A Worm! a God! — I tremble at myself,
And in myself am lost! At home a Stranger,
Thought wanders up and down, surpriz'd, aghast,
And wond'ring at her *own:* How Reason reels?
O what a Miracle to man is Man,
85 Triumphantly distress'd? what Joy, what Dread?
Alternately transported, and alarm'd!
What can preserve my Life? or what destroy?
An Angel's arm can't snatch me from the Grave:
Legions of Angels can't confine me There.
90   'Tis past Conjecture; all things rise in proof:
While o'er my limbs *Sleep's* soft dominion spread,
What, tho' my Soul phantastic Measures trod,
O'er Fairy Fields; or mourn'd along the gloom
Of pathless Woods; or down the craggy Steep
95 Hurl'd headlong, swam with pain the mantled Pool;
Or scal'd the Cliff; or danc'd on hollow Winds,
With antic Shapes, wild Natives of the Brain?
Her ceaseless Flight, tho' devious, speaks her Nature
Of subtler Essence than the trodden Clod;
100 Active, aërial, tow'ring, unconfin'd,
Unfetter'd with her gross Companion's fall.
Ev'n silent Night proclaims my Soul *immortal;*
Ev'n silent Night proclaims eternal Day.
For human weal, Heaven husbands all events,
105 Dull sleep instructs, nor sport vain Dreams in vain.
    Why then *their* Loss deplore, that are not lost?
Why wanders wretched Thought their tombs around
In infidel Distress? Are *Angels* there?
Slumbers, rak'd up in dust, Etherial fire?
110 They live! they greatly live a life on earth
Unkindled, unconceiv'd; and from an eye

Of Tenderness, let heavenly pity fall
On me, more justly number'd with the Dead.
This is the Desart, *this* the Solitude:
115   How populous? how vital, is the Grave?
This is Creation's melancholy Vault,
The Vale funereal, the sad *Cypress* gloom;
The land of Apparitions, empty Shades!
All, all on earth is *Shadow,* all beyond
120   Is *Substance;* the reverse is Folly's *creed:*
How solid all, where Change shall be no more?
    This is the bud of Being, the dim Dawn,
The twilight of our Day, the Vestibule.
Life's Theater as yet is shut, and Death,
125   Strong Death alone can heave the massy Bar,
This gross impediment of Clay remove,
And make us Embryos of Existence free.
From *real* life, but little more remote
Is *He,* not yet a candidate for Light,
130   The *future* Embryo, slumb'ring in his Sire.
Embryos we must be, till we burst the Shell,
Yon ambient, azure shell, and spring to Life,
The life of Gods: O Transport! and of Man.
Yet man, fool man! *here* burys all his Thoughts;
135   Inters celestial Hopes without one Sigh.
Prisoner of Earth, and pent beneath the Moon,
Here pinions all his Wishes; wing'd by Heaven
To fly at Infinite; and reach it there,
Where *Seraphs* gather Immortality,
140   On life's fair Tree, fast by the throne of God.
What golden Joys ambrosial clust'ring glow
In HIS full beam, and ripen for the Just,
Where momentary Ages are no more?
Where Time, and Pain, and Chance, and Death expire?
145   And is it in the Flight of threescore years,
To push Eternity from human Thought,
And smother souls immortal in the Dust?
A soul immortal, spending all her Fires,
Wasting her strength in strenuous Idleness,
150   Thrown into Tumult, raptur'd, or alarm'd,
At ought this scene can threaten, or indulge,
Resembles *Ocean* into Tempest wrought,
To waft a Feather, or to drown a Fly.
Where falls this Censure? It o'erwhelms myself.

155 How was my Heart encrusted by the World?
O how self-fetter'd was my groveling Soul?
How, like a Worm, was I wrapt round and round
In silken thought, which reptile *Fancy* spun,
Till darken'd *Reason* lay quite clouded o'er
160 With soft conceit of endless Comfort *here,*
Nor yet put forth her Wings to reach the skies!
　　Night-visions may befriend, (as sung above)
Our *waking* Dreams are fatal. How I dreamt
Of things Impossible? (could Sleep do more?)
165 Of Joys perpetual in perpetual Change?
Of stable Pleasures on the tossing Wave?
Eternal Sunshine in the Storms of life?
How richly were my noon-tide Trances hung
With gorgeous Tapestries of pictur'd joys?
170 Joy behind joy, in endless perspective!
Till at Death's Toll, whose restless Iron tongue
Calls daily for his Millions at a meal,
Starting I woke, and found myself undone.
Where now my Frenzy's pompous Furniture?
175 The *cobweb'd* Cottage, with its ragged wall
Of mould'ring Mud, is *Royalty* to me!
The *Spider's* most attenuated Thread
Is Cord, is Cable, to man's tender Tie
On earthly Bliss; it breaks at every Breeze.
180 　　O ye blest scenes of *permanent* Delight!
Full, above measure! lasting, beyond bound!
A *Perpetuity* of Bliss, is Bliss.
Could you, so rich in rapture, fear an End,
That ghastly Thought would drink up all your Joy,
185 And quite unparadise the realms of Light.
Safe are you lodg'd above these rowling Spheres;
The baleful influence of whose giddy Dance
Sheds sad Vicissitude on all beneath.
Here teems with Revolutions every Hour;
190 And rarely for the better; or the best,
More mortal than the common births of Fate.
Each *Moment* has its Sickle, emulous
Of *Time's* enormous Scythe, whose ample Sweep
Strikes Empires from the root; each *Moment* plays
195 His little weapon in the narrower sphere
Of sweet domestick Comfort, and cuts down
The fairest bloom of sublunary Bliss.

Bliss! sublunary bliss! — proud words, and vain!
Implicit Treason to divine Decree!
200 A bold invasion of the rights of Heaven!
I clasp'd the Phantoms, and I found them Air.
O had I weigh'd it ere my fond Embrace,
What darts of Agony had miss'd my heart!
　　Death! great Proprietor of all! 'tis thine
205 To tread out Empire, and to quench the Stars.
The Sun himself by thy permission shines;
And, one day, thou shalt pluck him from his sphere;
Amid such mighty plunder, why exhaust
Thy *partial* Quiver on a mark so *mean?*
210 Why thy *peculiar* Rancor wreak'd on *me?*
Insatiate Archer! could not *One* suffice?
Thy shaft flew *thrice;* and *thrice* my peace was slain;
And thrice, ere thrice yon Moon had fill'd her Horn.
O *Cynthia!* why so pale? Dost thou lament
215 Thy wretched Neighbour? Grieve, to see thy wheel
Of ceaseless change outwhirl'd in human Life?
How wanes my *borrow'd* bliss! from *Fortune's* smile,
Precarious Courtesy! not *Virtue's* sure,
Self-given, *solar,* ray of sound Delight.
220 　　In every vary'd Posture, Place, and Hour,
How widow'd every Thought of every Joy!
Thought, busy Thought! too busy for my Peace!
Thro' the dark Postern of Time long elaps'd,
Led softly, by the stillness of the Night,
225 Led, like a Murderer, (and such it proves!)
Strays, (wretched Rover!) o'er the pleasing *Past;*
In quest of wretchedness perversely strays;
And finds all Desart *now;* and meets the Ghosts
Of my departed Joys, a numerous Train!
230 I rue the Riches of my former Fate;
Sweet Comfort's blasted Clusters I lament;
I tremble at the Blessings once so dear;
And ev'ry Pleasure pains me to the Heart.
　　Yet why *complain?* or why complain for One?
235 Hangs out the Sun his Lustre but for me,
The *single* Man? are Angels all beside?
I mourn for Millions: 'tis the common Lot;
In *this* shape or in *that,* has Fate entail'd
The Mother's throws on all of woman born,
240 Not more the Children, than sure Heirs of *Pain.*

War, Famine, Pest, Volcano, Storm, and Fire,
Intestine Broils, *Oppression,* with her heart
Wrapt up in tripple Brass, besiege mankind.
God's Image, disinherited of Day,
245   *Here,* plung'd in Mines, forgets a Sun was made.
There, Beings deathless as their haughty Lord,
Are hammer'd to the galling Oar for life;
And plough the Winter's wave, and reap Despair.
Some, for hard Masters, broken under Arms,
250   In battle lopt away, with half their limbs,
Beg bitter bread thro' realms their Valour sav'd,
If so the Tyrant, or his Minion, doom.
Want, and incurable *Disease,* (fell Pair!)
On hopeless Multitudes remorseless seize
255   At once; and make a Refuge of the Grave.
How groaning *Hospitals* eject their dead?
What numbers groan for sad Admission there?
What numbers once in *Fortune*'s lap high-fed,
Sollicit the cold hand of Charity?
260   To shock us more, sollicit it in vain?
Ye silken Sons of Pleasure! since in Pains
You rue more modish visits, visit *here,*
And breathe from your Debauch: Give, and reduce
Surfeit's Dominion o'er you: but so great
265   Your Impudence, you blush at what is Right!
    Happy! did Sorrow seize on *such* alone.
Not *Prudence* can defend, or *Virtue* save;
Disease invades the chastest Temperance;
And Punishment the Guiltless; and Alarm
270   Thro' thickest shades pursues the fond of Peace.
Man's Caution often into Danger turns,
And, his Guard falling, crushes him to death.
Not *Happiness* itself makes good her name;
Our very Wishes give us not our wish.
275   How distant oft the Thing we doat on most,
From that for which we doat, *Felicity?*
The *smoothest* course of Nature has its Pains;
And *truest* Friends, thro' Error, wound our Rest.
Without Misfortune, what Calamities?
280   And what Hostilities, without a Foe?
Nor are Foes wanting to the best on earth.
But endless is the list of human Ills,
And Sighs might sooner fail, than Cause to sigh.

A Part how small of the terraqueous Globe
285 Is tenanted by man? the rest a *Waste,*
Rocks, Desarts, frozen Seas, and burning Sands;
Wild haunts of Monsters, Poison, Stings, and Death,
Such is Earth's melancholy Map! But far
More sad! this Earth is a true Map of *Man.*
290 So bounded are its haughty Lord's *Delights*
To *Woe*'s wide empire; where deep *Troubles* toss,
Loud *Sorrows* howl, envenom'd *Passions* bite,
Ravenous *Calamities* our vitals seize,
And threat'ning *Fate,* wide-opens to devour.
295 What then am I, who sorrow for *myself?*
In Age, in Infancy, from other's aid
Is all our Hope; to teach us to be *kind.*
That, Nature's *first, last* Lesson to mankind;
The selfish heart deserves the pain it feels.
300 More generous Sorrow, while it sinks, exalts,
And conscious Virtue mitigates the Pang.
Nor Virtue, more than *Prudence,* bids me give
Swoln thought a *second* channel; who divide,
They weaken too, the Torrent of their grief.
305 Take then, O World! thy much-indebted Tear;
How sad a Sight is human Happiness,
To those whose Thought can pierce beyond an Hour?
O thou, whate'er thou art, whose Heart exults!
Would'st thou I should congratulate thy Fate?
310 I know thou would'st; thy Pride demands it from me.
Let thy Pride pardon, what thy nature needs,
The salutary Censure of a friend.
Thou happy *Wretch!* by Blindness thou art blest;
By Dotage dandled to perpetual Smiles.
315 Know, *Smiler!* at thy peril art thou pleas'd;
Thy Pleasure is the promise of thy Pain.
Misfortune, like a Creditor severe,
But rises in demand for her Delay;
She makes a scourge of past Prosperity,
320 To sting thee more, and double thy Distress.
Lorenzo, Fortune makes her Court to thee,
Thy fond Heart dances, while the *Syren* sings.
Dear is thy Welfare; think me not unkind;
I would not damp, but to secure thy joys.
325 Think not that *Fear* is sacred to the Storm,
Stand on thy guard against the *Smiles* of Fate.

Is Heaven tremendous in its Frowns? most sure;
And in its Favours formidable too;
Its favours here are Tryals, not Rewards;
330   A call to Duty, not discharge from Care;
And should alarm us, full as much as Woes;
Awake us to their *Cause,* and *Consequence;*
And make us tremble, weigh'd with our Desert;
Awe Nature's Tumult, and chastise her Joys,
337   Lest, while we clasp, we kill them; nay invert
To worse than *simple* misery, their Charms.
Revolted Joys, like foes in civil war,
Like bosom friendships to resentment sour'd,
With rage envenom'd rise against our Peace.
340   Beware what Earth calls Happiness; beware
All joys, but joys that never can expire.
Who builds on less than an *immortal* Base,
Fond as he seems, condemns his joys to Death.
    Mine dy'd with thee, *Philander!* thy last Sigh
345   Dissolv'd the charm; the disenchanted Earth
Lost all her Lustre. Where, her glittering Towers?
Her golden Mountains, where? all darken'd down
To naked Waste; a dreary Vale of Tears;
The great Magician's dead! Thou poor, pale Piece
350   Of out-cast earth, in Darkness! what a Change
From yesterday! Thy darling Hope so near,
(Long-labour'd Prize!) O how Ambition flush'd
Thy glowing cheek? Ambition truly great,
Of virtuous Praise. Death's subtle seed within,
(Sly, treach'rous Miner!) working in the Dark,
355   Smil'd at thy well-concerted scheme, and beckon'd
The Worm to riot on that Rose so red,
Unfaded e'er it fell; one moment's Prey!
    Man's Foresight is *conditionally* wise.
360   *Lorenzo!* Wisdom into Folly turns,
Oft, the first instant, its Idea fair
To labouring Thought is born. How dim our eye?
The *present* Moment terminates our sight;
Clouds, thick as those on Doomsday, drown the *next;*
365   We penetrate, we prophesy in vain.
Time is dealt out by Particles; and each,
E'er mingled with the streaming sands of Life,
By Fate's inviolable oath is sworn
Deep silence, "Where Eternity begins."

370   By Nature's Law, what may be, may be *now;*
There's no Prerogative in human Hours.
In human hearts what bolder Thought can rise,
Than man's Presumption on To-morrow's dawn?
Where is To-morrow? In another world.

375   For numbers this is certain, the Reverse
Is sure to none; and yet on this *perhaps,*
This *peradventure,* infamous for lies,
As on a rock of Adamant we build
Our mountain Hopes; spin out eternal schemes,

380   As we the Fatal Sisters cou'd out-spin,
And, big with life's Futurities, expire.
      Not even *Philander* had bespoke his shroud.
Nor had he cause, a Warning was deny'd;
How Many fall as sudden, not as safe?

385   As sudden, tho' for Years admonisht home.
Of human Ills the last Extreme beware,
Beware, *Lorenzo!* a *slow-sudden* Death.
How dreadful that deliberate Surprize?
Be wise to-day; 'tis madness to defer;

390   Next day the fatal Precedent will plead;
Thus on, 'till Wisdom is push'd out of life.
Procrastination is the Thief of Time,
Year after year it steals, till all are fled,
And to the mercies of a Moment leaves

395   The vast Concerns of an Eternal scene.
If not so frequent, would not This be strange?
That 'tis so frequent, *This* is stranger still.
      Of Man's miraculous Mistakes, this bears
The Palm, "That all Men are about to live,"

400   For ever on the Brink of being born.
All pay themselves the compliment to think
They, one day, shall not drivel; and their Pride
On this Reversion takes up ready Praise;
At least, their own; their future selves applauds;

405   How excellent that Life they *ne'er* will lead?
Time lodg'd in their *own* hands is *Folly*'s Vails;
That lodg'd in *Fate*'s to *Wisdom* they consign;
The thing they can't but *purpose,* they *postpone;*
'Tis not in *Folly,* not to scorn a Fool;

410   And scarce in human *Wisdom* to do more.
All *Promise* is poor dilatory man,
And that thro' every Stage: When young, indeed.

In full content we, sometimes, nobly rest,
Unanxious for *ourselves*; and only wish,
415   As duteous sons, our *Fathers* were more Wise.
At *thirty* man *suspects* himself a Fool;
Knows it at *forty*, and reforms his Plan;
At *fifty* chides his infamous Delay,
Pushes his prudent Purpose to *Resolve;*
420   In all the magnanimity of Thought
Resolves; and re-resolves; then dies the same.
    And why? Because he thinks himself Immortal.
All men think all men mortal, but Themselves;
Themselves, when some alarming shock of Fate
425   Strikes thro' their wounded hearts the sudden Dread;
But their hearts wounded, like the wounded Air,
Soon close, where past the shaft, no Trace is found.
As, from the *Wing* no scar the Sky retains;
The parted Wave no furrow from the *Keel*;
430   So dies in human hearts the Thought of Death.
Even with the tender Tear which Nature sheds
O'er those we love, we drop it in their Grave.
Can I forget *Philander?* That were strange;
O my full Heart! — But should I give it vent,
435   The longest Night, tho' longer far, would fail,
And the *Lark* listen to my *midnight* Song.
    The Spritely *Lark's* shrill Mattin wakes the Morn;
Grief's sharpest Thorn hard-pressing on my Breast,
I strive, with wakeful Melody to chear
440   The sullen Gloom, sweet *Philomel!* like Thee,
And call the Stars to listen: Every star
Is deaf to mine, enamoured of thy Lay.
Yet be not vain; there are, who thine excell,
And charm thro' distant Ages: Wrapt in Shade,
445   Prisoner of Darkness! to the silent *Hours,*
How often I repeat their Rage divine,
To lull my Griefs, and steal my heart from Woe?
I roll their Raptures, but not catch their Flames,
Dark, tho' not blind, like thee *Maeonides!*
450   Or *Milton!* thee; ah cou'd I reach your Strain!
Or *His,* who made *Maeonides* our Own.
Man too He sung: *Immortal* man I sing;
Oft bursts my Song beyond the bounds of Life;
What, *now,* but Immortality can please?
455   O had He press'd his Theme, pursued the track,

Which opens out of Darkness into Day!
O had he mounted on his wing of Fire,
Soar'd, where I sink, and sung *Immortal* man!
How had it blest mankind, and rescued me?

William Shenstone

THE SCHOOL-MISTRESS

IN IMITATION OF SPENSER

Auditae voces, vagitus & ingens,
Infantumque animae flentes in limine primo.   Virgil.

AH me! full sorely is my heart forlorn,
To think how modest worth neglected lies;
While partial fame doth with her blasts adorn
Such deeds alone, as pride and pomp disguise;
5   Deeds of ill sort, and mischievous emprize:
Lend me thy clarion, goddess! let my try
To sound the praise of merit, ere it dies;
Such as I oft have chaunced to espy,
Lost in the dreary shades of dull obscurity.

10   In ev'ry village mark'd with little spire,
Embow'r'd in trees, and hardly known to fame,
There dwells, in lowly shed and mean attire,
A matron old, whom we school-mistress name;
Who boasts unruly brats with birch to tame;
15   They grieven sore, in piteous durance pent,
Aw'd by the pow'r of this relentless dame;
And oft-times, on vagaries idly bent,
For unkempt hair, or task unconn'd, are sorely shent.

And all in sight doth rise a birchen tree,
20   Which learning near her little dome did stowe;
Whilom a twig of small regard to see,
Tho' now so wide its waving branches flow;

And work the simple vassals mickle woe;
For not a wind might curl the leaves that blew,
25   But their limbs shudder'd, and their pulse beat low;
And as they look'd they found their horror grew,
And shap'd it into rods, and tingled at the view.

So have I seen (who has not, may conceive,)
A lifeless phantom near a garden plac'd;
30   So doth it wanton birds of peace bereave,
Of sport, of song, of pleasure, of repast;
They start, they stare, they wheel, they look aghast;
Sad servitude! such comfortless annoy
May no bold Briton's riper age e'er taste!
35   Ne superstition clog his dance of joy,
Ne vision empty, vain, his native bliss destroy.

Near to this dome is found a patch so green,
On which the tribe their gambols do display;
And at the door impris'ning board is seen,
40   Lest weakly wights of smaller size should stray;
Eager, perdie, to bask in sunny day!
The noises intermix'd, which thence resound,
Do learning's little tenement betray:
Where sits the dame, disguis'd in look profound,
45   And eyes her fairy throng, and turns her wheel around.

Her cap, far whiter than the driven snow,
Emblem right meet of decency does yield:
Her apron dy'd in grain, as blue, I trowe,
As is the hare-bell that adorns the field:
50   And in her hand, for scepter, she does wield
Tway birchen sprays; with anxious fear entwin'd,
With dark distrust, and sad repentance fill'd;
And stedfast hate, and sharp affliction join'd,
And fury uncontroul'd, and chastisement unkind.

55   Few but have ken'd, in semblance meet pourtray'd,
The childish faces of old Eol's train;
LIBS, NOTUS, AUSTER: these in frowns array'd,
How then would fare or earth, or sky, or main,
Were the stern god to give his slaves the rein?
60   And were not she rebellious breasts to quell,
And were not she her statutes to maintain,

The cot no more, I ween, were deem'd the cell,
Where comely peace of mind, and decent order dwell.

A russet stole was o'er her shoulders thrown;
65   A russet kirtle fenc'd the nipping air;
'Twas simple russet, but it was her own;
'Twas her own country bred the flock so fair;
'Twas her own labour did the fleece prepare;
And, sooth to say, her pupils, rang'd around,
70   Thro' pious awe, did term it passing rare;
For they in gaping wonderment abound,
And think, no doubt, she been the greatest wight on ground.

Albeit ne flatt'ry did corrupt her truth,
Ne pompous title did debauch her ear;
75   Goody, good-woman, gossip, n'aunt, forsooth,
Or dame, the sole additions she did hear;
Yet these she challeng'd, these she held right dear:
Ne would esteem him act as mought behove,
Who should not honour'd eld with these revere:
80   For never title yet so mean could prove,
But there was eke a mind which did that title love.

One ancient hen she took delight to feed,
The plodding pattern of the busy dame;
Which, ever and anon, impell'd by need,
85   Into her school, begirt with chickens, came;
Such favour did her past deportment claim:
And, if neglect had lavish'd on the ground
Fragment of bread, she would collect the same;
For well she knew, and quaintly could expound,
90   What sin it were to waste the smallest crumb she found.

Herbs too she knew, and well of each could speak
That in her garden sip'd the silv'ry dew;
Where no vain flow'r disclos'd a gaudy streak;
But herbs for use, and physick, not a few,
95   Of grey renown, within those borders grew:
The tufted basil, pun-provoking thyme,
Fresh baum, and mary-gold of chearful hue;
The lowly gill, that never dares to climb;
And more I fain would sing, disdaining here to rhyme.

100 Yet euphrasy may not be left unsung,
  That gives dim eyes to wander leagues around;
  And pungent radish, biting infant's tongue;
  And plantain ribb'd, that heals the reaper's wound;
  And marj'ram sweet, in shepherds posie found;
105 And lavender, whose spikes of azure bloom
  Shall be, ere-while, in arid bundles bound,
  To lurk amidst the labours of her loom,
And crown her kerchiefs clean with mickle rare perfume.

  And here trim rosemarine, that whilom crown'd
110 The daintiest garden of the proudest peer;
  Ere, driven from its envy'd site, it found
  A sacred shelter for its branches here;
  Where edg'd with gold its glitt'ring skirts appear.
  Oh wassel days! O customs meet and well!
115 Ere this was banish'd from its lofty sphere:
  Simplicity then sought this humble cell,
Nor ever would she more with thane and lordling dwell.

  Here oft the dame, on sabbath's decent eve,
  Hymned such psalms as STERNHOLD forth did mete,
120 If winter 'twere, she to her hearth did cleave;
  But in her garden found a summer seat:
  Sweet melody! to hear her then repeat
  How ISRAEL's sons, beneath a foreign king,
  While taunting foe-men did a song intreat,
125 All, for the nonce, untuning ev'ry string,
Uphung their useless lyres — small heart had they to sing.

  For she was just, and friend to virtuous lore,
  And pass'd much time in truly virtuous deed;
  And, in those elfins' ears, would oft deplore
130 The times, when truth by popish rage did bleed;
  And tortious death was true devotion's meed;
  And simple faith in iron chains did mourn,
  That nould on wooden image place her creed;
  And lawny saints in smould'ring flames did burn:
135 Ah! dearest Lord, forefend, thilk days should e'er return.

  In elbow chair, like that of Scottish stem
  By the sharp tooth of cank'ring eld defac'd,

In which, when he receives his diadem,
Our sov'reign prince and liefest liege is plac'd,
140   The matron sate; and some with rank she grac'd,
(The source of children's and of courtier's pride!)
Redress'd affronts, for vile affronts there pass'd;
And warn'd them not the fretful to deride,
But love each other dear, whatever them betide.

145   Right well she knew each temper to descry;
To thwart the proud, and the submiss to raise;
Some with vile copper prize exalt on high,
And some entice with pittance small of praise;
And other some with baleful sprig she 'frays:
150   Ev'n absent, she the reins of pow'r doth hold,
While with quaint arts the giddy crowd she sways;
Forewarn'd, if little bird their pranks behold,
'Twill whisper in her ear, and all the scene unfold.

Lo now with state she utters the command!
155   Eftsoons the urchins to their tasks repair;
Their books of stature small they take in hand.
Which with pellucid horn secured are;
To save from finger wet the letters fair:
The work so gay, that on their back is seen,
160   ST. GEORGE's high atchievements does declare:
On which thilk wight that has y-gazing been
Kens the forth-coming rod, unpleasing sight, I ween!

Ah luckless he, and born beneath the beam
Of evil star! it irks me whilst I write!
165   As erst the bard by MULLA's silver stream,
Oft, as he told of deadly dolorous plight,
Sigh'd as he sung, and did in tears indite.
For brandishing the rod, she doth begin
To loose the brogues, the stripling's late delight!
170   And down they drop; appears his dainty skin,
Fair as the furry coat of whitest ermilin.

O ruthful scene! when from a nook obscure,
His little sister doth his peril see:
All playful as she sate, she grows demure;
175   She finds full soon her wonted spirits flee;
She meditates a pray'r to set him free:

Nor gentle pardon could this dame deny,
(If gentle pardon could with dames agree)
To her sad grief that swells in either eye,
180   And wrings her so that all for pity she could die.

No longer can she now her shrieks command;
And hardly she forbears thro' aweful fear,
To rushen forth, and, with presumptuous hand,
To stay harsh justice in its mid career.
185   On thee she calls, on thee her parent dear!
(Ah! too remote to ward the shameful blow!)
She sees no kind domestic visage near,
And soon a flood of tears begins to flow;
And gives a loose at last to unavailing woe.

190   But ah! what pen his piteous plight may trace?
Or what device his loud laments explain?
The form uncouth of his disguised face?
The pallid hue that dyes his looks amain?
The plenteous show'r that does his cheek distain?
195   When he, in abject wise, implores the dame,
Ne hopeth aught of sweet reprieve to gain;
Or when from high she levels well her aim,
And, thro' the thatch, his cries each falling stroke
   proclaim.

The other tribe, aghast, with sore dismay,
200   Attend, and conn their tasks with mickle care:
By turns, astony'd, ev'ry twig survey,
And, from their fellow's hateful wounds, beware;
Knowing, I wist, how each the same may share;
'Till fear has taught them a performance meet,
205   And to the well-known chest the dame repair;
Whence oft with sugar'd cates she doth 'em greet,
And ginger-bread y-rare; now, certes, doubly sweet!

See to their seats they hye with merry glee,
And in beseemly order sitten there;
210   All but the wight of bum y-galled, he
Abhorreth bench and stool, and fourm, and chair;
(This hand in mouth y-fix'd, that rends his hair;)
And eke with snubs profound, and heaving breast,
Convulsions intermitting! does declare

112

215His grievous wrong; his dame's unjust behest;
And scorns her offer'd love, and shuns to be caress'd.

His face besprent with liquid crystal shines,
His blooming face that seems a purple flow'r,
Which low to earth its drooping head declines,
220All smear'd and sully'd by a vernal show'r.
O the hard bosoms of despotic pow'r!
All, all, but she, the author of his shame,
All, all, but she, regret this mournful hour:
Yet hence the youth, and hence the flow'r, shall claim,
225If so I deem aright, transcending worth and fame.

Behind some door, in melancholy thought,
Mindless of food, he, dreary caitiff! pines;
Ne for his fellow's joyaunce careth aught,
But to the wind all merriment resigns;
230And deems it shame, if he to peace inclines;
And many a sullen look ascance is sent,
Which for his dame's annoyance he designs;
And still the more to pleasure him she's bent,
The more doth he, perverse, her haviour past resent.

235Ah me! how much I fear lest pride it be!
But if that pride it be, which thus inspires,
Beware, ye dames, with nice discernment see,
Ye quench not too the sparks of nobler fires:
Ah! better far than all the muses' lyres,
240All coward arts, is valour's gen'rous heat;
The firm fixt breast which fit and right requires,
Like VERNON's patriot soul; more justly great
Than craft that pimps for ill, or flow'ry false deceit.

Yet nurs'd with skill, what dazzling fruits appear!
245Ev'n now sagacious foresight points to show
A little bench of heedless bishops here,
And there a chancellour in embryo,
Or bard sublime, if bard may e'er be so,
As MILTON, SHAKESPEAR, names that ne'er shall die!
250Tho' now he crawl along the ground so low,
Nor weeting how the muse shou'd soar on high,

Wisheth, poor starv'ling elf! his paper kite may fly.

And this perhaps, who, cens'ring the design,
Low lays the house which that of cards doth build,
255   Shall DENNIS be! if rigid fates incline,
And many an epic to his rage shall yield;
And many a poet quit th'Aonian field;
And, sour'd by age, profound he shall appear,
As he who now with 'sdainful fury thrill'd
260   Surveys mine work; and levels many a sneer,
And furls his wrinkly front, and cries, "What stuff
is here?"

But now DAN PHOEBUS gains the middle skie,
And liberty unbars her prison-door;
And like a rushing torrent out they fly,
265   And now the grassy cirque han cover'd o'er
With boist'rous revel-rout and wild uproar;
A thousand ways in wanton rings they run,
Heav'n shield their short-liv'd pastimes, I implore!
For well may freedom, erst so dearly won,
270   Appear to British elf more gladsome than the sun.

Enjoy, poor imps! enjoy your sportive trade,
And chase gay flies, and cull the fairest flow'rs;
For when my bones in grass-green sods are laid;
For never may ye taste more careless hours
275   In knightly castles, or in ladies bow'rs.
O vain to seek delight in earthly thing!
But most in courts where proud ambition tow'rs;
Deluded wight! who weens fair peace can spring
Beneath the pompous dome of kesar or of king.

280   See in each sprite some various bent appear!
These rudely carol most incondite lay;
Those saunt'ring on the green, with jocund leer
Salute the stranger passing on his way;
Some builden fragile tenements of clay;
285   Some to the standing lake their courses bend,
With pebbles smooth at duck and drake to play;
Thilk to the huxter's sav'ry cottage tend,
In pastry kings and queens th'allotted mite to spend.

114

Here, as each season yields a different store,
290   Each season's stores in order ranged been;
Apples with cabbage-net y-cover'd o'er,
Galling full sore th'unmoney'd wight, are seen;
And goose-b'rie clad in liv'ry red or green;
And here of lovely dye, the cath'rine pear,
295   Fine pear! as lovely for thy juice, I ween:
O may no wight e'er pennyless come there,
Lest smit with ardent love he pine with hopeless
        care!

See! cherries here, ere cherries yet abound,
With thread so white in tempting posies ty'd,
300   Scatt'ring like blooming maid their glances round,
With pamper'd look draw little eyes aside;
And must be bought, tho' penury betide.
The plumb all azure and the nut all brown,
And here each season, do those cakes abide,
305   Whose honour'd names th'inventive city own,
Rend'ring thro' Britain's isle Salopia's praises known.

Admir'd SALOPIA! that with venial pride
Eyes her bright form in SEVERN's ambient wave,
Fam'd for her loyal cares in perils try'd,
310   Her daughters lovely, and her striplings brave:
Ah! midst the rest, may flowers adorn his grave,
Whose art did first these dulcet cates display!
A motive fair to learning's imps he gave,
Who chearless o'er her darkling region stray;
315   'Till reason's morn arise, and light them on their
        way.

John Byrom

A DIALOGUE BETWEEN SIR JOHN JOBSON AND HARRY HOMESPUN, OCCASIONED BY THE MARCH OF THE HIGHLANDERS INTO LANCASHIRE IN THE YEAR 1745

Sir John. WAS ye not sadly frighten'd, honest *Harry*,
To see those *Highland* Fellows —
                Harry. *Not I, marry,* –
Sir J. No! how comes that? –
                H. *Whoy, Sur, I conno' see*
What theer wur in 'um that shid freeten me –
5   *Sir J.* So many armed Ruffians as came here,
Was there not cause enough for all to fear? –
H. *Aw whoa, Sur* John*? it happen mit be so*
Wi' sich foine loardly Gentlemen as yo:
But we poor Foke –
           Sir J. Why, prithee, poor or rich,
10   Is it not much the same?
                H. *nou, not so mich;*
We warken hard, as't iz, for meeat and clooas,
And connot eem to be so feert, God knooas.
Sir J. But, *Harry*, to see Fire and Sword advance!
To have such Enemies as *Rome* and *France!*
15   Shou'd not this move alike both Rich and Poor,
To drive impending Ruin from their Door?
H. *As for the Rich, Sur* John, *I conno' tell,*
But for the Poor, I'll onser for mysel;
If Fire shid come, I ha' nout for it to brun,
20   *Nor wark to find for oather Swooard, or Gun:*
For France *and* Rome *my feering is no greater,*
They lyen, I think, o'th'tother Side o'th Weater.
Sir J. You don't consider what may be the End
Of such a strange Indifference, my Friend;

116

25   Pray, whether you have more or less to lose,
       Wou'd you not guard your Country from its Foes?
       H. *My Country, Sur? I have, yo' understand,*
       In aw the Country not one Inch o' Lond:
       They that wood'n feight, and ha' Mon's Blood be spilt,
30   *May if they win, but whoy mun I be kilt?*
       Sir J. Your Country, Friend, is not the Ground alone;
       There is the King, that sits upon the Throne;
       The *Protestant Succession* lies at Stake,
       That bloody-minded *Papists* want to shake:
35   Now you have some Religion left, I hope,
       And wou'd not tamely give it to the *Pope.*
       H. *He wou'd no' have it, happen if I wou'd,*
       Th'oud Mon beloike mit think his ooan as gud;
       And true Religion, Sur, if I have onny,
40   *No Mon i'th' Ward con tak it fro me, con he?*
       Sir J. If you but knew, Friend *Harry,* what a Scene
       Of Mischiefs happen'd in King *James's* Reign;
       How, but for *Orange's* immortal Prince,
       The *Protestants* had all been kill'd long since;
45   If I should tell you —
                  H. *Nay, we aw, Sur* John,
       Known weel enough that yo're a larnid Mon;
       So wus my Gronfayther, and ore his Ale
       Monny a Toime has toud another Tale:
       And I darr say mi Gronfayther toud true;
50   *For, lukko me, th'oud Felly wus no Foo,*
       Nor Rebbil noather —
               Sir J. And what was't he tou'd?
       H. *Whoy! moor a deeal than my Brainpon con houd.*
       Its like yo known as haoo Sur, th'Oliverians
       Cut off th' King's Hyead —
                 Sir J. Yes.
                    H. *And haoo th'Presbyterians*
55   *Turnt aoot his Son, and maden a Rebelution.*
       Sir J. They did it Man to save the Constitution;
       'Twas Churchmen too that brought King *William* in,
       As well as they —
                H. *Whoy, be they whoa they winn,*
       One Egg, he sed, wus ne'er moor loik another,
60   *Than thooas two mac o' Foke, wurn like tone tother:*
       They wurn at aw toimes En'mies to th'blood Royal,
       And naoo woud'n ha' it, that none but hom are loyal:

Haoo con that be Sur?
   Sir J. Why, I'll tell thee how —
H. *Nay, but yo connot —*
   Sir J. Well, but hear me now —
Our Kings are Stewards —
    H. *Sur, yo meean they wurn,*
For Things, yo known, han tan another Turn;
The Stuarts *Race is —*
   Sir J. Poh! thou takes me wrong —
H. *Haoo mun I tak o'reet?*
   Sir J. I say, so long
As Kings are our Protectors —
    H. *Luk ye theer!*
70 *Oud* Oliver *agen —*
   Sir J. Nay, prithee hear,
And keep thy Nonsense in, till I have done —
H. *Weel, weel, I'zt hear yoars first then, if I mun.*
Sir J. The People, *Harry,* when they all agree —
H. *Aw Sur!*
   Sir J. Be quiet — choose them a Trustee,
75 And call him King: now, if he break his Trust,
They have a Right to turn him out, and must;
Unless they wou'd be ruin'd; dost thou think
For one Man's swimming all the rest shou'd sink?
H. *Yo lov'n a King, Sur, waintly; sink or swim,*
80 *No Mon, I foind, is to be draoont but him.*
This chozzen King mit happen draoon yo furst,
Then yo mit sink him after, an yo durst.
If Folks may tak whot Kings they han a Moind,
Whot Faut wi' aw theese Scotchmen *con yo foind?*
85 *Sir J.* Hang 'em all — have they not a King already,
That keeps his Contract with the People steady?
Rebels!
   H. *Whoy, ay, that's reet, for they wur byetten;*
They lost the Feight; but, haoo, if they had getten,
Wou'd yo ha' lik't it, Sur, if an Heelander
90 *Had toud o'* Sauce for th'Goose wur Sauce for th'Gonder
Sir J. Thou'rt a sly Tyke, I'll talk with thee no more —
H. *Whoy, if yo pleeasen then, Sur, ween give ore,*
Wishing that e'ry Mon may have his Reet,
Feight as feight winn, and so, Sur John, *good Neet.*
95 *Sir J.* Thou'lt look, I find, to thy own Carcass still —
H. *Yoi, Sur, as lung as ere I con, I will —*

James Macpherson

OITHÓNA:

A POEM

DARKNESS dwells around Dunlathmon, though the moon shews half her face on the hill. The daughter of night turns her eyes away; for she beholds the grief that is coming. — The son of Morni is on the plain; but there is no sound in the hall. No long streaming beam of light comes trembling through the gloom. The voice of Oithóna is not heard amidst the noise of the streams of Duvranna. —

WHITHER art thou gone in thy beauty, dark-haired daughter of Nuäth? Lathmon is in the field of the valiant, but thou didst promise to remain in the hall; thou didst promise to remain in the hall till the son of Morni returned. Till he returned from Strumon, to the maid of his love. The tear was on the cheek at his departure: the sigh rose in secret in thy breast. But thou dost not come to meet him, with songs, with the lightly-trembling sound of the harp. —

SUCH were the words of Gaul, when he came to Dunlathmon's towers. The gates were open and dark. The winds were blustering in the hall. The trees strewed the threshold with leaves; and the murmur of night was abroad. — Sad and silent, at a rock, the son of Morni sat: his soul trembled for the maid; but he knew not whither to turn his course. The son of Leth stood at a distance, and heard the winds in his bushy hair. But he did not raise his voice, for he saw the sorrow of Gaul.

SLEEP descended on the heroes. The visions of night arose. Oithóna stood in a dream, before the eyes of

119

Morni's son. Her dark hair was loose and disordered: her lovely eye rolled in tears. Blood stained her snowy arm. The robe half hid the wound of her breast. She stood over the chief, and her voice was heard.

SLEEPS the son of Morni, he that was lovely in the eyes of Oithóna? Sleeps Gaul at the distant rock, and the daughter of Nuäth low? The sea rolls round the dark isle of Tromáthon; I sit in my tears in the cave. Nor do I sit alone, O Gaul, the dark chief of Cuthal is there. He is there in the rage of his love. — And what can Oithóna do?

A ROUGHER blast rushed through the oak. The dream of night departed. Gaul took his aspen spear; he stood in the rage of wrath. Often did his eyes turn to the east, and accuse the lagging light. — At length the morning came forth. The hero lifted up the sail. The winds came rustling from the hill; and he bounded on the waves of the deep. — On the third day arose Tromáthon, like a blue shield in the midst of the sea. The white wave roared against its rocks; sad Oithóna sat on the coast. She looked on the rolling waters, and her tears descend. — But when she saw Gaul in his arms, she started and turned her eyes away. Her lovely cheek is bent and red; her white arm trembles by her side. — Thrice she strove to fly from his presence; but her steps failed her as she went.

DAUGHTER of Nuäth, said the hero, why dost thou fly from Gaul? Do my eyes send forth the flame of death? Or darkens hatred in my soul? Thou art to me the beam of the east rising in a land unknown. But thou coverest thy face with sadness, daughter of high Dunlathmon! Is the foe of Oithóna near? My soul burns to meet him in battle. The sword trembles on the side of Gaul, and longs to glitter in his hand. — Speak, daughter of Nuäth, dost thou not behold my tears?

CAR-BORNE chief of Strumon, replied the sighing maid, why comest thou over the dark-blue wave to Nuäth's mournful daughter? Why did I not pass away in secret, like the flower of the rock, that lifts its fair head unseen, and strews its withered leaves on the blast? Why didst thou come, O Gaul, to hear my departing sigh? I pass away in my youth; and my name shall not be heard. Or it will be heard with sorrow, and the tears of Nuäth

shall fall. Thou wilt be sad, son of Morni, for the fallen
fame of Oithóna. But she shall sleep in the narrow tomb,
far from the voice of the mourner. – Why didst thou
come, chief of Strumon, to the sea-beat rocks of Tromáthon?

I CAME to meet thy foes, daughter of car-borne
Nuäth! the death of Cuthal's chief darkens before me; or
Morni's son shall fall. – Oithóna! when Gaul is low,
raise my tomb on that oozy rock; and when the dark-
bounding ship shall pass, call the sons of the sea; call
them, and give this sword, that they may carry it to
Morni's hall; that the gray-haired hero may cease to look
towards the desart for the return of his son.

AND shall the daughter of Nuäth live, she replied
with a bursting sigh? Shall I live in Tromáthon, and the
son of Morni low? My heart is not of that rock; nor my
soul careless as that sea, which lifts its blue waves to
every wind, and rolls beneath the storm. The blast which
shall lay thee low, shall spread the branches of Oithóna
on earth. We shall wither together, son of car-borne
Morni! – The narrow house is pleasant to me, and the
gray stone of the dead: for never more will I leave thy
rocks, sea-surrounded Tromáthon! – Night came on with
her clouds, after the departure of Lathmon, when he
went to the wars of his fathers, to the moss-covered
rock of Duthórmoth; night came on, and I sat in the hall,
at the beam of the oak. The wind was abroad in the trees.
I heard the sound of arms. Joy rose in my face; for I
thought of thy return. It was the chief of Cuthal, the
red-haired strength of Dunrommath. His eyes rolled in
fire: the blood of my people was on his sword. They
who defended Oithóna fell by the gloomy chief. What
could I do? My arm was weak; it could not lift the spear.
He took me in my grief, amidst my tears he raised the
sail. He feared the returning strength of Lathmon, the
brother of unhappy Oithóna. – But behold, he comes
with his people! the dark wave is divided before him! –
Whither wilt thou turn thy steps, son of Morni? Many are
the warriors of Dunrommath!

MY steps never turned from battle, replied the hero
as he unsheathed his sword; and shall I begin to fear,
Oithóna, when thy foes are near? Go to thy cave,
daughter of Nuäth, till our battle cease. Son of Leth,

bring the bows of our fathers; and the sounding quiver of Morni. Let our three warriors bend the yew. Ourselves will lift the spear. They are an host on the rock; but our souls are strong.

THE daughter of Nuäth went to the cave: a troubled joy rose on her mind, like the red path of the lightning on a stormy cloud. — Her soul was resolved, and the tear was dried from her wildly-looking eye. — Dunrommath slowly approached; for he saw the son of Morni. Contempt contracted his face, a smile is on his dark-brown cheek; his red eye rolled, half-concealed, beneath his shaggy brows.

WHENCE are the sons of the sea, begun the gloomy chief? Have the winds driven you to the rocks of Tromáthon? Or come you in search of the white-handed daughter of Nuäth? The sons of the unhappy, ye feeble men, come to the hand of Dunrommath. His eye spares not the weak, and he delights in the blood of strangers. Oithóna is a beam of light, and the chief of Cuthal enjoys it in secret: wouldst thou come on its loveliness, like a cloud, son of the feeble hand! — Thou mayest come, but shalt thou return to the halls of thy fathers?

DOST thou not know me, said Gaul, red-haired chief of Cuthal? Thy feet were swift on the heath, in the battle of car-borne Lathmon: when the sword of Morni's son pursued his host in Morven's woody land. Dunrommath! thy words are mighty, for thy warriors gather behind thee. But do I fear them, son of pride? I am not of the race of the feeble.

GAUL advanced in his arms; Dunrommath shrunk behind his people. But the spear of Gaul pierced the gloomy chief, and his sword lopped off his head, as it bended in death. — The son of Morni shook it thrice by the lock; the warriors of Dunrommath fled. The arrows of Morven pursued them: ten fell on the mossy rocks. The rest lift the sounding sail, and bound on the echoing deep.

GAUL advanced towards the cave of Oithóna. He beheld a youth leaning against a rock. An arrow had pierced his side; and his eye rolled faintly beneath his helmet. — The soul of Morni's son is sad, he came and spoke the words of peace.

CAN the hand of Gaul heal thee, youth of the

mournful brow? I have searched for the herbs of the mountains; I have gathered them on the secret banks of their streams. My hand has closed the wound of the valiant, and their eyes have blessed the son of Morni. Where dwelt thy fathers, warrior? Were they of the sons of the mighty? Sadness shall come, like night on thy native streams; for thou art fallen in thy youth. —

MY fathers, replied the stranger, were of the race of the mighty; but they shall not be sad; for my fame is departed like morning mist. High walls rise on the banks of Duvranna; and see their mossy towers in the stream; a rock ascends behind them with its bending firs. Thou mayest behold it far distant. There my brother dwells. He is renowned in battle: give him this glittering helmet.

THE helmet fell from the hand of Gaul; for it was the wounded Oithóna. She had armed herself in the cave, and came in search of death. Her heavy eyes are half-closed; the blood pours from her side. —

SON of Morni, she said, prepare the narrow tomb. Sleep comes, like a cloud, on my soul. The eyes of Oithóna are dim. O had I dwelt at Duvranna, in the bright beam of my fame! then had my years come on with joy; and the virgins would bless my steps. But I fall in my youth, son of Morni, and my father shall blush in his hall. —

SHE fell pale on the rock of Tromáthon. The mournful hero raised her tomb. He came to Morven; but we saw the darkness of his soul. Ossian took the harp in the praise of Oithóna. The brightness of the face of Gaul returned. But his sigh rose, at times, in the midst of his friends, like blasts that shake their unfrequent wings, after the stormy winds are laid.

Charles Churchill

THE ROSCIAD

ROSCIUS deceas'd, each high aspiring Play'r
Push'd all his int'rest for the vacant chair.
The buskin'd Heroes of the mimic stage
No longer whine in love, and rant in rage;
5   The monarch quits his throne, and condescends
Humbly to court the favour of his friends;
For pity's sake tells undeserv'd mishaps,
And, their applause to gain, recounts his claps.
Thus the victorious chiefs of ancient Rome,
10   To win the mob, a suppliant's form assume,
In pompous strain fight o'er th'extinguish'd war,
And shew where honour bled in ev'ry scar.
    But though bare Merit might in Rome appear
The strongest plea for favour, 'tis not here;
15   We form our judgment in another way;
And they will best succeed, who best can pay:
Those, who would gain the votes of British tribes,
Must add to force of Merit, force of Bribes.
    What can an actor give? in ev'ry age
20   Cash hath been rudely banish'd from the stage;
Monarchs themselves, to grief of ev'ry play'r,
Appear as often as their image there:
They can't, like candidate for other seat,
Pour seas of wine, and mountains raise of meat.
25   Wine! they could bribe you with the world as soon,
And of roast beef, they only know the tune:
But what they have they give; could CLIVE do more,
Though for each million he had brought home four?
    SHUTER keeps open house at Southwark fair,
30   And hopes the friends of humour will be there;

In Smithfield, YATES prepares the rival treat
For those who laughter love, instead of meat;
FOOTE, at Old House, for even FOOTE will be,
In self-conceit, an actor, bribes with tea;
35   Which WILKINSON at second-hand receives,
And at the New, pours water on the leaves.
    The town divided, each runs sev'ral ways,
As passion, humour, int'rest, party sways.
Things of no moment, colour of the hair,
40   Shape of a leg, complexion brown or fair,
A dress well chosen, or a patch misplac'd,
Conciliate favour, or create distaste.
    From galleries loud peals of laughter roll,
And thunder SHUTER's praises, — he's so *droll.*
45   *Embox'd,* the ladies must have something smart,
PALMER! Oh! PALMER tops the janty part.
Seated in pit, the dwarf, with aching eyes,
Looks up, and vows that BARRY's out of size;
Whilst to six feet the vig'rous stripling grown,
50   Declares that GARRICK is another COAN.
    When place of judgment is by whim supply'd,
And our opinions have their rise in pride;
When, in discoursing on each mimic elf,
We praise and censure with an eye to self;
55   All must meet friends, and ACKMAN bids as fair
In such a court, as GARRICK, for the chair.
    At length agreed, all squabbles to decide,
By some one judge the cause was to be try'd;
But this their squabbles *did* afresh renew,
60   Who should be judge in such a trial: — Who?
    For JOHNSON some, but JOHNSON, it was fear'd,
Would be too grave; and STERNE too gay appear'd:
Others for FRANKLIN votes; but 'twas known,
He sicken'd at all triumphs but his own;
65   For COLMAN many, but the peevish tongue
Of prudent Age found out that he was Young.
For MURPHY some few *pilf'ring* wits declar'd,
Whilst FOLLY clap'd her hands, and WISDOM star'd.
    To mischief train'd, e'en from his mother's womb,
70   Grown old in fraud, tho' yet in manhood's bloom,
Adopting arts, by which gay villains rise,
And reach the heights, which honest men despise;
Mute at the bar, and in the senate loud,

Dull 'mongst the dullest, proudest of the proud;
75   A pert, prim Prater of the *northern* race,
      Guilt in his heart, and famine in his face,
      Stood forth, — and thrice he wav'd his lilly hand —
      And thrice he twirl'd his Tye — thrice strok'd his band —
           "At Friendship's call (thus oft with trait'rous aim,
80   Men, void of faith, usurp faith's sacred name)
      "At Friendship's call I come, by MURPHY sent,
      "Who thus by me *developes* his intent.
      "But lest, *transfus'd,* the Spirit should be lost,
      "That Spirit, which in storms of *Rhet'ric* tost,
85   "Bounces about, and flies like bottled beer,
      "In his own words his own intentions hear.
           "Thanks to my friends. — But to vile fortunes born,
      "No robes of fur these shoulders must adorn.
      "Vain your applause, no aid from thence I draw;
90   "Vain all my wit, — for what is wit in law?
      "Twice (curs'd rememb'rance!) twice I strove to gain
      "Admittance 'mongst the law-instructed train,
      "Who, in the TEMPLE and GRAYS-INN, prepare
      "For client's wretched feet the legal snare;
95   "Dead to those arts, which polish and refine,
      "Deaf to all worth, because that worth was *Mine,*
      "Twice did those blockheads startle at my name,
      "And foul rejection gave me up to shame.
      "To laws and lawyers then I bad adieu,
100   "And plans of far more lib'ral note pursue.
      "Who will may be a Judge — my kindling breast
      "Burns for that Chair which ROSCIUS once possess'd.
      "*Here* give your votes, your int'rest *here* exert,
      "And let Success for *once* attend Desert."
105   With sleek appearance, and with ambling pace,
      And, type of vacant head, with vacant face,
      The Proteus HILL put in his *modest* plea, —
      "Let Favour speak for others, Worth for me." —
      For who, like him, his various pow'rs could call
110   Into so many shapes, and shine in all?
      Who could so nobly grace the motley list,
      Actor, Inspector, Doctor, Botanist?
      Knows any one so well — sure no one knows, —
      At once to *play, prescribe, compound, compose?*
115   Who can — But WOODWARD came, — HILL slipp'd away,

126

Melting, like ghosts, before the rising day.
    With that *low* CUNNING, which in fools supplies,
And amply too, the place of being wise,
Which Nature, kind indulgent parent, gave
120 To qualify the Blockhead for a Knave;
    With that *smooth* FALSHOOD, whose appearance charms,
And reason of each wholsome doubt disarms,
Which to the lowest depths of guile descends,
By vilest means pursues the vilest ends,
125 Wears Friendship's mask for purposes of spite,
Fawns in the day, and Butchers in the night;
    With that *malignant* ENVY, which turns pale,
And sickens, even if a friend prevail,
Which merit and success pursues with hate,
130 And damns the worth it cannot imitate;
    With the *cold* CAUTION of a coward's spleen,
Which fears not guilt, but always seeks a screen,
Which keeps this maxim ever in her view —
What's *basely* done, should be done *safely* too;
135 With that *dull, rooted, callous* IMPUDENCE,
Which, dead to shame, and ev'ry nicer sense,
Ne'er blush'd, unless, in spreading VICE's snares,
She blunder'd on some Virtue *unawares;*
    With all these blessings, which we seldom find
140 Lavish'd by Nature on *one* happy mind,
A Motley Figure, of the FRIBBLE Tribe,
Which Heart can scarce conceive, or pen describe,
Came *simp'ring* on; to ascertain whose sex
Twelve, sage, *impannell'd* Matrons would perplex.
145 Nor *Male,* nor *Female; Neither,* and yet both;
Of *Neuter* Gender, tho' of *Irish* growth;
A six-foot suckling, mincing in *Its* gait;
Affected, peevish, prim, and delicate;
Fearful *It* seem'd, tho' of Athletic make,
150 Lest *brutal breezes* should too roughly shake
Its tender form, and *savage* motion spread,
O'er *Its* pale cheeks, the horrid manly red.
    Much did *It* talk in *Its* own *pretty* phrase,
Of Genius and of Taste, of Play'rs and Plays;
155 Much too of writings, which *Itself* had wrote,
Of special merit, tho' of little note;
For Fate, in a strange humour, had decreed
That what *It* wrote, none but *Itself* should read;

Much too *It* chatter'd of *Dramatic* Laws,
160   Misjudging Critics, and misplac'd applause,
Then, with a self-complacent jutting air,
It smil'd, It smirk'd, It wriggled to the chair;
And, with an aukward briskness not *its* own,
Looking around, and *perking* on the throne,
165   Triumphant seem'd, when that strange savage Dame,
Known but to few, or only known by name,
Plain COMMON SENSE appear'd, by Nature there
Appointed, with plain TRUTH, to guard the Chair.
The Pageant saw, and blasted with her frown,
170   To *Its* first state of Nothing melted down.
    Nor shall the MUSE (for even there the pride
Of this *vain Nothing* shall be mortified)
Nor shall the MUSE (should Fate ordain her rimes,
Fond, pleasing thought! to live in after-times)
175   With such a Trifler's name her pages blot;
Known be the Character, the *Thing* forgot;
Let *It,* to disappoint each future aim,
Live without Sex, and die without a name!
    Cold-blooded critics, by enervate sires
180   Scarce hammer'd out, when nature's feeble fires
Glimmer'd their last; whose sluggish blood, half froze,
Creeps lab'ring thro' the veins; whose heart ne'er glows
With fancy-kindled heat:— A servile race,
Who, in mere want of fault, all merit place;
185   Who blind obedience pay to ancient schools,
Bigots to Greece, and slaves to musty rules;
With solemn consequence declar'd that none
Could judge that cause but SOPHOCLES alone.
Dupes to their fancied excellence, the crowd,
190   Obsequious to the sacred dictate, bow'd.
    When, from amidst the throng, a Youth stood forth,
Unknown his person, not unknown his worth;
His looks bespoke applause; alone he stood,
Alone he stemm'd the mighty critic flood.
195   He talk'd of ancients, as the man became
Who priz'd our own, but envied not their fame;
With noble rev'rence spoke of Greece and Rome,
And scorn'd to tear the laurel from the tomb.
    "But more than just to other countries grown,
200   "Must we turn base apostates to our own?
"Where do these words of Greece and Rome excel,

"That England may not please the ear as well?
"What mighty magic's in the place or air,
"That all perfection needs must centre there?
205 "In states, let strangers blindly be preferr'd;
"In state of letters, Merit should be heard.
"Genius is of no country, her pure ray
"Spreads all abroad, as gen'ral as the day:
"Foe to restraint, from place to place she flies,
210 "And may hereafter e'en in Holland rise.
"May not (to give a pleasing fancy scope,
"And chear a patriot heart with patriot hope)
"May not some great extensive genius raise
"The name of Britain 'bove Athenian praise;
215 "And, whilst brave thirst of fame his bosom warms,
"Make England great in Letters as in Arms?
"There may – there hath – and SHAKESPEARE's
        muse aspires
"Beyond the reach of Greece; with native fires
"Mounting aloft, he wings his daring flight,
220 "Whilst SOPHOCLES below stands trembling at his
        height.
    "Why should we then abroad for judges roam,
"When abler judges we may find at home?
"Happy in tragic and in comic pow'rs,
"Have we not SHAKESPEARE? – Is not JOHNSON ours?
225 "For them, your nat'ral judges, Britons, vote;
"They'll judge like Britons, who like Britons wrote."
    He said, and conquer'd. – Sense resum'd her sway,
And disappointed pedants stalk'd away.
SHAKESPEARE and JOHNSON, with deserv'd applause,
230 Joint-judges were ordain'd to try the cause.
Mean-time the stranger ev'ry voice employ'd,
To ask or tell his name. – Who is it? – LLOYD.
    Thus, when the aged friends of JOB stood mute,
And, tamely prudent, gave up the dispute,
235 ELIHU, with the decent warmth of youth,
Boldly stood forth the advocate of Truth;
Confuted Falshood, and disabled pride,
Whilst baffled age stood snarling at his side.
    The day of tryal's fix'd, nor any fear
240 Lest day of tryal should be put off here.
Causes but seldom for delay can call
In courts where forms are few, fees none at all.

The morning came, nor find I that the sun,
As he on other great events hath done,
245   Put on a brighter robe than what he wore
To go his journey in the day before.
     Full in the centre of a spacious plain,
On plan entirely new, where nothing vain,
Nothing magnificent appear'd, but Art,
250   With decent modesty perform her part,
Rose a tribunal: from no other court
It borrow'd ornament, or sought support:
No juries here were pack'd to kill or clear,
No bribes were taken, nor oaths broken here;
255   No gownsmen, partial to a client's cause,
To their own purpose tun'd the pliant laws.
Each judge was true and steady to his trust,
As MANSFIELD wise, and as old FOSTER just.
     In the first seat, in robe of various dyes,
260   A noble wildness flashing from his eyes,
Sat SHAKESPEARE. — In one hand a wand he bore,
For mighty wonders fam'd in days of yore;
The other held a globe, which to his will
Obedient turn'd, and own'd the master's skill:
265   Things of the noblest kind his genius drew,
And look'd through Nature at a single view:
A loose he gave to his unbounded soul,
And taught new lands to rise, new seas to roll;
Call'd into being scenes unknown before,
270   And, passing Nature's bounds, was something more.
     Next JOHNSON sat, in antient learning train'd,
His rigid Judgment Fancy's flights restrain'd,
Correctly prun'd each wild luxuriant thought,
Mark'd out her course, nor spar'd a glorious fault.
275   The book of man he read with nicest art,
And ransack'd all the secrets of the heart;
Exerted Penetration's utmost force,
And trac'd each passion to its proper source;
Then, strongly mark'd, in liveliest colours drew,
280   And brought each foible forth to public view.
The Coxcomb felt a lash in ev'ry word,
And fools, hung out, their brother fools deterr'd.
His comic humour kept the world in awe,
And Laughter frightened Folly more than Law.
285   But, hark! — The trumpet sounds, the crowd gives way

And the procession comes in just array.
    Now should I, in some sweet poetic line,
Offer up incense at APOLLO's shrine;
Invoke the muse to quit her calm abode,
290   And waken mem'ry with a sleeping ode.
For how should mortal man, in mortal verse,
Their titles, merits, or their names rehearse?
But give, kind DULLNESS, memory and rime,
We'll put off Genius till another time.
295   First, ORDER came, — with solemn step, and slow.
In measur'd time his feet were taught to go.
Behind, from time to time, he cast his eye,
Lest This should quit his place, That step awry.
Appearances to save his only care;
300   So things seem right, no matter what they are.
In him his parents saw themselves renew'd,
Begotten by *Sir* CRITIC on *Saint* PRUDE.
    Then came *Drum, Trumpet, Hautboy, Fiddle, Flute;*
Next *Snuffer, Sweeper, Shifter, Soldier, Mute:*
305   Legions of Angels all in *white* advance;
Furies, all *fire,* come forward in a dance:
Pantomime figures then are brought to view,
    Fools hand in hand with Fools, go two by two.
Next came the Treasurer of either house;
310   One with full purse, t'other with not a sous.
    Behind a group of figures awe create,
Set off with all th'impertinence of state;
By lace and feather consecrate to fame,
Expletive Kings, and Queens without a name.
315   Here HAVARD, all serene, in the same strains,
Loves, hates and rages, triumphs, and complains;
His easy vacant face proclaim'd a heart
Which could not feel emotions, nor impart.
With him came mighty DAVIES. On my life,
320   That DAVIES hath a very pretty wife! —
Statesman all over! — In plots famous grown! —
He mouthes a sentence, as curs mouthe a bone.
    Next HOLLAND came. — With truly tragic stalk,
He creeps, he flies. — A Hero should nòt walk.
325   As if with heav'n he warr'd his eager eyes
Planted their batteries against the skies,
Attitude, Action, Air, Pause, Start, Sigh, Groan,
He borrow'd, and made use of as his own.

By fortune thrown on any other stage,
330   He might, *perhaps*, have pleas'd an easy age;
But now appears a copy, and no more,
Of something better we have seen before.
The actor who would build a solid fame,
Must imitation's servile arts disclaim;
335   Act from himself, on his own bottom stand;
I hate e'en GARRICK thus at second-hand.

    Behind came KING. — Bred up in modest lore,
Bashful and young he sought Hibernia's shore;
Hibernia, fam'd, 'bove ev'ry other grace,
340   For matchless intrepidity of face.
From Her his Features caught the gen'rous flame,
And bid defiance to all sense of shame:
Tutor'd by Her all rivals to surpass,
'Mongst DRURY'S sons he comes, and shines in BRASS.

345   Lo YATES! — Without the least finesse of art
He gets applause! — I wish he'd get his part.
When hot impatience is in full career,
How vilely "Hark'e! Hark'e!" grates the ear?
When active fancy from the brain is sent,
350   And stands on tip-toe for some wish'd event,
I hate those careless blunders which recall
Suspended sense, and prove it fiction all.

    In characters of low and vulgar mould,
Where nature's coarsest features we behold,
355   Where, destitute of ev'ry decent grace,
Unmanner'd jests are blurted in your face,
There YATES with justice strict attention draws,
Acts truly from himself, and gains applause.
But when, to please himself or charm his wife,
360   He aims at something in politer life,
When, blindly thwarting Nature's stubborn plan,
He treads the stage, by way of gentleman,
The Clown, who no one touch of breeding knows,
Looks like TOM ERRAND dress'd in CLINCHER's
    cloaths.
365   Fond of his dress, fond of his person grown,
Laugh'd at by all, and to himself unknown,
From side to side he struts, he smiles, he prates,
And seems to wonder what's become of YATES.

    WOODWARD, endow'd with various tricks of face,
370   Great master in the science of grimace,

From Ireland ventures, fav'rite of the town,
Lur'd by the pleasing prospect of renown;
A speaking Harlequin, made up of whim,
He twists, he twines, he tortures ev'ry limb,
375   Plays to the eye with a mere monkey's art,
And leaves to sense the conquest of the heart.
We laugh indeed, but on reflection's birth,
We wonder at ourselves, and curse our mirth.
His walk of parts he fatally misplac'd,
380   And inclination fondly took for taste;
Hence hath the town so often seen display'd
Beau in Burlesque, High Life in Masquerade.
      But when bold Wits, not such as patch up plays,
Cold and correct, in these insipid days,
385   Some comic character, strong-featur'd, urge
To probability's extremest verge,
Where modest judgment her decree suspends,
And for a time, nor censures, nor commends,
Where critics can't determine on the spot,
390   Whether it is in Nature found or not,
There WOODWARD safely shall his pow'rs exert,
Nor fail of favour where he shews desert.
Hence he in Bobadil such praises bore,
Such worthy praises, Kitely scarce had more.
395   By turns transform'd into all kind of shapes,
Constant to none, FOOTE laughs, cries, struts, and
        scrapes:
Now in the centre, now in van or rear,
The Proteus shifts, *Bawd, Parson, Auctioneer.*
His strokes of humour, and his bursts of sport
400   Are all contain'd in this one word, *Distort.*
Doth a man stutter, look a-squint, or halt?
Mimics draw humour out of Nature's fault:
With personal defects their mirth adorn,
And hang misfortunes out to public scorn.
405   E'en I, whom Nature cast in hideous mould,
Whom, having made, she trembled to behold,
Beneath the load of mimicry may groan,
And find that Nature's errors are my own.
      Shadows behind of FOOTE and WOODWARD came;
410   WILKINSON this, OBRIEN was that name.
Strange to relate, but wonderfully true,
That even shadows have their shadows too!

With not a single comic pow'r endu'd,
The first a mere mere mimic's mimic stood.
415   The last, by Nature form'd to please, who shows,
In JOHNSON's Stephen, which way Genius grows,
Self quite put off, affects, with too much art,
To put on WOODWARD in each mangled part;
Adopts his shrug, his wink, his stare; nay, more,
420   His voice, and croaks; for WOODWARD croak'd before.
When a dull copier simple grace neglects,
And rests his Imitation in Defects,
We readily forgive; but such vile arts
Are double guilt in men of real parts.
425   By Nature form'd in her perversests mood,
With no one requisite of Art endu'd,
Next JACKSON came — Observe that settled glare,
Which better speaks a Puppet than a Play'r;
List to that voice — did ever DISCORD hear
430   Sounds so well fitted to her untun'd ear?
When, to enforce some very tender part,
The right hand sleeps by instinct on the heart,
His soul, of every other thought bereft,
Is anxious only where to place the left;
435   He sobs and pants to sooth his weeping spouse,
To sooth his weeping mother, turns and bows.
Aukward, embarrass'd, stiff, without the skill
Of moving gracefully, or standing still,
One leg, as if suspicious of his brother,
440   Desirous seems to run away from t'other.
      Some errors, handed down from age to age,
Plead Custom's force, and still possess the stage.
That's vile — should we a parent's faults adore,
And err, because our fathers err'd before?
445   If, inattentive to the author's mind,
Some actors made the jest they could not find,
If by low tricks they marr'd fair Nature's mien,
And blurr'd the graces of the simple scene,
Shall we, if reason rightly is employ'd,
450   Not see their faults, or seeing not avoid?
When FALSTAFF stands detected in a lye,
Why, without meaning, rowls LOVE's glassy eye?
Why? — There's no cause — at least no cause we know —
It was the Fashion twenty years ago.
455   Fashion — a word which knaves and fools may use

Their knavery and folly to excuse.
To copy beauties, forfeits all pretence
To fame — to copy faults, is want of sense.
   Yet (tho' in some particulars he fails,
460   Some few particulars, where MODE prevails)
If in these hallow'd times, when sober, sad,
All GENTLEMEN are melancholy mad,
When 'tis not deem'd so great a crime by half
To violate a vestal, as to laugh,
465   Rude mirth may hope presumptuous to engage
An Act of Toleration for the stage,
And courtiers will, like reasonable creatures,
Suspend vain Fashion, and unscrew their features,
Old FALSTAFF, play'd by LOVE, shall please once more,
470   And humour set the audience in a roar.
   Actors I've seen, and of no vulgar name,
Who, being from one part possess'd of fame,
Whether they are to laugh, cry, whine, or bawl,
Still introduce that fav'rite part in all.
475   Here, LOVE, be cautious — ne'er be thou betray'd
To call in that wag FALSTAFF's dang'rous aid;
Like GOTHS of old, howe'er he seems a friend,
He'll seize that throne, you wish him to defend.
In a peculiar mould by HUMOUR cast,
480   For FALSTAFF fram'd — Himself the First and Last, —
He stands aloof from all — maintains his state,
And scorns, like *Scotsmen,* to assimilate.
Vain all disguise — too plain we see the trick,
Tho' the Knight wears the weeds of DOMINIC,
485   And BONIFACE, disgrac'd, betrays the smack,
In ANNO DOMINI, of FALSTAFF's sack.
   Arms cross'd, brows bent, eyes fix'd, feet marching slow,
A band of malecontents with spleen o'erflow;
Wrapt in conceit's impenetrable fog,
490   Which Pride, like Phoebus, draws from ev'ry bog,
They curse the managers, and curse the town,
Whose partial favour keeps such merit down.
But if some man, more hardy than the rest,
Should dare attack these *gnatlings* in their nest;
495   At once they rise with impotence of rage,
Whet their small stings, and buzz about the stage.
" 'Tis breach of privilege! — Shall any dare
"To arm satyric truth against a play'r?

"Prescriptive rights we plead time out of mind;
500   "Actors, unlash'd themselves, may lash mankind."
      What! shall Opinion then, of nature free
And lib'ral as the vagrant air, agree
To rust in chains like these, impos'd by Things
Which, less than nothing, ape the pride of kings?
505   No — though half-poets with half-players join
To curse the freedom of each honest line;
Though rage and malice dim their faded cheek;
What the muse freely thinks, she'll freely speak.
With just disdain of ev'ry paltry sneer,
510   Stranger alike to flattery and fear,
In purpose fix'd, and to herself a rule,
Public Contempt shall wait the Public Fool.
      AUSTIN would always glisten in French silks,
ACKMAN would Norris be, and PACKER Wilks.
515   For who, like ACKMAN, can with humour please;
Who can, like PACKER, charm with sprightly ease?
Higher than all the rest, see BRANSBY strut:
A mighty Gulliver in Lilliput!
Ludicrous nature! which at once could shew
520   A man so very High, so very Low.
      If I forget thee, BLAKES, or if I say
Aught hurtful, may I never see thee play.
Let critics, with a supercilious air,
Decry thy various merit, and declare
525   Frenchman is still at top; — but scorn that rage
Which, in attacking thee, attacks the age.
French follies, universally embrac'd,
At once provoke our mirth, and form our taste.
      Long, from a nation ever hardly us'd,
530   At random censur'd, wantonly abus'd,
Have BRITONS drawn their sport, with partial view
Form'd gen'ral notions from the rascal few;
Condemn'd a people, as for vices known,
Which, from their country banish'd, seek our own.
535   At length, howe'er, the slavish chain is broke,
And Sense, awaken'd, scorns her ancient yoke:
Taught by thee, MOODY, we now learn to raise
Mirth from their foibles; from their virtues, praise.
      Next came the legion, which our *Summer* BAYES,
540   From Alleys, here and there, contriv'd to raise,
Flush'd with vast hopes, and certain to succeed,

With WITS who cannot write, and scarce can read.
Vet'rans no more support the rotten cause,
No more from ELLIOT's worth they reap applause,
545 Each on himself determines to rely,
Be YATES disbanded, and let ELLIOT fly.
Never did play'rs so well an Author Fit,
To Nature dead, and foes declar'd to Wit.
So loud each tongue, so empty was each head,
550 So much they talk'd, so very little said,
So wond'rous dull, and yet so wond'rous vain,
At once so willing, and unfit to reign,
That Reason swore, nor would the oath recall,
Their mighty Master's soul inform'd them all.
555   As one with various disappointments sad,
Whom Dullness only kept from being mad,
Apart from all the rest great MURPHY came —
Common to fools and wits, the rage of fame.
What tho' the sons of Nonsense hail him SIRE,
560 AUDITOR, AUTHOR, MANAGER, and SQUIRE,
His restless soul's ambition stops not there,
To make his triumphs perfect, dubb him PLAY'R.
    In person tall, a figure form'd to please,
If Symmetry could charm, depriv'd of ease;
565 When motionless he stands, we all approve;
What pity 'tis the THING was made to move.
    His voice, in one dull, deep, unvaried sound,
Seems to break forth from caverns under ground.
From hollow chest the low sepulchral note
570 Unwilling heaves, and struggles in his throat.
    Could authors butcher'd give an actor grace,
All must to him resign the foremost place.
When he attempts, in some one fav'rite part,
To ape the feelings of a manly heart,
575 His honest features the disguise defy,
And his face loudly gives his tongue the lye.
    Still in extremes, he knows no happy mean,
Or raving mad, or stupidly serene,
In cold-wrought scenes the lifeless actor flags,
580 In passion, tears the passion into rags.
Can none remember? Yes — I know all must —
When in the MOOR he ground his teeth to dust,
When o'er the stage he Folly's standard bore,
Whilst COMMON-SENSE stood trembling at the door.

585   How few are found with real talents bless'd,
       Fewer with Nature's gifts contented rest.
       Man from his sphere eccentric starts astray;
       All hunt for fame; but most mistake the way.
       Bred at St. OMER's to the Shuffling trade,
590   The hopeful youth a Jesuit might have made,
       With various readings stor'd his empty skull,
       Learn'd without sense, and venerably dull;
       Or at some Banker's desk, like many more,
       Content to tell that two and two make four,
595   His name had stood in CITY ANNALS fair,
       And PRUDENT DULLNESS mark'd him for a MAYOR.
          What then could tempt thee, in a critic age,
       Such blooming hopes to forfeit on a stage?
       Could it be worth thy wond'rous waste of pains
600   To publish to the world thy lack of brains?
       Or might not reason e'en to thee have shewn
       Thy greatest praise had been to live *unknown?*
       Yet let not vanity, like thine, despair:
       Fortune makes Folly her peculiar care.
605   A vacant throne high-plac'd in SMITHFIELD view,
       To sacred DULLNESS and her FIRST-BORN due,
       Thither with haste in happy hour repair,
       Thy birth-right claim, nor fear a rival there.
       SHUTER himself shall own thy juster claim,
610   And VENAL LEDGERS puff their MURPHY's name,
       Whilst VAUGHAN or DAPPER, call him which you will,
       Shall blow the trumpet, and give out the bill.
          There rule secure from critics and from sense,
       Nor once shall GENIUS rise to give offence;
615   Eternal peace shall bless the happy shore,
       And LITTLE FACTIONS break thy rest no more.
          From COVENT-GARDEN crowds promiscuous go,
       Whom the muse knows not, nor desires to know.
       Vet'rans they seem'd, but knew of arms no more
620   Than if, till that time, arms they never bore:
       Like Westminster militia train'd to fight,
       They scarcely knew the left hand from the right.
       Asham'd among such troops to shew the head,
       Their Chiefs were scatter'd, and their Heroes fled.
625   SPARKS at his glass sat comfortably down
       To sep'rate frown from smile, and smile from frown.
       SMITH, the genteel, the airy, and the smart,

SMITH was just gone to school to say his part;
ROSS (a misfortune which we often meet)
630 Was fast asleep at dear STATIRA's feet;
STATIRA, with her hero to agree,
Stood on her feet as fast asleep as he;
MACKLIN, who largely deals in half-form'd sounds,
Who wantonly transgresses Nature's bounds,
635 Whose Acting's hard, affected, and constrain'd,
Whose features, as each other they disdain'd,
At variance set, inflexible and coarse,
Ne'er know the workings of united force,
Ne'er kindly soften to each other's aid,
640 Nor shew the mingled pow'rs of light and shade,
No longer for a thankless stage concern'd,
To worthier thoughts his mighty Genius turn'd,
Harangu'd, gave Lectures, made each simple elf
Almost as good a speaker as himself;
645 Whilst the whole town, mad with mistaken zeal,
An aukward rage for ELOCUTION feel;
Dull CITS and grave DIVINES his praise proclaim,
And join with SHERIDAN's their MACKLIN's name.
SHUTER, who never car'd a single pin
650 Whether he left out nonsense, or put in,
Who aim'd at wit, tho', levell'd in the dark,
The random arrow seldom hit the mark,
At Islington, all by the placid stream
Where city swains in lap of Dullness dream,
655 Where, quiet as her strains their strains *do* flow,
That all the patron by the bards may know;
Secret as night, with ROLT's experienc'd aid,
The plan of future operations laid,
Projected schemes the summer months to chear,
660 And spin out happy Folly through the year.
But think not, though these dastard-chiefs are fled,
That COVENT-GARDEN troops shall want a head:
HARLEQUIN comes their chief! — see from afar,
The hero seated in fantastic car!
665 Wedded to *Novelty,* his only arms
Are wooden swords, wands, talismans, and charms;
On one side Folly sits, by some call'd Fun,
And on the other, his arch-patron, LUN.
Behind, for liberty a-thirst in vain,
670 SENSE, helpless captive, drags the galling chain.

Six rude mis-shapen beasts the chariot draw,
Whom Reason loaths, and Nature never saw,
Monsters, with tails of ice, and heads of fire;
Gorgons, and Hydras, and Chymaeras dire.
675   Each was bestrode by full as monstrous wight,
Giant, Dwarf, Genius, Elf, Hermaphrodite.
The Town, as usual, met him in full cry;
The Town, as usual, knew no reason why.
But Fashion so directs, and Moderns raise
680   On Fashion's mould'ring base their transient praise.
    Next, to the field a band of females draw
Their force; for Britain owns no Salique Law:
Just to their worth, we female rights admit,
Nor bar their claim to empire or to wit.
685   First, giggling, plotting chamber-maids arrive,
Hoydens and romps, led on by Gen'ral CLIVE.
In spite of outward blemishes, she shone
For Humour fam'd, and Humour all her own.
Easy as if at Home the stage she trod,
690   Nor sought the critic's praise, nor fear'd his rod.
Original in spirit and in ease,
She pleas'd by hiding all attempts to please.
No comic actress ever yet could raise,
On Humour's base, more merit or more praise.
695   With all the native vigour of sixteen,
Among the merry troop conspicuous seen,
See lively POPE advance in *jig,* and *trip*
Corinna, Cherry, Honeycomb, and Snip.
Not without Art, but yet to Nature true,
700   She charms the town with humour just, yet new.
Chear'd by her promise, we the less deplore
The fatal time when CLIVE shall be no more.
    Lo! VINCENT comes — with simple grace array'd,
She laughs at paltry arts, and scorns parade.
705   Nature through her is by reflection shewn,
Whilst GAY once more knows POLLY for his own.
    Talk not to me of diffidence and fear —
I see it all, but must forgive it here.
Defects like these, which *modest* terrors cause,
710   From Impudence itself extort applause.
Candour and Reason still take Virtue's part;
We love e'en foibles in so good an heart.
    Let TOMMY ARNE, with usual pomp of stile,

Whose chief, whose only merit's to compile,
715 Who, meanly pilf'ring here and there a bit,
Deals music out as MURPHY deals out Wit,
Publish proposals, laws for taste prescribe,
And chant the praise of an ITALIAN tribe;
Let him reverse kind Nature's first decrees,
720 And teach e'en BRENT a method not to please;
But never shall a TRULY BRITISH Age
Bear a vile race of EUNUCHS on the stage.
The boasted work's call'd NATIONAL in vain,
If one ITALIAN voice pollutes the strain.
725 Where tyrants rule, and slaves with joy obey,
Let slavish minstrils pour th'enervate lay;
To BRITONS far more noble pleasures spring,
In native notes whilst BEARD and VINCENT sing.
  Might figure give a title unto fame,
730 What rival should with YATES dispute her claim?
But justice may not partial trophies raise,
Nor sink the Actress in the Woman's praise.
Still hand in hand her words and actions go,
And the heart feels more than the features show:
735 For, through the regions of that beauteous face,
We no variety of passions trace;
Dead to the soft emotions of the heart,
No kindred softness can those eyes impart;
The brow, still fix'd in sorrow's sullen frame,
740 Void of distinction, marks all parts the same.
  What's a fine person, or a beauteous face,
Unless deportment gives them decent grace?
Bless'd with all other requisites to please,
Some want the striking elegance of Ease;
745 The curious eye their aukward movement tires;
They seem like puppets led about by wires.
Others, like statues, in one posture still,
Give great ideas of the workman's skill;
Wond'ring, his art we praise the more we view,
750 And only grieve he gave not motion too.
Weak of themselves are what we beauties call,
It is the manner which gives strength to all.
This teaches ev'ry beauty to unite,
And brings them forward in the noblest light.
755 Happy in this, behold, amidst the throng,
With transient gleam of grace, HART sweeps along.

141

If all the wonders of external grace,
A person finely turn'd, a mould of face,
Where, Union rare, Expression's lively force
760 With Beauty's softest magic holds discourse,
Attract the eye; if feelings, void of art,
Rouze the quick passions, and enflame the heart;
If music, sweetly breathing from the tongue,
Captives the ear, BRIDE must not pass unsung.
765 When fear, which rank ill-nature terms conceit,
By time and custom conquer'd, shall retreat;
When judgment, tutor'd by experience sage,
Shall shoot abroad, and gather strength from age;
When heav'n in mercy shall the stage release
770 From the dull slumbers of a still-life piece;
When some stale flow'r, disgraceful to the walk,
Which long hath hung, tho' wither'd, on the stalk,
Shall kindly drop, then BRIDE shall make her way,
And merit find a passage to the day;
775 Brought into action she at once shall raise
Her own renown, and justify our praise.
  Form'd for the tragic scene, to grace the stage,
With rival excellence of Love and Rage,
Mistress of each soft art, with matchless skill
780 To turn and wind the passions as she will;
To melt the heart with sympathetic woe,
Awake the sigh, and teach the tear to flow;
To put on Frenzy's wild distracted glare,
And freeze the soul with horror and despair;
785 With just desert enroll'd in endless fame,
Conscious of worth superior, CIBBER came.
  When poor Alicia's madd'ning brains are rack'd,
And strongly imag'd griefs her mind distract;
Struck with her grief, I catch the madness too!
790 My brain turns round, the headless trunk I view!
The roof cracks, shakes, and falls! — New horrors rise,
And Reason buried in the ruin lies.
  Nobly disdainful of each slavish art,
She makes her first attack upon the heart:
795 Pleas'd with the summons, it receives her laws,
And all is silence, sympathy, applause.
But when, by fond ambition drawn aside,
Giddy with praise, and puff'd with female pride,
She quits the tragic scene, and, in pretence

142

800   To comic merit, breaks down Nature's fence;
   I scarcely can believe my ears or eyes,
   Or find out CIBBER through the dark disguise.
      PRITCHARD, by Nature for the stage design'd,
   In person graceful, and in sense refin'd;
805   Her art as much as Nature's friend became,
   Her voice as free from blemish as her fame.
   Who knows so well in majesty to please,
   Attemper'd with the graceful charms of ease?
      When Congreve's favour'd pantomime to grace,
810   She comes a captive queen of Moorish race;
   When Love, Hate, Jealousy, Despair and Rage,
   With wildest tumults in her breast engage;
   Still equal to herself is Zara seen;
   Her passions are the passions of a Queen.
815   When she to murther whets the tim'rous Thane,
   I feel ambition rush through ev'ry vein;
   Persuasion hangs upon her daring tongue,
   My heart grows flint, and ev'ry nerve's new strung.
      In Comedy — "Nay, there," cries Critic, "hold.
820   "PRITCHARD's for Comedy too fat and old.
   "Who can, with patience, bear the grey coquette,
   "Or force a laugh with over-grown Julett?
   "Her Speech, Look, Action, Humour, all are just;
   "But then, her age and figure give disgust."
825   Are Foibles then, and Graces of the mind,
   In real life, to size or age confin'd?
   Do spirits flow, and is good-breeding plac'd
   In any set circumference of waist?
   As we grow old, doth affectation cease,
830   Or gives not age new vigour to caprice?
   If in originals these things appear,
   Why should we bar them in the copy here?
   The nice punctilio-mongers of this age,
   The grand minute reformers of the stage,
835   Slaves to propriety of ev'ry kind,
   Some standard-measure for each part should find,
   Which when the best of Actors shall exceed,
   Let it devolve to one of smaller breed.
   All actors too upon the back should bear
840   Certificate of birth; — time, when; — place, where.
   For how can critics rightly fix their worth,
   Unless they know the minute of their birth?

An audience too, deceiv'd, may find too late
That they have clapp'd an actor out of date.
845   Figure, I own, at first may give offence,
And harshly strike the eye's too curious sense:
But when perfections of the mind break forth,
Humour's chaste sallies, Judgment's solid worth;
When the pure genuine flame, by Nature taught,
850 Springs into Sense, and ev'ry action's Thought;
Before such merit all objections fly;
PRITCHARD's genteel, and GARRICK six feet high.
    Oft have I, PRITCHARD, seen thy wond'rous skill,
Confess'd thee great, but find thee greater still.
855 That worth, which shone in scatter'd rays before,
Collected now, breaks forth with double pow'r.
The JEALOUS WIFE! — On that thy trophies raise,
Inferior only to the Author's praise.
    From Dublin, fam'd in legends of Romance
860 For mighty magic of enchanted lance,
With which her heroes arm'd victorious prove,
And like a flood rush o'er the land of Love;
MOSSOP and BARRY came. — Names ne'er design'd
By fate in the same sentence to be join'd.
865 Rais'd by the breath of popular acclaim,
They mounted to the pinnacle of Fame;
There the weak brain, made giddy with the height,
Spurr'd on the rival chiefs to mortal fight.
Thus sportive boys, around some bason's brim,
870 Behold the pipe-drawn bladders circling swim:
But if, from lungs more potent, there arise
Two bubbles of a more than common size,
Eager for honour they for fight prepare,
Bubble meets bubble, and both sink to air.
875   MOSSOP, attach'd to military plan,
Still kept his eye fix'd on his right-hand man.
Whilst the mouth measures words with seeming skill;
The right-hand labours, and the left lies still;
For he resolv'd on scripture-grounds to go,
880 What the right doth, the left-hand shall not know.
With studied impropriety of speech,
He soars beyond the hackney critic's reach;
To epithets allots emphatic state,
Whilst principals, ungrac'd, like lacquies wait;
885 In ways first trodden by himself excels,

And stands alone in indeclinables:
CONJUNCTION, PREPOSITION, ADVERB, join
To stamp new vigour on the nervous line:
In monosyllables his thunders roll,
890 HE, SHE, IT, AND, WE, YE, THEY, fright the soul.
  In person taller than the common size,
Behold where BARRY draws admiring eyes!
When lab'ring passions, in his bosom pent,
Convulsive rage, and struggling heave for vent;
895 Spectators, with imagin'd terrors warm,
Anxious expect the bursting of the storm:
But, all unfit in such a pile to dwell,
His voice comes forth, like Echo from her cell;
To swell the tempest needful aid denies,
900 And all a-down the stage in feeble murmurs dies.
  What man, like BARRY, with such pains, can err
In elocution, action, character?
What man could give, if BARRY was not here,
Such well-applauded tenderness to Lear?
905 Who else can speak so very, very fine,
That sense may kindly end with ev'ry line?
  Some dozen lines before the ghost is there,
Behold him for the solemn scene prepare.
See how he frames his eyes, poises each limb,
910 Puts the whole body into proper trim, —
From whence we learn, with no great stretch of art,
Five lines hence comes a ghost, and, Ha! a start.
  When he appears most perfect, still we find
Something which jars upon, and hurts the mind,
915 Whatever lights upon a part are thrown,
We see too plainly they are not his own.
No flame from Nature ever yet he caught,
Nor knew a feeling which he was not taught;
He rais'd his trophies on the base of art,
920 And conn'd his passions, as he conn'd his part.
  QUIN, from afar, lur'd by the scent of fame,
A Stage Leviathan, put in his claim,
Pupil of BETTERTON and BOOTH. Alone,
Sullen he walk'd, and deem'd the chair his own.
925 For how should Moderns, mushrooms of the day,
Who ne'er those masters knew, know how to play?
Grey-bearded vet'rans, who, with partial tongue,
Extol the times when they themselves were young;

Who, having lost all relish for the stage,
930 See not their own defects, but lash the age,
Receiv'd, with joyful murmurs of applause,
Their darling chief, and lin'd his fav'rite cause.
    Far be it from the candid muse to tread
Insulting o'er the ashes of the dead,
935 But, just to living merit, she maintains,
And dares the test, whilst GARRICK's Genius reigns;
Ancients, in vain, endeavour to excel,
Happily prais'd, if they could act as well.
But, though prescription's force we disallow,
940 Nor to antiquity submissive bow;
Though we deny imaginary grace,
Founded on accidents of time and place;
Yet real worth of ev'ry growth shall bear
Due praise, nor must we, QUIN, forget thee there.
945   His words bore sterling weight, nervous and strong,
In manly tides of sense they roll'd along.
Happy in art, he chiefly had pretence
To keep up numbers, yet not forfeit sense.
No actor ever greater heights could reach
950 In all the labour'd artifice of speech.
Speech! Is that all? — And shall an actor found
An universal fame on partial ground?
Parrots themselves speak properly by rote,
And, in six months, my dog shall howl by note.
955 I laugh at those, who, when the stage they tread,
Neglect the heart, to compliment the head;
With strict propriety their care's confin'd
To weigh out words, while passion halts behind.
To Syllable-dissectors they appeal,
960 Allow them accent, cadence, — Fools may feel;
But, Spite of all the criticising elves,
Those who would make us feel, must feel themselves.
    His eyes, in gloomy socket taught to roll,
Proclaim'd the sullen habit of his soul.
965 Heavy and phlegmatic he trod the stage,
Too proud for Tenderness, too dull for Rage.
When Hector's lovely widow shines in Tears,
Or Rowe's gay Rake dependant Virtue jeers,
With the same cast of features he is seen
970 To chide the Libertine, and court the Queen.
From the tame scene, which without passion flows,

With just desert his reputation rose;
Nor less he pleas'd, when, on some surly plan,
He was, at once, the Actor and the Man.
975 In Brute he shone unequall'd: all agree
GARRICK's not half so great a brute as he.
When Cato's labour'd scenes are brought to view,
With equal praise the Actor labour'd too,
For still you'll find, trace passions to their root,
980 Small diff'rence 'twixt the Stoic and the Brute.
In fancied scenes, as in life's real plan,
He could not, for a moment, sink the Man.
In whate'er cast his character was laid,
Self still, like oil, upon the surface play'd.
985 Nature, in spite of all his skill, crept in:
Horatio, Dorax, Falstaff, — still 'twas QUIN.
   Next follows SHERIDAN. — A doubtful name,
As yet unsettled in the rank of fame.
This, fondly lavish in his praises grown,
990 Gives him all merit: That allows him none.
Between them both, we'll steer the middle course,
Nor, loving praise, rob judgment of her force.
   Just his conceptions, natural and great:
His feelings strong, his words enforc'd with weight.
995 Was speech-fam'd QUIN himself to hear him speak,
Envy would drive the colour from his cheek:
But step-dame Nature, niggard of her grace,
Deny'd the social pow'rs of voice and face.
Fix'd in one frame of features, glare of eye,
1000 Passions, like chaos, in confusion lie:
In vain the wonders of his skill are try'd
To form distinctions Nature hath deny'd.
His voice no touch of harmony admits,
Irregularly deep, and shrill by fits:
1005 The two extremes appear like man and wife,
Coupled together for the sake of strife.
   His action's always strong, but sometimes such
That Candour must declare he acts too much.
Why must impatience fall three paces back?
1010 Why paces three return to the attack?
Why is the right leg too forbid to stir,
Unless in motion semicircular?
Why must the hero with the Nailor vie,
And hurl the close-clench'd fist at nose or eye?

147

1015   In royal John, with Philip angry grown,
    I thought he would have knock'd poor DAVIES down.
    Inhuman tyrant! was it not a shame,
    To fright a king so harmless and so tame?
    But, spite of all defects, his glories rise;
1020   And Art, by Judgment form'd, with Nature vies;
    Behold him sound the depth of HUBERT's soul,
    Whilst in his own contending passions roll;
    View the whole scene, with critic judgment scan,
    And then deny him Merit if you can.
1025   Where he falls short, 'tis Nature's fault alone;
    Where he succeeds, the Merit's all his own.
        Last GARRICK came. — Behind him throng a train
    Of snarling critics, ignorant as vain.
        One finds out, — "He's of stature somewhat low, —
1030   "Your Hero always should be tall you know. —
    "True nat'ral greatness all consists in height."
    Produce your voucher, Critic — "Sergeant KYTE."
        Another can't forgive the paltry arts,
    By which he makes his way to shallow hearts;
1035   Mere pieces of finesse, traps for applause. —
    "Avaunt, unnat'ral Start, affected Pause."
        For me, by Nature form'd to judge with phlegm,
    I can't acquit by wholesale, nor condemn.
    The best things carried to excess are wrong:
1040   The start may be too frequent, pause too long;
    But, only us'd in proper time and place,
    Severest judgment must allow them Grace.
        If Bunglers, form'd on Imitation's plan,
    Just in the way that monkies mimic man,
1035   Their copied scene with mangled arts disgrace,
    And pause and start with the same vacant face;
    We join the critic laugh; those tricks we scorn,
    Which spoil the scenes they mean them to adorn.
    But when, from Nature's pure and genuine source,
1050   These strokes of Acting flow with gen'rous force,
    When in the features all the soul's portray'd,
    And passions, such as GARRICK's are display'd,
    To me they seem from quickest feelings caught:
    Each start is Nature; and each pause is Thought.
1055   When Reason yields to Passion's wild alarms,
    And the whole state of man is up in arms;
    What, but a Critic, could condemn the Play'r,

For pausing here, when Cool Sense pauses there?
Whilst, working from the Heart, the fire I trace,
1060 And mark it strongly flaming to the Face;
Whilst, in each sound, I hear the very man;
I can't catch words, and pity those who can.
    Let wits, like spiders, from the tortur'd brain
Fine-draw the critic-web with curious pain;
1065 The gods, — a kindness I with thanks must pay, —
Have form'd me of a coarser kind of clay;
Nor stung with envy, nor with Spleen diseas'd,
A poor dull creature, still with Nature pleas'd;
Hence to thy praises, GARRICK, I agree,
1070 And, pleas'd with Nature, must be pleas'd with Thee.
    Now might I tell, how silence reign'd throughout,
And deep attention hush'd the rabble rout:
How ev'ry claimant, tortur'd with desire,
Was pale as ashes, or as red as fire:
1075 But, loose to Fame, the muse more simply acts,
Rejects all flourish, and relates mere facts.
    The Judges, as the sev'ral parties came,
With temper heard, with Judgment weigh'd each Claim,
And, in their sentence happily agreed,
1080 In name of both, Great SHAKESPEARE thus decreed:
    "If manly Sense; if Nature link'd with Art;
"If thorough knowledge of the Human Heart;
"If Pow'rs of acting vast and unconfin'd;
"If fewest Faults with greatest Beauties join'd;
1085 "If strong Expression, and strange Pow'rs, which lie
"Within the magic circle of the Eye;
"If feelings which few hearts, like his, can know,
"And which no face so well as His can show;
"Deserve the Pref'rence; — GARRICK take the Chair;
1090 "Nor quit it — till Thou place an Equal there."

Christopher Smart

A SONG TO DAVID

I

O THOU, that sit'st upon a throne,
With harp of high majestic tone,
   To praise the King of kings;
And voice of heav'n-ascending swell,
5   Which, while its deeper notes excell,
   Clear, as a clarion, rings:

II

To bless each valley, grove and coast,
And charm the cherubs to the post
   Of gratitude in throngs;
10   To *keep* the days on Zion's mount,
And send the year to his account,
   With dances and with songs:

III

O Servant of God's holiest charge,
The minister of praise at large,
15   Which thou may'st now receive;
From thy blest mansion hail and hear,
From topmost eminence appear
   To this the wreath I weave.

IV

Great, valiant, pious, good, and clean,
20   Sublime, contemplative, serene,
   Strong, constant, pleasant, wise!
Bright effluence of exceeding grace;
Best man! — the swiftness and the race,
   The peril, and the prize!

V

25 Great — from the lustre of his crown,
From Samuel's horn and God's renown,
    Which is the people's voice;
For all the host, from rear to van,
Applauded and embrac'd the man —
30   The man of God's own choice.

VI

Valiant — the word, and up he rose —
The fight — he triumph'd o'er the foes,
    Whom God's just laws abhor;
And arm'd in gallant faith he took
35 Against the boaster, from the brook,
    The weapons of the war.

VII

Pious — magnificent and grand;
'Twas he the famous temple plan'd:
    (The seraph in his soul)
40 Foremost to give the Lord his dues,
Foremost to bless the welcome news,
    And foremost to condole.

VIII

Good — from Jehudah's genuine vein,
From God's best nature good in grain,
45   His aspect and his heart;
To pity, to forgive, to save,
Witness En-gedi's conscious cave,
    And Shimei's blunted dart.

IX

Clean — if perpetual prayer be pure,
50 And love, which could itself innure
    To fasting and to fear —
Clean in his gestures, hands, and feet,
To smite the lyre, the dance compleat,
    To play the sword and spear.

X

55 Sublime — invention ever young,
Of vast conception, tow'ring tongue,
  To God th'eternal theme;
Notes from yon exaltations caught,
Unrivall'd royalty of thought,
60   O'er meaner strains supreme.

XI

Contemplative — on God to fix
His musings, and above the six
  The sabbath-day he blest;
'Twas then his thoughts self-conquest prun'd,
65 And heavenly melancholy tun'd,
  To bless and bear the rest.

XII

Serene — to sow the seeds of peace,
Rememb'ring, when he watch'd the fleece,
  How sweetly Kidron purl'd —
70 To further knowledge, silence vice,
And plant perpetual paradise
  When God had calm'd the world.

XIII

Strong — in the Lord, who could defy
Satan, and all his powers that lie
75   In sempiternal night;
And hell, and horror, and despair
Were as the lion and the bear
  To his undaunted might.

XIV

Constant — in love to God THE TRUTH,
80 Age, manhood, infancy, and youth —
  To Jonathan his friend
Constant, beyond the verge of death;
And Ziba, and Mephibosheth,
  His endless fame attend.

XV

85 Pleasant — and various as the year;
Man, soul, and angel, without peer,

Priest, champion, sage and boy;
In armour, or in ephod clad,
His pomp, his piety was glad;
90   Majestic was his joy.

XVI

Wise — in recovery from his fall,
Whence rose his eminence o'er all,
   Of all the most revil'd;
The light of Israel in his ways,
95 Wise are his precepts, prayer and praise,
   And counsel to his child.

XVII

His muse, bright angel of his verse,
Gives balm for all the thorns that pierce,
   For all the pangs that rage;
100 Blest light, still gaining on the gloom,
The more than Michal of his bloom,
   Th'Abishag of his age.

XVIII

He sung of God — the mighty source
Of all things — the stupendous force
105   On which all strength depends;
From whose right arm, beneath whose eyes,
All period, pow'r, and enterprize
   Commences, reigns, and ends.

XIX

Angels — their ministry and meed,
110 Which to and fro with blessings speed,
   Or with their citterns wait;
Where Michael with his millions bows,
Where dwells the seraph and his spouse,
   The cherub and her mate.

XX

115 Of man — the semblance and effect
Of God and Love — the Saint elect
   For infinite applause —
To rule the land, and briny broad,
To be laborious in his laud,
120   And heroes in his cause.

XXI

The world — the clustring spheres he made,
The glorious light, the soothing shade,
    Dale, champaign, grove, and hill;
The multitudinous abyss,
125   Where secrecy remains in bliss,
    And wisdom hides her skill.

XXII

Trees, plants, and flow'rs — of virtuous root;
Gem yielding blossom, yielding fruit,
    Choice gums and precious balm;
130   Bless ye the nosegay in the vale,
And with the sweetners of the gale
    Enrich the thankful psalm.

XXIII

Of fowl — e'en ev'ry beak and wing
Which chear the winter, hail the spring,
135   That live in peace or prey;
They that make music, or that mock,
The quail, the brave domestic cock,
    The raven, swan, and jay.

XXIV

Of fishes — ev'ry size and shape,
140   Which nature frames of light escape,
    Devouring man to shun:
The shells are in the wealthy deep,
The shoals upon the surface leap,
    And love the glancing sun.

XXV

145   Of beasts — the beaver plods his task;
While the sleek tygers roll and bask,
    Nor yet the shades arouse:
Her cave the mining coney scoops;
Where o'er the mead the mountain stoops,
150   The kids exult and brouse.

XXVI

Of gems — their virtue and their price,
Which hid in earth from man's device,
   Their darts of lustre sheathe;
The jasper of the master's stamp,
155   The topaz blazing like a lamp
     Among the mines beneath.

XXVII

Blest was the tenderness he felt
When to his graceful harp he knelt,
   And did for audience call;
160   When satan with his hand he quell'd,
And in serene suspence he held
     The frantic throes of Saul.

XXVIII

His furious foes no more malign'd
165   As he such melody divin'd,
   And sense and soul detain'd;
Now striking strong, now soothing soft,
He sent the godly sounds aloft,
     Or in delight refrain'd.

XXIX

When up to heav'n his thoughts he pil'd,
170   From fervent lips fair Michal smil'd,
   As blush to blush she stood;
And chose herself the queen, and gave
Her utmost from her heart, "so brave,
     "And plays his hymns so good."

XXX

175   The pillars of the Lord are seven,
Which stand from earth to topmost heav'n;
   His wisdom drew the plan;
His WORD accomplish'd the design,
From brightest gem to deepest mine,
180   From CHRIST enthon'd to man.

XXXI

Alpha, the cause of causes, first
In station, fountain, whence the burst

Of light, and blaze of day;
Whence bold attempt, and brave advance,
185   Have motion, life, and ordinance,
        And heav'n itself its stay.

XXXII

Gamma supports the glorious arch
On which angelic legions march,
        And is with sapphires pav'd;
190   Thence the fleet clouds are sent adrift
And thence the painted folds, that lift
        The crimson veil, are wav'd.

XXXIII

Eta with living sculpture breathes,
With verdant carvings, flow'ry wreathes
195   Of never-wasting bloom;
In strong relief his goodly base
All instruments of labour grace,
        The trowel, spade, and loom.

XXXIV

Next Theta stands to the Supreme —
200   Who form'd, in number, sign, and scheme,
        Th'illustrious lights that are;
And one address'd his saffron robe,
And one, clad in a silver globe,
        Held rule with ev'ry star.

XXXV

205   Iota's tun'd to choral hymns
Of those that fly, while he that swims
        In thankful safety lurks;
And foot, and chapitre, and niche,
The various histories enrich
210   Of God's recorded works.

XXXVI

Sigma presents the social droves,
With him that solitary roves,
        And man of all the chief;
Fair on whose face, and stately frame,
215   Did God impress his hallow'd name,
        For ocular belief.

XXXVII

OMEGA! GREATEST and the BEST,
Stands sacred to the day of rest,
    For gratitude and thought;
220   Which bless'd the world upon his pole,
And gave the universe his goal,
    And clos'd th'infernal draught.

XXXVIII

O DAVID, scholar of the Lord!
Such is thy science, whence reward
225   And infinite degree;
O strength, O sweetness, lasting ripe!
God's harp thy symbol, and thy type
    The lion and the bee!

XXXIX

There is but One who ne'er rebell'd,
230   But One by passion unimpell'd,
    By pleasures unintice't;
He from himself his semblance sent,
Grand object of his own content,
    And saw the God in CHRIST.

XL

235   Tell them I am, JEHOVA said
To MOSES; while earth heard in dread,
    And smitten to the heart,
At once above, beneath, around,
All nature, without voice or sound,
240   Replied, O Lord, THOU ART.

XLI

Thou art — to give and to confirm,
For each his talent and his term;
    All flesh thy bounties share:
Thou shalt not call thy brother fool;
245   The porches of the Christian school
    Are meekness, peace, and pray'r.

XLII

Open, and naked of offence,
Man's made of mercy, soul, and sense;
   God arm'd the snail and wilk;
250   Be good to him that pulls thy plough;
Due food and care, due rest, allow
   For her that yields thee milk.

XLIII

Rise up before the hoary head,
And God's benign commandment dread,
255   Which says thou shalt not die:
"Not as I will, but as thou wilt,"
Pray'd He whose conscience knew no guilt;
   With whose bless'd pattern vie.

XLIV

Use all thy passions! — love is thine,
260   And joy, and jealousy divine;
   Thine hope's eternal fort,
And care thy leisure to disturb,
With fear concupiscence to curb,
   And rapture to transport.

XLV

265   Act simply, as occasion asks;
Put mellow wine in season'd casks;
   Till not with ass and bull:
Remember thy baptismal bond;
Keep from commixtures foul and fond,
270   Nor work thy flax with wool.

XLVI

Distribute: pay the Lord his tithe,
And make the widow's heart-strings blithe;
   Resort with those that weep:
As you from all and each expect,
275   For all and each thy love direct,
   And render as you reap.

XLVII

The slander and its bearer spurn,
And propagating praise sojourn

To make thy welcome last;
280　Turn from old Adam to the New;
By hope futurity pursue;
　　Look upwards to the past.

XLVIII
Controul thine eye, salute success,
Honour the wiser, happier bless,
285　　And for thy neighbour feel;
Grutch not of mammon and his leaven,
Work emulation up to heaven
　　By knowledge and by zeal.

XLIX
O DAVID, highest in the list
290　Of worthies, on God's ways insist,
　　The genuine word repeat:
Vain are the documents of men,
And vain the flourish of the pen
　　That keeps the fool's conceit.

L
295　PRAISE above all — for praise prevails;
Heap up the measure, load the scales,
　　And good to goodness add:
The gen'rous soul her Saviour aids,
But peevish obloquy degrades;
300　　The Lord is great and glad.

LI
For ADORATION all the ranks
Of angels yield eternal thanks,
　　And DAVID in the midst;
With God's good poor, which, last and least
305　In man's esteem, thou to thy feast,
　　O blessed bride-groom, bidst.

LII
For ADORATION seasons change,
And order, truth, and beauty range,
　　Adjust, attract, and fill:
310　The grass the polyanthus cheques;
And polish'd porphyry reflects,
　　By the descending rill.

159

LIII

Rich almonds colour to the prime
For ADORATION; tendrils climb,
    And fruit-frees pledge their gems;
And Ivis with her gorgeous vest
Builds for her eggs her cunning nest,
    And bell-flowers bow their stems.

315

LIV

With vinous syrup cedars spout;
From rocks pure honey gushing out,
    For ADORATION springs:
All scenes of painting croud the map
Of nature; to the mermaid's pap
    The scaled infant clings.

320

LV

The spotted ounce and playsome cubs
Run rustling 'mongst the flow'ring shrubs,
    And lizards feed the moss;
For ADORATION beasts embark,
While waves upholding halcyon's ark
    No longer roar and toss.

325

330

LVI

While Israel sits beneath his fig,
With coral root and amber sprig
    The wean'd advent'rer sports;
Where to the palm the jasmin cleaves,
For ADORATION 'mongst the leaves
    The gale his peace reports.

335

LVII

Increasing days their reign exalt,
Nor in the pink and mottled vault
    Th'opposing spirits tilt;
And, by the coasting reader spied,
The silverlings and crusions glide
    For ADORATION gilt.

340

LVIII

For ADORATION rip'ning canes
And cocoa's purest milk detains
    The western pilgrim's staff;
Where rain in clasping boughs inclos'd,
And vines with oranges dispos'd,
    Embow'r the social laugh.

LIX

Now labour his reward receives,
For ADORATION counts his sheaves
    To peace, her bounteous prince;
The nectarine his strong tint imbibes,
And apples of ten thousand tribes,
    And quick peculiar quince.

LX

The wealthy crops of whit'ning rice,
'Mongst thyine woods and groves of spice,
    For ADORATION grow;
And, marshall'd in the fenced land,
The peaches and pomegranates stand,
    Where wild carnations blow.

LXI

The laurels with the winter strive;
The crocus burnishes alive
    Upon the snow-clad earth:
For ADORATION myrtles stay
To keep the garden from dismay,
    And bless the sight from dearth.

LXII

The pheasant shows his pompous neck;
And ermine, jealous of a speck,
    With fear eludes offence:
The sable, with his glossy pride,
For ADORATION is descried,
    Where frosts the wave condense.

LXIII

The chearful holly, pensive yew,
And holy thorn, their trim renew;

375   The squirrel hoards his nuts:
All creatures batten o'er their stores,
And careful nature all her doors
        For ADORATION shuts.

LXIV

For ADORATION, DAVID'S psalms
380   Lift up the heart to deeds of alms;
        And he, who kneels and chants,
Prevails his passions to controul,
Finds meat and med'cine to the soul,
        Which for translation pants.

LXV

385   For ADORATION, beyond match,
The scholar bulfinch aims to catch
        The soft flute's iv'ry touch;
And, careless on the hazle spray,
The daring redbreast keeps at bay
390   The damsel's greedy clutch.

LXVI

For ADORATION, in the skies,
The Lord's philosopher espies
        The Dog, the Ram, and Rose;
The planets ring, Orion's sword;
395   Nor is his greatness less ador'd
        In the vile worm that glows.

LXVII

For ADORATION on the strings
The western breezes work their wings,
        The captive ear to sooth. —
400   Hark! 'tis a voice — how still, and small —
That makes the cataracts to fall,
        Or bids the sea be smooth.

LXVIII

For ADORATION, incense comes
From bezoar, and Arabian gums;
405   And on the civet's furr.
But as for prayer, or e're it faints,
Far better is the breath of saints
        Than galbanum and myrrh.

LXIX

For ADORATION from the down,
Of dam'sins to th'anana's crown,
   God sends to tempt the taste;
And while the luscious zest invites,
The sense, that in the scene delights,
   Commands desire be chaste.

LXX

For ADORATION, all the paths
Of grace are open, all the baths
   Of purity refresh;
And all the rays of glory beam
To deck the man of God's esteem,
   Who triumphs o'er the flesh.

LXXI

For ADORATION, in the dome
Of Christ the sparrow's find an home;
   And on his olives perch:
The swallow also dwells with thee,
O man of God's humility,
   Within his Saviour's CHURCH.

LXXII

Sweet is the dew that falls betimes,
And drops upon the leafy limes;
   Sweet Hermon's fragrant air:
Sweet is the lilly's silver bell,
And sweet the wakeful tapers smell
   That watch for early pray'r.

LXXIII

Sweet the young nurse with love intense,
Which smiles o'er sleeping innocence;
   Sweet when the lost arrive:
Sweet the musician's ardour beats,
While his vague mind's in quest of sweets
   The choicest flow'rs to hive.

LXXIV

Sweeter in all the strains of love,
440   The language of thy turtle dove,
        Pair'd to thy swelling chord;
Sweeter with ev'ry grace endu'd,
The glory of thy gratitude,
        Respir'd unto the Lord.

LXXV

445   Strong is the horse upon his speed;
Strong in pursuit the rapid glede,
        Which makes at once his game:
Strong the tall ostrich on the ground;
Strong thro' the turbulent profound
450   Shoots xiphias to his aim.

LXXVI

Strong is the lion — like a coal
His eye-ball — like a bastion's mole
        His chest against the foes:
Strong, the gier-eagle on his sail,
455   Strong against tide, th'enormous whale
        Emerges as he goes.

LXXVII

But stronger still, in earth and air,
And in the sea, the man of pray'r;
        And far beneath the tide;
460   And in the seat to faith assign'd,
Where ask is have, where seek is find,
        Where knock is open wide.

LXXVIII

Beauteous the fleet before the gale;
Beauteous the multitudes in mail,
465   Rank'd arms and crested heads:
Beauteous the garden's umbrage mild,
Walk, water, meditated wild,
        And all the bloomy beds.

LXXIX

Beauteous the moon full on the lawn;
470   And beauteous, when the veil's withdrawn,

The virgin to her spouse:
Beauteous the temple deck'd and fill'd,
When to the heav'n of heav'ns they build
    Their heart-directed vows.

LXXX
475 Beauteous, yea beauteous more than these,
The shepherd king upon his knees,
    For his momentous trust;
With wish of infinite conceit,
For man, beast, mute, the small and great,
480   And prostrate dust to dust.

LXXXI
Precious the bounteous widow's mite;
And precious, for extream delight,
    The largess from the churl:
Precious the ruby's blushing blaze,
485 And alba's blest imperial rays,
    And pure cerulean pearl.

LXXXII
Precious the penitential tear;
And precious is the sigh sincere,
    Acceptable to God:
490 And precious are the winning flow'rs,
In gladsome Israel's feast of bow'rs,
    Bound on the hallow'd sod.

LXXXIII
More precious that diviner part
Of David, ev'n the Lord's own heart,
495   Great, beautiful, and new:
In all things where it was intent,
In all extreams, in each event,
    Proof — answ'ring true to true.

LXXXIV
Glorious the sun in mid career;
500 Glorious th'assembled fires appear;
    Glorious the comet's train:
Glorious the trumpet and alarm;
Glorious th'almighty stretch'd-out arm;
    Glorious th'enraptur'd main:

LXXXV

505   Glorious the northern lights astream;
Glorious the song, when God's the theme;
    Glorious the thunder's roar:
Glorious hosanna from the den;
Glorious the catholic amen;
510   Glorious the martyr's gore:

LXXXVI

Glorious — more glorious is the crown
Of Him that brought salvation down
    By meekness, call'd thy Son:
Thou that stupendous truth believ'd,
515   And now the matchless deed's atchiev'd,
    DETERMINED, DARED, and DONE.

John Cunningham

NEWCASTLE BEER

I

WHEN Fame brought the news of Great Britain's success,
    And told at Olympus each Gallic defeat;
Glad Mars sent by Mercury orders express,
    To summon the deities all to a treat:
        Blithe Comus was plac'd
        To guide the gay feast,
And freely declar'd there was choice of good cheer;
        Yet vow'd to his thinking,
        For exquisite drinking,
Their Nectar was nothing to Newcastle Beer.

II

The great God of War, to encourage the fun
    And humour the taste of his whimsical guest,
Sent a message that moment to Moor's for a tun
    Of Stingo, the stoutest, the brightest, and best:
        No Gods — they all swore,
        Regal'd so before,
With liquor so lively — so potent, and clear:
        And each deified fellow
        Got jovially mellow,
In honour, brave boys, of our Newcastle Beer.

III

Apollo, perceiving his talents refine,
    Repents he drank Helicon Water so long:
He bow'd, being ask'd by the musical Nine,
    And gave the gay board an extempore song;
        But 'ere he began,

He toss'd off his cann:
There's nought like good liquor the fancy to clear:
Then sang with great merit,
The flavour and spirit,
30 His godship had found in the Newcastle Beer.

IV

'Twas Stingo like this made Alcides so bold;
It brac'd up his nerves, and enliven'd his pow'rs;
And his mystical club, that did wonders of old,
Was nothing, my lads, but such liquor as ours.
35 The horrible crew
That Hercules slew,
Were Poverty — Calumny — Trouble — and Fear:
Such a club would you borrow,
To drive away sorrow,
40 Apply for a *quantum* of Newcastle Beer.

V

Ye youngsters, so diffident, languid and pale!
Whom Love, like the cholic, so rudely infests;
Take a cordial of this, 'twill *probatum* prevail,
And drive the cur Cupid away from your breasts:
45 Dull whining despise,
Grow rosy and wise,
Nor longer the jest of good fellows appear;
Bid adieu to your folly,
Get drunk and be jolly,
50 And smoke o'er a tankard of Newcastle Beer.

VI

Ye fanciful folk, for whom *Physic* prescribes,
Whom bolus and potion have harrass'd to death!
Ye wretches, whom *Law* and her ill-looking tribes
Have hunted about 'till you're quite out of breath!
55 Here's shelter and ease,
No craving for fees,
No danger, — no doctor, — no bailiff is near!
Your spirits this raises,
It cures your diseases,
60 There's freedom and health in our Newcastle Beer.

Mark Akenside

THE BEGINNING OF THE FOURTH BOOK OF THE

PLEASURES OF THE IMAGINATION

ONE effort more, one cheerful sally more,
Our destin'd course will finish; and in peace
Then, for an offering sacred to the powers
Who lent us gracious guidance, we will then
5   Inscribe a monument of deathless praise,
O my adventurous song. With steady speed
Long hast thou, on an untried voyage bound,
Sail'd between earth and heaven: hast now survey'd,
Stretch'd out beneath thee, all the mazy tracts
10   Of passion and opinion; like a waste
Of sands and flowery lawns and tangling woods,
Where mortals roam bewilder'd: and hast now,
Exulting soar'd among the worlds above,
Or hover'd near the eternal gates of heaven,
15   If haply the discourses of the Gods,
A curious, but an unpresuming guest,
Thou might'st partake, and carry back some strain
Of divine wisdom, lawful to repeat,
And apt to be conceiv'd of man below.
20   A different task remains; the secret paths
Of early genius to explore: to trace
Those haunts where Fancy her predestin'd sons,
Like to the Demigods of old, doth nurse
Remote from eyes profane. Ye happy souls
25   Who now her tender discipline obey,
Where dwell ye? What wild river's brink at eve
Imprint your steps? What solemn groves at noon
Use ye to visit, often breaking forth

In rapture 'mid your dilatory walk,
30   Or musing, as in slumber, on the green?
— Would I again were with you! — O ye dales
Of Tyne, and ye most ancient woodlands; where,
Oft as the giant flood obliquely strides,
And his banks open, and his lawns extend,
35   Stops short the pleased traveller to view
Presiding o'er the scene some rustic tower
Founded by Norman or by Saxon hands:
O ye Northumbrian shades, which overlook
The rocky pavement and the mossy falls
40   Of solitary Wensbeck's limpid stream;
How gladly I recall your well-known seats
Belov'd of old, and that delightful time
When all alone, for many a summer's day,
I wander'd through your calm recesses, led
45   In silence by some powerful hand unseen.
     Nor will I e'er forget you; nor shall e'er
The graver tasks of manhood, or the advice
Of vulgar wisdom, move me to disclaim
Those studies which possess'd me in the dawn
50   Of life, and fix'd the colour of my mind
For every future year: whence even now
From sleep I rescue the clear hours of morn,
And, while the world around lies overwhelm'd
In idle darkness, am alive to thoughts
55   Of honourable fame, of truth divine
Or moral, and of minds to virtue won
By the sweet magic of harmonious verse;
The themes which now expect us. For thus far
On general habits, and on arts which grow
60   Spontaneous in the minds of all mankind,
Hath dwelt our argument; and how self-taught,
Though seldom conscious of their own imploy,
In nature's or in fortune's changeful scene
Men learn to judge of beauty, and acquire
65   Those forms set up, as idols in the soul
For love and zealous praise. Yet indistinct,
In vulgar bosoms, and unnotic'd lie
These pleasing stores, unless the casual force
Of things external prompt the heedless mind
70   To recognize her wealth. But some there are
Conscious of nature, and the rule which man

O'er nature holds: some who, within themselves
Retiring from the trivial scenes of chance
And momentary passion, can at will
75   Call up these fair exemplars of the mind;
Review their features; scan the secret laws
Which bind them to each other: and display
By forms, or sounds, or colors, to the sense
Of all the world their latent charms display:
80   Even as in nature's frame (if such a word,
If such a word, so bold, may from the lips
Of man proceed) as in this outward frame
Of things, the great artificer pourtrays
His own immense idea. Various names
85   These among mortals bear, as various signs
They use, and, by peculiar organs speak
To human sense. There are who by the flight
Of air through tubes with moving stops distinct,
Or by extended chords in measure taught
90   To vibrate, can assemble powerful sounds
Expressing every temper of the mind
From every cause, and charming all the soul
With passion void of care. Others mean time
The rugged mass of metal, wood, or stone
95   Patiently taming; or with easier hand
Describing lines, and with more ample scope
Uniting colors; can to general sight
Produce those permanent and perfect forms,
Those characters of heroes and of gods,
100   Which from the crude materials of the world
Their own high minds created. But the chief
Are poets; eloquent men, who dwell on earth
To clothe whate'er the soul admires or loves
With language and with numbers. Hence to these
105   A field is open'd wide as nature's sphere;
Nay, wider: various as the sudden acts
Of human wit, and vast as the demands
Of human will. The bard nor length, nor depth,
Nor place, nor form controuls. To eyes, to ears,
110   To every organ of the copious mind,
He offereth all its treasures. Him the hours,
The seasons him obey: and changeful Time
Sees him at will keep measure with his flight,
At will outstrip it. To enhance his toil,

115   He summoneth, from the uttermost extent
           Of things which God hath taught him, every form
           Auxiliar, every power; and all beside
           Excludes imperious. His prevailing hand
           Gives, to corporeal essence, life and sense
120   And every stately function of the soul.
           The soul itself to him obsequious lies,
           Like matter's passive heap; and as he wills,
           To reason and affection he assigns
           Their just alliances, their just degrees:
125   Whence his peculiar honours: whence the race
           Of men who people his delightful world,
           Men genuine and according to themselves,
           Transcend as far the uncertain sons of earth,
           As earth itself to his delightful world
130   The palm of spotless beauty doth resign.

Thomas Chatterton

AN EXCELENTE BALADE OF CHARITIE: AS

WROTEN BIE THE GODE PRIESTE THOMAS ROWLEY, 1464

IN Virgyne the sweltrie sun gan sheene,
And hotte upon the mees did caste his raie;
The apple rodded from its palie greene,
And the mole peare did bende the leafy spraie;
5   The peede chelandri sunge the livelong daie;
'Twas nowe the pride, the manhode of the yeare,
And eke the grounde was dighte in its mose defte aumere.

The sun was glemeing in the midde of daie,
Deadde still the aire, and eke the welken blue,
10   When from the sea arist in drear arraie
A hepe of cloudes of sable sullen hue,
The which full fast unto the woodlande drewe,
Hiltring attenes the sunnis fetive face,
And the blacke tempeste swolne and gatherd up apace.

15   Beneathe an holme, faste by a pathwaie side,
Which did unto Seyncte Godwine's covent lede,
A hapless pilgrim moneynge did abide,
Pore in his viewe, ungentle in his weede,
Longe bretful of the miseries of neede,
20   Where from the hail-stone coulde the almer flie?
He had no housen theere, ne anie covent nie.

Look in his glommed face, his sprighte there scanne;
Howe woe-be-gone, how withered, forwynd, deade!
Haste to thie church-glebe-house, ashrewed manne!
25   Haste to thie kiste, thie onlie dortoure bedde.

173

Cale, as the claie whiche will gre on thie hedde,
Is Charitie and Love aminge highe elves;
Knightis and Barons live for pleasure and themselves.

The gatherd storme is rype; the bigge drops falle;
30   The forswat meadowes smethe, and drenche the raine;
The comyng ghastness do the cattle pall,
And the full flockes are drivynge ore the plaine;
Dashde from the cloudes the waters flott againe;
The welkin opes; the yellow levynne flies;
35 And the hot fierie smothe in the wide lowings dies.

Liste! now the thunder's rattling clymmynge sound
Cheves slowlie on, and then embollen clangs,
Shakes the hie spyre, and losst, dispended, drown'd,
Still on the gallard eare of terroure hanges;
40   The windes are up; the lofty elmen swanges;
Again the levynne and the thunder poures,
And the full cloudes are braste attenes in stonen showers.

Spurreynge his palfrie oere the watrie plaine,
The Abbote of Seyncte Godwynes convente came;
45   His chapournette was drented with the reine,
And his pencte gyrdle met with mickle shame;
He ayneward tolde his bederoll at the same;
The storme encreasen, and he drew aside,
With the mist almes craver neere to the holme to bide.

50   His cope was all of Lyncolne clothe so fyne,
With a gold button fasten'd neere his chynne;
His autremete was edged with golden twynne,
And his shoone pyke a loverds mighte have binne;
Full well it shewn he thoughten coste no sinne:
55   The trammels of the palfrye pleasde his sighte,
For the horse-millanare his head with roses dighte.

An almes, sir prieste! the droppynge pilgrim saide,
O! let me waite within your covente dore,
Till the sunne sheneth hie above our heade,
60   And the loude tempeste of the aire is oer;
Helpless and ould am I alas! and poor;
No house, ne friend, ne moneie in my pouche;
All yatte I call my owne is this my silver crouche.

174

Varlet, replyd the Abbatte, cease your dinne;
65   This is no season almes and prayers to give;
Mie porter never lets a faitour in;
None touch mie rynge who not in honour live.
And now the sonne with the black cloudes did stryve,
And shettynge on the grounde his glairie raie,
70   The Abbatte spurrde his steede, and eftsoons roadde awaie.

Once moe the skie was blacke, the thounder rolde;
Faste reyneynge oer the plaine a prieste was seen;
Ne dighte full proude, ne buttoned up in golde;
His cope and jape were graie, and eke were clene;
75   A Limitoure he was of order seene;
And from the pathwaie side then turned hee,
Where the pore almer laie binethe the holmen tree.

An almes, sir priest! the droppynge pilgrim sayde,
For sweete Seyncte Marie and your order sake.
80   The Limitoure then loosen'd his pouche threade,
And did thereoute a groate of silver take;
The mister pilgrim dyd for halline shake.
Here take this silver, it maie eathe thie care;
We are Goddes stewards all, nete of oure owne we bare.

85   But ah! unhailie pilgrim, lerne of me,
Scathe anie give a rentrolle to their Lorde.
Here take my semescope, thou art bare I see;
Tis thyne; the Seynctes will give me mie rewarde.
He left the pilgrim, and his waie aborde.
90   Virgynne and hallie Seyncte, who sitte yn gloure,
Or give the mittee will, or give the gode man power.

Robert Fergusson

HALLOW-FAIR

AT *Hallowmas,* whan nights grow lang,
 And *starnies* shine fu' clear,
Whan fock, the nippin cald to bang,
 Their winter *hap-warms* wear,
5 Near Edinbrough a fair there hads,
  I wat there's nane whase name is,
For strappin dames and sturdy lads,
  And cap and stoup, mair famous
   Than it that day.

10 Upo' the tap o' ilka lum
  The sun began to keek,
And bid the trig made maidens come
  A sightly joe to seek
At *Hallow-fair,* whare browsters rare
15 Keep gude yale on the gantries,
And dinna scrimp ye o' a skair
  O' kebbucks frae their pantries,
   Fu' saut that day.

Here country *John* in bannet blue,
20 An' eke his Sunday's clais on,
Rins after *Meg* wi' *rokelay* new,
  An' sappy kisses lays on;
She'll tauntin say, Ye silly coof!
  Be o' your gab mair sparin;
25 He'll tak the hint, and criesh her loof
  Wi' what will buy her fairin,
   To chew that day.

Here chapmen billies tak their stand,
    An' shaw their *bonny wallies;*
30   Wow, but they lie fu' gleg aff hand
        To trick the silly fallows:
Heh, Sirs! what cairds and tinklers come,
    An' *ne'er-do weel* horse-coupers,
An' spae-wives fengying to be dumb,
35   Wi' a' siclike landloupers,
            To thrive that day.

Here Sawny cries, frae Aberdeen;
    "Come ye to me fa need:
"The brawest *shanks* that e'er were seen
40   "I'll sell ye cheap an' guid.
"I wyt they are as protty hose
    "As come frae *weyr* or *leem:*
"Here tak a rug, and shaw's your pose:
    "Forseeth, my ain's but teem
45   "An' light this day."

Ye wives, as ye gang thro' the fair,
    O mak your bargains hooly!
O' a' thir wylie lowns beware,
    Or fegs they will ye spulzie.
50   For fairn-year *Meg Thamson* got,
    Frae thir mischievous villains,
A scaw'd bit o' a penny note,
    That lost a score o' shillins
            To her this day.

55   The dinlin drums alarm our ears,
    The serjeant screechs fu' loud,
"A' gentlemen and volunteers
    "That wish your country gude,
"Come here to me, and I sall gie
60   "Twa guineas and a crown,
"A bowl o' *punch*, that like the sea,
    "Will soum a lang dragoon
            "Wi' ease that day."

Without, the cussers prance and nicker,
65   An' our the ley-rig scud;
In tents the carls bend the bicker,

And rant and roar like wud.
Then there's sic yellowchin and din,
   Wi' wives and wee-anes gablin,
70   That ane might true they were a-kin
   To a' the tongues at Babylon,
      Confus'd that day.

Whan *Phoebus* ligs in *Thetis* lap,
   Auld Reikkie gi'es them shelter,
75   Whare cadgily they kiss the cap,
   An' ca'd round helter skelter.
Jock Bell gaed furth to play his friaks,
   Great cause he had to rue it,
For frae a stark Lockaber aix
80   He gat a *clamihewit*
      Fu' sair that night.

"Ohon!" quo' he, "I'd rather be
   "By *sword* or *bagnet* stickit,
"Than hae my crown or body wi'
85   "Sic deadly weapons nicket."
Wi' that he gat anither straik
   Mair weighty than before,
That gar'd his feckless body aik,
   An' spew the reikin gore,
90   Fu' red that night.

He peching on the cawsey lay,
   O' kicks and cuffs weel saird;
A *Highland* aith the serjeant ga'e,
   "She maun be see our guard."
95   Out spak the weirlike corporal,
   "Pring in ta drunken sot."
They trail'd him ben, an' by my saul,
   He paid his drunken groat
      For that neist day.

100   Good fock, as ye come frae the fair,
   Bide yont frae this black squad;
There's nae sic canker'd pack elsewhere
   Allow'd to wear cockade.
Than the strong lion's hungry maw,
105   Or tusk o' Russian bear,

Frae their wanruly fellin paw
    Mair cause ye ha'e to fear
        Your death that day.

A wee soup drink dis unco weel
    To had the heart aboon;
It's gude as lang's a canny chiel
    Can stand steeve in his shoon.
But gin a birkie's our weel saird
    It gars him aften stammer
To *pleys* that bring him to the guard,
    An' eke the *Council-chawmir*,
        Wi' shame that day.

110

115

John Langhorne

BORN with a gentle Heart, and born to please
    With native Goodness, of no Fortune vain,
The social Aspect of inviting Ease,
    The kind Opinion, and the Sense humane;

5   To Thee, my CRACROFT, whom, in early Youth,
    With lenient Hand, and anxious Love I led
Thro' Paths where Science points to manly Truth,
    And Glory gilds the Mansions of the Dead:

To Thee this Offering of maturer Thought,
10   That, since wild FANCY flung the Lyre aside,
With heedful Hand the MORAL MUSE hath wrought,
    That Muse devotes, and bears with honest Pride.

Yet not that Period of the human Year,
    When FANCY reign'd, shall we with Pain review,
15   All NATURE'S Seasons different Aspects wear,
    And now her Flowers, and now her Fruits are due.

Not that in Youth we rang'd the smiling Meads,
    On Essex' Shores the trembling Angle play'd,
Urging at Noon the slow Boat in the Reeds,
20   That wav'd their green Uncertainty of Shade.

Nor yet the Days consum'd in HACKTHORN'S Vale,
    That lonely on the Heath's wild Bosom lies,
Should we with stern Severity bewail,
    And all the *lighter* Hours of Life despise.

25   For Nature's Seasons different Aspects wear,
        And now her Flowers, and now her Fruits are due;
Awhile she freed us from the Scourge of CARE,
    But told us *then* — for social Ends we grew.

To find some Virtue trac'd on Life's short Page,
30   Some Mark of Service paid to human Kind,
Alone can cheer the wintry Paths of Age,
    Alone support the far-reflecting Mind.

Oh! often thought — when SMITH'S discerning Care
    To further Days prolong'd this failing Frame!
35   To die, was little — But what Heart could bear
    To die, and leave an undistinguish'd Name?

Blagdon-House,
22 Feb. 1775.

PROTECTION OF THE POOR

YET, while thy Rod restrains the needy Crew,
Remember that Thou art their Monarch too.
KING OF THE BEGGARS! — Lov'st Thou not the Name?
40   O, great from GANGES to the golden TAME!
Far-ruling Sovereign of this begging Ball,
Low at thy Footstool other Thrones shall fall.
His Alms to Thee the whisker'd Moor convey,
And PRUSSIA'S sturdy Beggar own thy Sway;
45   Courts, Senates — all to BAAL that bend the Knee,
King of the Beggars, these are Fiefs to Thee!
    But still, forgot the Grandeur of thy Reign,
Descend to Duties meaner Crowns disdain;
That worst Excrescency of Power forego,
50   That *Pride* of Kings, Humanity's first Foe.
    Let Age no longer toil with feeble Strife,
Worn by long Service in the War of Life;
Nor leave the Head, that Time hath whiten'd, bare
To the rude Insults of the searching Air;

55   Nor bid the Knee, by Labour harden'd, bend,
O Thou, the poor Man's Hope, the poor Man's Friend!
    If, when from Heav'n severer Seasons fall,
Fled from the frozen Roof, and mouldering Wall,
Each face the Picture of a Winter-Day,
60   More strong than *Teniers'* Pencil could pourtray; —
If then to Thee resort the shivering Train,
Of cruel Days, and cruel Man complain,
Say to thy Heart (remembering Him who said)
These people come from far, and have no Bread.
65   Nor leave they venal Clerk empower'd to hear;
The Voice of Want is sacred to *thy* Ear.
He, where no Fees his sordid Pen invite,
Sports with their Tears, too indolent to write;
Like the fed Monkey in the Fable, vain
70   To hear more helpless Animals complain.
    But chief thy notice shall One Monster claim,
A Monster furnish'd with a human Frame,
    The Parish-Officer! — tho' VERSE disdain
Terms that deform the Splendour of the Strain;
75   It stoops to bid Thee bend the Brow severe
On the sly, pilfering, cruel Overseer;
The shuffling Farmer, faithful to no Trust,
Ruthless as Rocks, insatiate as the Dust!
    When the poor Hind, with Length of Years decay'd,
80   Leans feebly on his once subduing Spade,
Forgot the Service of his abler Days,
His profitable Toil, and honest Praise,
Shall this low Wretch abridge his scanty Bread,
This Slave, whose Board his former Labours spread?
85   When Harvest's burning Suns and sickening Air
From Labour's unbrac'd Hand the grasp'd Hook tear,
Where shall the helpless Family be fed,
That vainly languish for a Father's Bread?
See the pale Mother, sunk with Grief and Care,
90   To the proud Farmer fearfully repair;
Soon to be sent with Insolence away,
Referr'd to Vestries, and a distant Day!
Referr'd — to perish! — Is my verse severe?
Unfriendly to the human Character?
95   Ah! to this Sigh of sad Experience trust:
The Truth is rigid, but the Tale is just.
    If in thy Courts this Caitiff Wretch appear,

Think not, that Patience were a Virtue here.
His low-born Pride with honest Rage controul;
100 Smite his hard Heart, and shake his Reptile Soul.
    But, hapless! oft thro' Fear of future Woe,
And certain Vengeance of th'insulting Foe,
Oft, ere to Thee the Poor prefer their Pray'r,
The last Extremes of Penury they bear.
105   Wouldst Thou then raise thy Patriot Office higher,
To something more than Magistrate aspire?
And, left each poorer, pettier Chace behind,
Step nobly forth, the Friend of Human Kind?
The Game I start courageously pursue!
110 Adieu to Fear! to Indolence adieu!
    And, first we'll range this Mountain's stormy Side,
Where the rude Winds the Shepherd's Roof deride,
As meet no more the wintry Blast to bear,
And all the wild Hostilities of Air.
115 — That Roof have I remember'd many a Year;
It once gave Refuge to a hunted Deer —
Here, in those Days, we found an aged Pair; —
But TIME untenants — Hah! what seest Thou there?
"Horror! — By Heav'n, extended on a Bed
120 "Of naked Fearn, two human Creatures dead!
"Embracing as alive! — ah, no! — no Life!
"Cold, breathless!"
            'Tis the Shepherd and his Wife.
I knew the Scene, and brought Thee to behold
What speaks more strongly than the story told.
125 They died thro' Want —
            "By every Power I swear,
"If the Wretch treads the Earth, or breathes the Air,
"Thro' whose Default of Duty, or Design,
"These Victims fell, he dies"
            They fell by thine.
"Infernal! — Mine! — by — "
            Swear on no Pretence:
130 A swearing Justice wants both Grace and Sense.
    When thy good Father held this wide Domain,
The Voice of Sorrow never mourn'd in vain.
Sooth'd by his Pity, by his Bounty fed,
The Sick found Medicine, and the Aged Bread.
135 He left their Interest to no Parish-Care,
No Bailiff urg'd his little Empire there:

183

No Village-Tyrant starv'd them, or oppress'd;
He learnt their Wants, and He those Wants redress'd.
  Ev'n these, unhappy! who, beheld too late,
140 Smote thy young Heart with Horror at their Fate,
His Bounty found, and destin'd here to keep
A small Detachment of his Mountain-Sheep.
Still pleas'd to see them from the annual Fair
Th'unwritten History of their Profits bear;
145 More nobly pleas'd those Profits to restore,
And, if their Fortune fail'd them, make it more.
  When Nature gave her Precept to remove
His kindred Spirit to the Realms of Love,
Afar their Anguish from thy distant Ear,
150 No Arm to save, and no Protection near,
Led by the Lure of unaccounted Gold,
Thy Bailiff seiz'd their little Flock, and sold,
  Their Want contending Parishes survey'd,
And this disown'd, and that refus'd to aid:
155 A while, who should *not* succour them, they tried,
And in that while the wretched Victims died.
    "I'll scalp that bailiff — sacrifice."
                       In vain
To rave at Mischief, if the Cause remain!
  O Days long lost to man in each Degree!
160 The golden Days of Hospitality!
When liberal Fortunes vied with liberal Strife
To fill the noblest Offices of Life;
When WEALTH was Virtue's Handmaid, and her Gate
Gave a free Refuge from the Wrongs of Fate;
165 The Poor at Hand their natural Patrons saw,
And Lawgivers were Supplements of Law!
  Lost are those Days, and FASHION'S boundless Sway
Has borne the Guardian Magistrate away.
Save in AUGUSTA'S Streets, on Gallia's Shore,
170 The Rural patron is beheld no more.
No more the Poor his kind Protection share,
Unknown their Wants, and unreceiv'd their Prayer.
  Yet has that Fashion, long so light and vain,
Reform'd at last, and led the moral Train?
175 Have her gay Vot'ries nobler worth to boast
For NATURE'S Love, for NATURE'S Virtue lost?
No — fled from these, the Sons of Fortune find
What poor Respect to Wealth remains behind.

The Mock Regard alone of menial Slaves,
180   The worship'd Calves of their outwitting Knaves!
      Foregone the social, hospitable Days,
When wide Vales echoed with their Owner's Praise,
Of all that *ancient Consequence* bereft,
What has the *modern Man of Fashion* left?
185   Does He, perchance, to rural Scenes repair,
And "waste his sweetness" on the essenc'd Air?
Ah! gently lave the feeble Frame he brings,
Ye scouring Seas! and ye sulphureous Springs!
      And thou, Brighthelmstone, where no Cits annoy,
190   (All borne to MARGATE, in the Margate-Hoy,)
Where, if the hasty Creditor advance,
Lies the light Skiff, and ever-bailing France,
Do Thou defend Him in the Dog-Day-Suns!
Secure in Winter from the Rage of Duns!
195   While the grim Catchpole, the grim Porter swear,
One that He is, and one, He is not there,
The tortur'd Us'rer, as he murmurs by,
Eyes the Venetian Blinds, and heaves a Sigh.
      O, from each Title Folly ever took,
200   Blood! Maccarone! Cicisbeo! or Rook!
From each low Passion, from each low Resort,
The thieving Alley, nay, the righteous Court,
From BERTIE'S, ALMACK'S, ARTHUR'S, and the Nest
Where JUDAH'S Ferrets earth with CHARLES unblest;—
205   From these and all the Garbage of the great,
At Honour's, Freedom's, Virtue's Call — retreat!
      Has the fair Vale, where REST, conceal'd in Flowers,
Lies in sweet Ambush for thy careless Hours,
The Breeze, that, balmy Fragrance to infuse,
210   Bathes it's soft Wing in Aromatic Dews,
The Stream, to sooth thine Ear, to cool thy Breast,
That mildly murmurs from it's crystal Rest;—
Have these less Charms to win, less Power to please,
Than Haunts of Rapine, Harbours of Disease?
215   Will no kind Slumbers o'er thine Eyelids creep,
Save where the sullen Watchman growls at Sleep?
Does Morn no sweeter, purer Breath diffuse
Than steams thro' Alleys from the Lungs of JEWS?
And is thy Water, pent in putrid Wood,
220   BETHESDA-like, when troubled *only* good?
      Is it thy Passion LINLEY'S Voice to hear,

And has no Mountain-Lark detain'd thine Ear?
Song marks alone the Tribes of Airy Wing;
For, trust Me, Man was never meant to sing:
225 And all his Mimic Organs e'er exprest,
Was but an imitative Howl at best.
        Is it on GARRICK'S Attitude you doat?
See on the pointed Cliff yon lordly Goat!
Like LEAR'S, his Beard descends in graceful Snow,
230 And wild He looks upon the World below.
        Superior *here* the Scene in every Part!
Here reigns great Nature, and there little Art!
Here let thy Life assume a nobler Plan,
To Nature faithful, and the Friend of Man!
235   Unnumber'd Objects ask thy honest Care,
Beside the Orphan's Tears, the Widow's prayer.
Far as thy Power can save, thy Bounty bless,
Unnumber'd Evils call for thy Redress.
        Seest Thou afar yon solitary Thorn,
240 Whose aged *Limbs* the Heath's wild Winds have torn?
While yet to cheer the homeward Shepherd's Eye,
A *few* seem straggling in the Evening Sky!
Not many Suns have hastened down the Day,
Or blushing Moons immers'd in Clouds their Way,
245 Since there a Scene, that stain'd their sacred Light,
With Horror stopp'd a Felon in his Flight;
A Babe just born that Signs of Life exprest,
Lay naked o'er the Mother's lifeless Breast.
The pitying Robber, conscious that, pursued,
250 He had no Time to waste, yet stood and view'd;
To the next Cot the trembling Infant bore,
And gave a Part of what He stole before;
Nor known to Him the Wretches were, nor dear,
He felt as Man, and dropp'd a human Tear.
253   Far other Treatment She who breathless lay,
Found from a viler Animal of Prey.
        Worn with long Toil on many a painful Road,
That Toil increas'd by Nature's growing Load,
When Evening brought the friendly Hour of Rest,
260 And all the Mother throng'd about her Breast,
The Ruffian Officer oppos'd her Stay,
And, cruel, bore her in her pangs, away,
So far beyond the Town's last Limits drove,
That to return were hopeless, had She strove.

265   Abandon'd there — with Famine, Pain, and Cold,
And Anguish, She expir'd — the rest I've told.
    "Now *let* me swear — For, by my Soul's last Sigh,
"That Thief shall live, that Overseer shall die."
    Too late! — His Life the generous Robber paid,
270   Lost by that Pity which his Steps delay'd!
No Soul-discerning MANSFIELD sate to hear,
No HERTFORD bore his Prayer to Mercy's Ear;
No liberal Justice first assign'd the Gaol,
Or urg'd, as CAMPLIN would have urg'd his Tale.
275   The living Object of thy honest Rage,
Old in Parochial Crimes, and *steel'd* with Age,
The grave Church-warden! — Unabash'd he bears
Weekly to Church his Book of wicked Prayers;
And pours, with all the Blasphemy of Praise,
280   His creeping Soul in Sternhold's creeping Lays!

Notes

JOHN POMFRET 1667-1702

Pomfret was born in Luton, where his father was vicar. He was educated at Bedford Grammar School and Queen's College, Cambridge. After taking orders, he was instituted in 1695 to the rectory of Maulden in Bedfordshire, and in 1702 to the rectory of Millbrook in the same county. The first edition of his *Poems on Several Occasions* was published in 1699. 'The Choice' appeared separately in 1700, went through four editions in 1701, and was included in a second edition of *Poems on Several Occasions* in 1702.

Pomfret's false-Pindaric odes on religious subjects, such as 'The General Conflagration and Ensuing Judgment', are sublime in intention but tedious in effect. His more numerous poems in decasyllabic couplets have the qualities defined by Johnson: 'the pleasure of smooth metre is afforded to the ear, and the mind is not oppressed with ponderous or entangled with intricate sentiment'. The shorter pieces are often pastoral or epistolary; and the versification is for the most part sweetly insipid. Among the longer pieces, 'Cruelty and Lust' recounts a sensational incident from the Monmouth rebellion, while 'Love Triumphant over Reason' is unusual for this period in following the dream-allegory convention.

p.1. The Choice.

'The Choice', which is Pomfret's only important work, may owe something to Swift's patron Sir William Temple. A writer in *The Gentleman's Magazine* 1757, page 489) asserted: '*Pomfret, in his little poem called the choice, is said to have given an exact description of Moor Park;* to have delineated Sir *Wm* in the account of his own fancy and taste; and to have taken his picture of the female friend and companion from Mrs *Johnson.*' Whatever its immediate inspiration, the poem reflects both a social mood and a literary tradition. Its predecessors and successors are discussed at length by Maren-Sofie Røstvig in *The Happy Man: Studies in the Metamorphoses of a Classical Ideal* (Oslo, 2 volumes, 1954 and 1958). The literary sources for Pomfret's ideal include the Horatian epode beginning

Beatus ille qui procul negotiis

but 'The Choice' is a simpler and more self-indulgent work, lacking the dramatic and ironic qualities of the Latin poem. The same theme was handled with more sophistication by other eighteenth-century writers, including the Countess of Winchilsea in 'The Petition for an Absolute Retreat'; yet Pomfret's version retained its position as a popular classic

189

for almost a century, Johnson commented in 1779: 'He ... has always been the favourite of that class of readers who, without vanity or criticism, seek only their amusement. His *Choice* exhibits a system of life adapted to common notions, and equal to common expectations; such a state as affords plenty and tranquillity, without exclusion of intellectual pleasures. Perhaps no composition in our language has been oftener perused than Pomfret's *Choice* ... He pleases many, and he who pleases many must have some species of merit.' These measured phrases, besides offering an antidote to intellectual snobbery, show the historical importance of Pomfret's work.

94.   *Caesar*   William III, to whom Pomfret had already paid tribute in 'A Pastoral Elegy on the Death of Queen Mary'.
157.   According to a story which Johnson repeats, this parenthesis was the cause of Pomfret's death. He had been presented to 'a living of considerable value': but objections were raised, because it was 'inferred that he considered happiness as more likely to be found in the company of a mistress than of a wife'. These objections were overcome, thanks to the fact that he was by then married; but they 'constrained his attendance in London', where he caught smallpox and died.

JOHN PHILIPS 1676-1709

Philips was born at Bampton in Oxfordshire, where his father was vicar. When he was a schoolboy at Winchester, 'his sovereign pleasure was to sit, hour after hour, while his hair was combed by somebody, whose service he found means to procure'. His other interests included ancient and modern poetry; and as a student at Christ Church, Oxford, 'he took much delight in natural history, of which botany was his favourite part'. His Miltonic burlesque, *The Splendid Shilling,* was published without his consent in 1701; and four years later, at the invitation of Harley and Bolingbroke, he wrote a serious poem in neo-Miltonic blank verse entitled *Blenheim,* in which he offered a Tory view of the victory Addison had celebrated in *The Campaign.* His longest and most successful work was a blank-verse georgic called *Cyder,* which appeared in January 1708; Gay's *Wine,* which appeared in May 1708, was the first of many imitations. Philips died in Hereford, and was buried in the cathedral there. Part of an unfinished poem about beer was published after his death under the title *Cerealia.*

The historical importance of Philips' poetry lies in its progressive adaptation of a Miltonic medium for contemporary purposes. Addison and Lady Winchilsea wrote imitations of Milton, and Watts composed blank verse of some distinction; but it was Philips, during the first quarter of the eighteenth century, who directly undertook the reconciliation of *Paradise Lost* with the post-Dryden literary tradition. Like the imitators of Spenser, he began cautiously with burlesque. When this was favourably received, he was persuaded to use the Miltonic style unironically to celebrate a politico-military triumph; but the results were unsatisfactory, because he lacked both the enthusiasm and the knowledge for this task. In *Cyder,* however, he tackled a subject which he understood and cared about; and he evolved for that subject a form of 'Miltonian verse' in which the heroic, mock-heroic and expository notes combine in an appropriate harmony. The poem was a model not only for other blank-verse georgics like Smart's *The Hop-Garden,* but also for *The Seasons;* and Thomson paid a fitting tribute to 'Pomona's bard' in lines 640-50 of 'Autumn'.

p.6. The Splendid Shilling.

'The Splendid Shilling' was described by Addison, soon after the 1707 Union, as 'the finest burlesque poem in the British language'. Its success arises not only from the consistency of its pseudo-Miltonic language and prosody but also from its graphic presentation of the poet's physical and economic state: the comic vitality generated by the imitating of Milton achieves a triumph over problems whose reality has been acknowledged.

6. *Junyper's Magpye, or Town-Hall* 'noted alehouses in Oxford'.
15. *Tiffy* a sip or little drink of punch or other diluted liquid.
21. *Mundungus* a bad-smelling tobacco.
23. *Cambro-Briton* a Welshman. Philips observes, in the projected dedication to the poem, that the similes 'are so full of geography, that you must get a Welshman to understand them'.
27. *Cestrian Cheese* Cheshire cheese.
29. *Arvonian Mart* presumably Caernarvon.
30. *Maridunum* Carmarthen.
31. *Brechinia* Brecon.
32. *Ariconium* a town in Roman Britain, traditionally identified with Hereford.
34. *Massic* named after a mountain in Campania, is mentioned by Horace and Virgil. The wine of Setia, a city in Latium, is mentioned by Martial and Pliny. Falernian wine, which came from Campania, is mentioned frequently by Horace.
58. *Catchpole* a bailiff employed in making arrests.
67. *Pallas* the goddess of arts, crafts and war and the patroness of Athens: came to the rescue of Hercules, Perseus and others.
74. *Grimalkin* name commonly given to a female cat.
77. *Protending* 'stretching forth'.
79. *Arachne* transformed by Minerva into a spider.
80. The phrase 'obvious to' is used in the Latin sense, and means 'so as to encounter'.
117; *John-Apple* said to keep for two years, and to be in perfection when shrivelled and withered.
119. *Medlar* a fruit resembling the apple, which is eaten only when decayed.
121. *Galligaskins* loose breeches. Philips' friend Edmund Smith wrote of these lines: 'This is admirably pathetical, and shows very well the vicissitudes of sublunary things.'
126. *Eurus* the east wind. *Auster* the south wind.
127. *Boreas* the north wind. *The Cronian Waves* those of the Arctic Ocean, as in *Paradise Lost* X.290.
132. The Lilybean promontory is on the coast of Sicily.
133. *Scylla ... Charybdis* the classical names for a rock and a whirlpool which face one another in the Straits of Messina.
140. *Lave* to bale.

ISAAC WATTS 1674-1748

Watts was born in Southampton. His father had been a tradesman, and was later to run a boarding-house; but in 1674 he was in prison because of his obstinate nonconformity. Watts received his early education at the Southampton Grammar School, whose headmaster was John Pinhorne: he began Latin at the age of four, and soon afterwards progressed to Greek and Hebrew. A Lawrentian critic, recording these facts 'with horror', describes Watts as an 'unfortunate infant'; but a Latin ode to Pinhorne written in 1694 shows that Watts was appropriately grateful. Because he would not conform to the Established Church, Watts proceeded not to Oxford or Cambridge but to Stoke Newington Academy. He was thus introduced to a Puritan aristocracy which had many links with the Cromwellian era; and in 1702 he became minister of an Independent Church in the City of London. Ill-health, however, soon forced him into retirement; and in 1712 he went to stay with Sir Thomas Abney, a leading Whig merchant, at his house in Hertfordshire. He lived with the Abney family for thirty-six years, first in Hertfordshire and then in London; and during this period, Johnson tells us, 'his life was no otherwise diversified than by successive publications'. His prose works include theological and educational treatises, the most celebrated being *The Improvement of the Mind;* but he is chiefly remembered for his four collections of religious verse: *Horae Lyricae, Hymns and Spiritual Songs, Divine Songs for the Use of Children,* and *The Psalms of David Imitated.* The first editions of these works appeared in 1706, 1707, 1715 and 1719 respectively; but some of the later editions were substantially altered, and included new material.

Much of Watts' verse, even in *Horae Lyricae,* is controlled by non-literary purposes. He composes religious and moral songs, hoping that they will 'incline children to make this part of their business a diversion'; and he is careful so to word these songs that 'children of high and low degree, of the church of England, or dissenters, baptized in infancy, or not, may all join together' in singing them. His hymns and psalms are contributions to the improvement of church services, and are meant in particular to introduce specifically Christian values into a region hitherto dominated by the Old Testament. But Watts belonged not only to the world of religious dissent but also to a literary culture guided by neo-classical principles; and he aims in the hymns, psalms and divine songs at the lucidity and order which were recommended by the Royal Society. These works become poetry, in strange and unpredictable ways, when the pressure of individual feeling overwhelms the merely practical process of religious verse-making. This happens in the most famous of the hymns,

<blockquote>When I survey the wondrous cross,</blockquote>

and in the great adaptation of Psalm 90,

<blockquote>'Our God, our help in ages past'.</blockquote>

It happens also in 'A Cradle Hymn', which was published along with the songs for children. The re-writing of this poem in Blake's *Songs of Innocence* is a critique of Watts' dogmatism; but it is also, like Blake's many re-creations of Miltonic works, an acknowledgement of visionary elements in the original. *Horae Lyricae,* whose preface gives a valuable statement of Watts' literary objectives, attempts to Christianize the contemporary poetic tradition. Here too the verse can be impressive in its authoritative simplicity:

<blockquote>Reason may grasp the massy hills,
And stretch from pole to pole,</blockquote>

But half thy name our spirit fills,
And overloads our soul.

But the book also shows Watts as a sophisticated artist willing to experiment with many forms. His free-Pindaric odes are spoilt by their formlessness; but the strong and unembarrassed blank verse of such poems as 'To Sarissa' and 'The Dacian Battle' offers an interesting contrast to John Philips' 'verse Miltonian'.

p. 10. The Day of Judgment.

'The Day of Judgment' is characteristic of *Horae Lyricae* in its curious blend of vision and dogma, and in its boldness as a prosodic experiment. The Sapphic stanza, which is common in Greek and Latin poetry, consists of three long lines of the pattern

$$- \cup - - - \cup \cup - \cup - \breve{\cup}$$

and one short line of the pattern

$$- \cup \cup - \breve{\cup}.$$

The form was used by Sidney in the sixteenth century and by Swinburne in the nineteenth; but a more interesting parallel to Watts' ode is afforded by a poem of Cowper's which begins

Hatred and vengeance, my eternal portion.

5.   Watts' grandfather was a naval captain.
15.   The mid-stanza transition is awkward.
29.   The comparative weakness of the final stanzas reveals the limitations of Watts' faith. Despite his formal convictions, and his desire to Christianize the metrical psalter, he finds damnation more imaginable than paradise.

AMBROSE PHILIPS 1674-1749

Philips was a native of Shropshire and was educated at Shrewsbury and Cambridge. The literary tasks which he undertook during the early part of his career included the abridging of a biography, and the translating of some 'Persian tales' from the French. Four of his pastorals were included in Fenton's *Oxford and Cambridge Miscellany* in 1706; and all six appeared in Tonson's *Poetical Miscellanies* in 1709. In 1712 his blank-verse adaptation of Racine's *Andromaque* was produced at Drury Lane under the title *The Distrest Mother*. Philips was by this time a close associate of Addison and Steele; and when Thomas Tickell, another Buttonian, wrote for *The Guardian* a series of essays on pastoral poetry, he associated Philips' work with that of Theocritus, Virgil and Spenser. Pope, whose own more sophisticated pastorals had been ignored, retaliated with devastating irony in the essay published on 27 April 1713. This attack, which can be found on pages 445-51 of John Butt's one-volume edition of Pope's poems, permanently damaged Philips' literary reputation; but in the years 1714-23 he published two political epistles, edited a periodical called *The Freethinker,* and had two new tragedies produced. Being 'a zealous Whig', he found the political climate more congenial after Queen Anne's death; and Pope was able to sum up the decline of cultural standards in a short message to posterity:

In George's Reign these fruitless lines were writ,
When Ambrose Philips was preferr'd for Wit.

Philips' patron was Hugh Boulter, who became Archbishop of Armagh in 1724. From then until 1748 Philips lived in Ireland, where he occupied a series of official posts and composed whimsical verses for the children of the Lord Lieutenant. On his return to London, four years after Pope's death, he published a collected edition of his poems, in which the pastorals were extensively revised.

Philips' pastorals achieve the 'sedate and quiet harmony' he thought appropriate to the genre; but they are important chiefly for their place in a complex and fascinating controversy which involved Addison, Steele, Pope, Swift and Gay. His *faux-naïf* poems to children, which provoked Henry Carey to satirise him as 'Namby Pamby', help one to appreciate the poise and wit of Marvell's 'Young Love' and Prior's 'To a Child of Quality Five Years Old'. His principal work as a translator has other faults, on which Johnson passed a definitive judgment: 'In his translations from Pindar, he found the art of reaching all the obscurity of the Theban bard, however he may fall below his sublimity; he will be allowed, if he has less fire, to have more smoke.' In two of his epistles, however, Philips' conversational manner enables him to avoid both childishness and pomposity, and to say something of interest.

p.12. To the Earl of Dorset.

The epistle 'From Holland, to a Friend in England, in the Year 1703' has received little praise; but it offers, in relaxed and unpretentious verse, a thoughtful statement about the relationship between private life and public affairs. The poem 'To the Earl of Dorset', which first appeared in *The Tatler,* has been generally and rightly admired. Steele introduced it as follows: 'The following poem comes from Copenhagen, and is as fine a winter-piece as we have ever had from any of the schools of the most learned painters. Such images as these give us a new pleasure in our sight, and fix upon our minds traces of reflection, which accompany us whenever the like objects occur.' Goldsmith, who considered the opening of this poem 'incomparably fine', described the latter part as 'tedious and trifling'; but he was referring to a revised version, which ended with an epic simile.

Title. The Earl of Dorset in 1709 was Lionel Cranfield Sackville, who had succeeded his more famous father in 1706. He was employed in 1714 as envoy-extraordinary to Hanover; and in 1718 Prior dedicated to him the folio edition of *Poems on Several Occasions.*

10. This line is echoed and transformed in lines 235-40 of Thomson's *Winter.*

JOHN GAY 1685-1732

Gay was born at Barnstaple in Devon, and educated at the local grammar school. He was apprenticed for a time to a silk mercer in London, but found the work uncongenial. His first poem, *Wine*, was published in 1708. In the years 1711-14, when he was closely associated with Swift and Pope, he produced two dramatic works; but his main publications of this period were a georgic called *Rural Sports,* a mock-epic called *The Fan,* and a volume of burlesque pastorals called *The Shepherd's Week.* The death of Queen Anne ended his hopes of preferment; but in the years 1715-17 he published a town-georgic entitled *Trivia* and had two plays performed at Drury Lane. In 1720 a collected edition of his poems brought in substantial profits; but he immediately invested in South Sea stock, which was soon worthless. In 1727 he published his most popular book of verse, a collection of Aesopic fables addressed to the young Duke of Cumberland; and in 1728 his masterpiece, *The Beggar's Opera,* began its triumphant progress at Lincoln's Inn Fields. The Walpole government prevented the performance of a sequel entitled *Polly;* but Gay's Tory friends ensured that the printed text sold well. His posthumously-published works included a ballad-opera, two comedies, and a second collection of fables.

Although *The Beggar's Opera* is very obviously Gay's masterpiece, his non-dramatic works are more consistently interesting than his plays. After the false start of *Wine,* which is much inferior to John Philips' *Cyder,* he established himself as a civilized and intelligent poet in a wide range of characteristic Scriblerian forms. *Rural Sports* is a lesser work than Pope's *Windsor Forest, The Fan* a much lesser work than the *The Rape of the Lock;* and the shorter poems, apart from the ballad-opera songs, are rarely more than agreeable light verse. On three occasions, however, Gay took up a minor genre and explored its potentialities more successfully than any other eighteenth-century poet. *The Shepherd's Week,* though conceived in burlesque terms as an attack on Ambrose Philips, advances beyond burlesque in a typically Augustan fashion, developing for its own sake the realism which it offers as criticism of a false ideal. The first series of fables, which blends satire and sentiment as tactfully as it seasons morality with wit, is the closest equivalent in English to the great collection of La Fontaine. And it was Gay who wrote the only major work in that town-georgic form whose potentialities were first indicated by Swift's 'A Description of a City Shower'.

p.42. Trivia.

Trivia or the Art of Walking the Streets of London is in the first place an imitation of Virgil's *Georgics;* and its verse-form is the heroic couplet, as used in Dryden's translation. John Philips and his successors imitated the *Georgics* in celebrating agricultural labour as part of a universal scheme; and poems like *Rural Sports* and Somerville's *The Chace* develop a sub-genre about country pastimes, for which there are Latin precedents. By transferring the scene from country to city, however, Gay introduces a burlesque element akin to that of the contemporary town-eclogues. Just as Augustan writers could not see the life of London's poor as Arcadian, so they could not easily feel that all the activities of their city were appropriate contributions to a universal order. The mock-georgic quality, which invites comparison with Popean and other mock-epics, is enforced by Gay's part-icular choice of subject. Whatever claims might be made for the activities celebrated in *The Fleece,* it could not be asserted without irony that urban perambulation was in itself a major contribution to human culture. But Gay, like Pope in *The Rape of the Lock,* is remarkably skilful in maintaining a dual attitude here. One is certainly conscious of an excessive and absurd solemnity in much of his advice; but one also feels that his accounts of urban perils, besides having a critical or satirical purpose, imply that qualities of courage and judgment may be as necessary in George I's London as they were in Virgil's Italian countryside. The expository and advisory sections of the poem, in which Gay focuses on the physical and social details of his London scene, sustain this complexity of purpose with great success. Much less successful, although justified by Virgilian precedents, is the narrative episode about the invention of pattens. In the second edition of *Trivia,* Gay introduced into Book II an equally tedious burlesque myth about the origin of bootblacks. The text reprinted here is that of 1716; but the advertisement, notes and index have been omitted.

Title. 'Trivia' is the feminine singular form of an adjective, and identifies Diana as the goddess of all places where three roads meet. It is also the plural form of a noun, and signifies 'matters appropriate to the elementary stages of education'. This pun in the title epitomizes the poem's mock-georgic strategy.

Epigraph. This is the opening line of Virgil's ninth eclogue. Dryden translates, rather noisily:

> Ho, Moeris! whither on thy way so fast?
> This leads to town.

I.15. *Kennels* gutters.
I.20. The City Poet, 'whose annual office was to describe the glories of the Mayor's day', is mentioned contemptuously in *The Dunciad.*
I.30. *Spanish ... Morocco* leather used in shoemaking.
I.32. *'scallop'd* the top of the dancer's shoe is ornamented in a manner which suggests scallop-shells.
I.43. *Doily* Thomas Doily, a London linen-draper, 'rais'd a Fortune by finding out Materials for such Stuffs as might at once be cheap and genteel'.
I.44. *Drugget* 'a sort of stuff, very thin, and narrow, usually all wool, and sometimes half wool and half silk'.
I.45. *Nap* The woolly substance of a material, usually removed from the surface by shearing. *Frieze* a coarse woollen cloth with a nap on one side or both.
I.46. *Camlet* an expensive material made from the hair of the Angora goat. Gay uses a Latin participial construction to say that rain quickly soaks this material, making its surface uneven or 'cockled'.
I.47. *Witney* a town in Oxfordshire, noted for the manufacture of a heavy woollen material often used for blankets. If the 'nap' of a piece of cloth is long and coarse, it can be called a 'shag'.
I.49. *Fence* here means 'protection'.
I.51. *Roquelaure* a fashionable cloak, named after the Duke of Roquelaure.
I.53. *Bavaroy* a cloak, perhaps of Bavarian origin.
I.58. *Surtout* an overcoat of traditional design. For Gay the word rhymes (appropriately) with 'foot'.
I.59. *Kersey* a coarse narrow cloth woven from long wool.
I.72. *White's* the reference, Gay explains, is to 'White's Chocolate-house in St. James's Street'.
I.104. An act of 1711 licensed 200 public sedan chairs, and an act of 1712 licensed 100 more.
I.145. *The Mall* a fashionable promenade between St. James' Palace and St. James' Park.
I.147. Young fallow-deer could be seen in St. James' Park.

NOTES

I.164.   *Tilts* the large rowing-boats used on the Thames were called 'tilt-boats', because each of them had a tilt or awning which could provide shelter from the weather.

I.168.   After the death of her children, Niobe could not stop weeping, even when she was turned to stone.

I.171.   *Common-shores* sewers.

I.177.   The festival of the conversion of St Paul is on 25 January.

I.183.   St Swithin's day is 15 July. A popular rhyme asserts:

> St. Swithin's day, if thou dost rain,
> For forty days it will remain,
> St. Swithin's day, if thou be fair,
> For forty days 'twill rain nae mair.

The 'welkin' is the sky.

I.199.   *Scud* a hurried movement.

I.201.   *scow'r* to move hastily (especially in search of something).

I.203.   *Alecto* one of the Erinnyes or Furies, who fell silent when Orpheus sang to them in the Underworld.

I.205.   The sea-god Glaucus wooed Scylla, rejecting the sorceress Circe. Circe poisoned the waters where Scylla bathed, and the girl was transformed into a rock.

I.212.   *Pattens* a patten is an overshoe or sandal, which raises ordinary shoes out of the mud. It consists of a wooden sole secured to the foot by a leather strap and mounted on an iron ring.

I.241.   *Vulcan ... Mulciber* a fire-god, often depicted as a blacksmith or master-craftsman. He was worshipped on Mount Moschylus in Lemnos. His wife, the goddess Aphrodite, was worshipped especially at Paphos in Cyprus.

II.10.   *Billingsgate* a famous fish-market below London Bridge.

II.13.   *Asses* asses' milk, recommended by doctors, was supplied very fresh to rich invalids.

II.14.   *arrogate* appropriate without just reason.

II.17.   Newly-married couples were commonly serenaded by drummers.

II.18.   *Vellom-Thunder* the noise of the drums, which are made (like parchment) from the skins of animals.

II.33.   Chimneys were cleaned by small boys, who climbed up inside them.

II.34.   Swift, in 'A Description of the Morning', refers to the 'cadence deep' of the small-coal-man, who sold coal suitable for domestic use.

II.66.   *the sworn Porter* one with an official licence.

II.73ff. At a point where seven streets met, in the parish of St Giles-in-the-Fields, there was a column with seven sundials.

II.83ff. After killing the Minotaur, Theseus had to find his way out of the labyrinth where the monster was kept. The help of Minos' daughter Ariadne enabled him to do this.

II.92.   *slabby* muddy.

II.100.   *the Board* of the pillory.

II.106.   In more civilized streets pedestrians were protected by a line of posts, which kept vehicles away from the wall.

II.115ff. *the Samian* the Greek philosopher Pythagoras, who believed in metempsychosis, was born in Samos.

II.123.   *that rugged Street* Thames Street

II.124.   Fleet Ditch flowed into the Thames near Blackfriars Wharf. Pope tells that it was full of dead dogs, and that the 'silver flood' was darkened by its black waters.

NOTES

II.132.   *Cornavian Cheese*   Cheshire cheese.

II.135.   Pall Mall (the name rhymes with 'smell') was originally an alley in which the game known as 'pall mall' was played. Vehicles were excluded from it, but the new sedan-chairs were admitted.

II.141.   *Sashes*   frames fitted with glass to form part of a window.

II.160.   Many prostitutes lived near Drury Lane.

II.166.   *the Meuse*   the royal stables near Charing Cross were known as the Mews or Meuse. *the Thimble's Cheats*   Gay explains that a trick was 'commonly practised in the streets with three thimbles and a little ball'.

II.167.   Presumably it is the horses pulling the drays which 'bound high'.

II.173ff.   Parthian horsemen were said to hurl missiles backwards while pretending to retreat.

II.176.   *Tea*   still a luxury; the word rhymed, for Pope, with 'obey'.

II.179.   This use of 'trivial' reminds us that the poem's title is ambiguous.

II.197.   *nitry*   frost was thought to be caused by nitre in the air.

II.206.   *ward*   equivalent to the modern 'ward off'.

II.211.   *spurn*   trip or stumble.

II.215.   *'Change*   the New Exchange was a shopping area on the Strand.

II.216.   *The Belgian Stove*   used to warm the feet.

II.217.   To 'whip' muslin is to ornament it with embroidery.

II.221.   St. Paul's Church in Covent Garden was built by Inigo Jones.

II.223.   There were elegant arcades on two sides of the Covent Garden piazza.

II.233ff.   The thrower's dexterity would make the broken window surprising, if his occupation did not provide a motive.

II.235ff.   During the winter of 1715-16, *The Historical Register* tells us, the frost continued from November to February 'with greater Severity than had been known in the Memory of Man'. The Thames 'was quite frozen up, and abundance of Booths were built upon it'.

II.239ff.   One function of the frost fair was to give employment to some of these watermen.

II.258.   *Philomela*   the nightingale.

II.271ff.   After failing to rescue Eurydice from Hades, Orpheus returned to Thrace. His body was torn apart by the Ciconian women, but his head and lyre floated down the River Hebrus, uttering plaintive sounds.

II.288.   Bear-baiting and bull-baiting were regular entertainments at Hockley-in-the-Hole.

II.292.   *Maid*   the skate.

II.299.   The accent in 'Balconies' falls on the second syllable.

II.310.   Mackerel, which goes bad quickly, could be sold on Sunday.

II.347.   *Upholder*   undertaker.

II.353.   William Fortescue was a lawyer, and a friend of both Gay and Pope.

II.361ff.   Stow's *Survey of London,* written in 1598, mentions among the great houses between London and Westminster those of the Earl of Arundel, the Earl of Essex, Sir Robert Cecil and the Earl of Bedford. The coming-together of the two cities, however, transformed the social character of this district; and by Gay's time these noblemen's mansions had been demolished. Arundel House, which once contained a famous collection of Greek statues and other works of art, was commemorated in Arundel Street.

II.365.   It was the custom for the bellman, who acted as night-watchman and town-crier, to compose verses every Easter and leave them at houses which he passed.

II.366.   John Overton, who died about 1708, was the leading seller of mezzotints in his day. He was succeeded by Henry Overton, who was probably his son.

II.367.   *Phidias*   a great Athenian sculptor.

II.371.   Richard Boyle, third Earl of Burlington, was a patron of architecture and the other arts. His Palladian reconstruction of the Piccadilly mansion erected by his great-grandfather began in 1716. Gay and Pope addressed verse-epistles to him; and Handel (Georg Friedrich Händel) lived for three years in his house.

II.382.   The Chairmen fit the poles of their sedan-chairs into slings, so that they are easier to carry.

II.413ff.   Phaëthon, offspring of the god Phoebus, took charge of his father's sun-chariot but could not control it. Jupiter therefore destroyed him with a thunderbolt.

II.418.   *Bills*   advertising leaflets.

II.419.   A doctor who was seventh son of a seventh son was believed to be infallible.

II.421ff.   The functions of the seven markets which Gay mentions are clearly defined in the text.

II.438.   *Stagyra's Sage*   Aristotle was born at Stagira.

II.439.   The tragic dramatist Thomas Otway was celebrated for his ability to evoke tears.

II.440.   The dramatist and critic John Dennis had engaged in controversy with various leading writers, including Pope.

II.442.   Squirt is the apothecary's boy in Sir Samuel Garth's mock-epic *The Dispensary*, an important precursor of *The Rape of the Lock*. An 'apozem' is a medicinal preparation.

II.443.   Bernard Lintot was the publisher of *Trivia*, and of other works by Gay and Pope.

II.452.   Heavy carriages were often drawn by horses from Flanders.

III.4.   Diana, who is named Trivia as goddess of three-road junctions, is named Cynthia as goddess of the moon.

III.17ff.   A narrow lane near St Clement Danes was known as the Pass of St Clement's.

III.45   *Ytene*   the New Forest.

III.64.   *Lurcher*   petty thief.

III.82.   *Cambrick*   Cambric is a type of linen originally made at Cambrai.

III.95ff.   Aeneas was separated from his wife Creüsa during the sack of Troy, and his attempts to find her were unsuccessful.

III.97ff.   During Aeneas' wars in Latium, the Trojan Nisus lost his way in the forest and was taken prisoner. When his companion Euryalus tried to rescue him, they were both killed.

III.122.   *steepy*   precipitous.

III.125.   *Huckster*   a pedlar operating from a booth or stall.

III.131ff.   The meaning must be 'Let no courts detain nor alewives bid'.

III.132.   *sneering*   simply 'grinning' or 'laughing foolishly'

III.137.   This concept is developed in *The Beggar's Opera.*

III.145.   *Augusta*   London.

III.183.   See the note on *The Splendid Shilling*, L.133.

III.185.   *Ostrea*   a pseudo-classical name for an oyster-seller.

III.186.   Thomas Flatman in 1674 declared that no one could prefer 'Wall fleet Oysters' to those from Colchester.

III.203.   *Morells*   a morel is an edible fungus.

III.211.   *Shed*   a projecting roof which offers shelter.

III.215ff. Oedipus of Thebes killed his royal father, whom he did not know, after a quarrel over the right of way at a crossroad. His later misfortunes included marriage to his mother and the loss of his eyes.

III.263.   *vagrant*   wandering. This refers to the poem's discursive method; but Gay is also aware that a vagrant is a wandering beggar.

III.270ff. *Manteau*   'a loose upper Garment ... generally worn by Women, instead of a straight-body'd Gown'. The prostitute's manteau is newly washed, but her manner suggests her occupation.

III.276.   *Pinners*   a pinner is a headdress with two flaps, one on each side, which are sometimes fastened at the breast. 'Muffled' may be a transferred epithet here; but in some dialects the word can mean 'covered with feathers'.

III.277.   *Bandbox*   with which the harlot masquerades as a milliner.

III.281.   *Sarsnet*   a fine silk material.

III.297.   *Round-house*   a place of detention for arrested persons.

III.300.   The pills are to cure venereal disease.

III.314.   *the scow'ring Crew*   the scourers, about whom Shadwell wrote a comedy, amused themselves by breaking windows and beating watchmen.

III.323.   *Nicker*   the nickers made a practice of breaking windows by throwing halfpence at them.

III.326.   *Mohock*   the mohocks, who figure in Gay's first dramatic work, are described by Swift as 'a race of rakes that play the devil about this town every night, slit people's noses, and beat them'.

III.330.   Snow Hill is in Holborn.

III.334.   Marcus Atilius Regulus, having been captured by the Carthaginians, was sent on parole to Rome. After persuading the Senate to refuse the terms of peace which he brought, he returned to Carthage, where he was tortured and killed.

III.345ff. The first Eddystone Lighthouse, built by Henry Winstanley in 1696-1700, was swept away by a storm in 1703.

III.368.   *The Dardan Hero*   Aeneas, who saved his father Anchises from the burning city of Troy.

III.381ff. A house is being destroyed with gunpowder in order to prevent the fire from spreading. In using 'grain' for gunpowder, Gay may be echoing *Paradise Lost* IV.817.

III.411.   Edward Ward was the author of *The London Spy*. Charles Gildon was a hack writer, and was attacked by Pope.

III.412ff. Unmarketable literature might be used for serving refreshments, or for re-covering milliners' boxes, or in the manufacture of fireworks.

III.415ff. Posts set up in the street were used to advertise new publications.

THOMAS PARNELL 1679-1718

Parnell's father, a supporter of the Commonwealth, left Cheshire for Ireland after the Restoration. Parnell was born and educated in Dublin, where he became a Master of Arts in 1700; and in 1706 he was made Archdeacon of Clogher in Tyrone. Despite his Whig background, he allied himself with the Harley-Bolingbroke ministry of 1710-14; and during those years he lived in London, on intimate terms with Swift and Pope in the Scriblerus Club. In 1716, on Swift's recommendation, he was made vicar of Finglas in County Dublin. The collected edition of his poems which appeared three years after his death included a dedicatory epistle addressed by Pope to Harley.

Parnell was the least gifted of the five Scriblerians, and his career was cut short by an early death; but many features of his work invite comparison with that of his friends. His translation of the Homeric *Batrachomuomachia* as *The Battle of the Frogs and Mice* has its importance for the student of Augustan mock-epic; and the associated prose works, including *The Life of Zoilus,* look forward to the editorial matter of *The Dunciad.* His most celebrated poem, 'The Hermit', presents a moral fable wholly inadequate to its apparent purpose; but the heroic couplets are Goldsmithian in their sweetness and elegance. 'Hesiod' and 'A Fairy Tale' are similarly unsatisfactory as narratives; but the former has an eloquently anti-feminist conclusion, and the latter is of historical interest as an imitation of Chaucer's 'Sir Topas'. The shorter poems, which are mainly narrative and lyrical, are in general relaxed and civilized though never strikingly original. One of the best is an imitation of Théodore de Bèze in which the speaker grandiloquently condemns a bookworm for attacking works by Swift, Pope and Gay.

p. 42. A Night-Piece on Death.

The eschatological theme and weighty octosyllabics of 'A Night-Piece on Death' recall an earlier age; but the poem is Augustan in its balanced precision, and looks forward to nocturnal and graveyard poems of the forties and fifties. Goldsmith praises it highly, implying that it is superior to Gray's *Elegy Written in a Country Churchyard;* but Johnson more judiciously concludes that 'Gray has the advantage in dignity, variety, and originality of sentiment'.

45.   *they* in this line refers to the rich and the great; in the following line refers to the marble tombs.
61.   *Darts* Death alludes here to the missiles with which he kills his victims.

MATTHEW PRIOR 1664-1721

Prior was born in Westminster, of a poor family with Dorset connections. He attended Westminster School, but after his father's death he was transferred to work in his uncle's tavern. The Earl of Dorset paid for the renewal of his education, and in 1682 he went to St. John's College Cambridge, where he took his bachelor's degree in 1686 and obtained a fellowship in 1688. In 1687, along with his friend Charles Montagu, he attacked Dryden's *The Hind and the Panther* in a satirical medley entitled *The Country Mouse and the City Mouse.* He won the favour of William III by his work as ambassador in the Hague, and as secretary in the negotiations leading to the Treaty of Ryswick; but in 1702 he allied himself with the Tories, thus establishing contact with Harley, Bolingbroke and Swift. He played a major role in the preparations for the Peace of Utrecht, which was popularly known as 'Matt's Peace'; but in 1714, when Queen Anne died and the Tory ministry fell, he was recalled to London. Having been interrogated by a committee under the chairmanship of Sir Robert Walpole, he was impeached in 1715, and spent two years in close confinement. His fortunes were partly restored in 1718 by the publication of his poems; and financial assistance from Harley enabled him to settle at Down Hall in Essex. He was buried in Westminster Abbey, 'at the feet of Spenser'.

Prior's career as a poet began in James II's reign, when he composed literary satires under the patronage of the Earl of Dorset. In William III's reign he celebrated the capture of Namur in a parody of Boileau, and looked forward to the new century in a 'Carmen Seculare'. The poems he published in 1708 included a heavy-handed re-writing of 'The Nut-Brown Maid' under the title 'Henry and Emma', and an ambitious work in three books entitled 'Solomon on the Vanity of the World', which is much indebted to *Ecclesiastes.* 'Alma or The Progress of the Mind' was first printed in the great folio of 1718. Much of Prior's best work, however, is to be found in his most casual and unpretentious pieces. Comic tales like 'Hans Carvel' and 'Paolo Purganti' were popular and much imitated during the eighteenth century; and as an epigrammatist he has few superiors in English. In his prose dialogues, notably that between Locke and Montaigne, he expresses the wary and sceptical vision which made him distrustful of social formality and large assertions. The same mood predominates in many of his love-poems and occasional poems, which use colloquial language and unemphatic rhythms to achieve the honest expression of a limited faith. Especially successful is the poem in anapaestic triplets entitled 'Jinny the Just', in which he pays a tactful, eloquent and entirely convincing tribute to his housekeeper and mistress.

p.45. Alma

'Alma' takes its title from Book II Canto 9 of *The Faerie Queene,* where the House of Alma is the human body and Alma herself is the intellectual reason. As in Butler's *Hudibras,* however, the Spenserian element is confined to the title; and *Hudibras,* to which tribute is paid in II 1-20, serves also as model for Prior's colloquial-burlesque octosyllabics. Composing not a narrative-poem but a conversation-piece, Prior evolves a mock-philosophical strategy analogous to the mock-heroic strategy of *The Rape of the Lock;* and he invokes the ghosts of Aristotle and Descartes as Pope invoked those of Homer and Virgil. Taking his cue from Montaigne's essay 'De l'Yvrognerie' he voices his scepticism about intellectual theorizing by propounding and justifying a theory which is self-evidently absurd. Like Sterne in *Tristram Shandy,* he uses an erratic and digressive presentation to show his distrust of systematic logic. The poem, which Pope described as 'a masterpiece', is a witty and sophisticated exploration of current intellectual controversies.

Epigraph. 'All is laughter, and all is dust, and all is nothing; for out of unreason is all that is.' In the *Greek Anthology,* this couplet is attributed to Glycon.

I.1.   Matthew is the poet. Richard is Richard Shelton, whom Prior described in a letter as 'the Partner of my inmost Soul'.
I.10.   The 1718 folio was published by Jacob Tonson.
I.15ff.   Aquinas, interpreting Aristotle, declares that the soul 'is wholly in the whole body and at the same time wholly in each part of the body'.
I.17.   *bonâ fide* 'in good faith' or 'truly'.
I.20.   Prior is recalling Hamlet I.140-46, probably from a stage production.
I.23.   The Aristotelian tradition was still powerful in Oxford.
I.24.   Cambridge intellectuals were much influenced by Descartes and the New Science.
I.25.   An 'ipse dixit' may be either a dogmatic assertion or, as in this context, the person who makes that assertion.

I.27.   *that old Greek*   Aristotle.
I.29.   This proverbial expression was used by Greene and Peele in the 1590's, and survived into the nineteenth century.
I.97.   *Ergo*   therefore.
I.113.   *ab Origine*   originally.
I.127.   *Num-scull's Self*   the brain, for which the Cartesian makes excessive claims.
I.136ff. Lucretius argues, in *De Rerum Natura* IV.823-57, that man's limbs and organs were created not for specific puposes but by chance.
I.137.   Thomas Creech published his translation of Lucretius in 1682.
I.163.   The reference is to the switch from couplets to alternate rhyme in I.152-9.
I.170.   Monmouth Street, where old clothes were sold, is also mentioned in *Trivia* II.427.
I.177.   *Pismire*   an ant.
I.190.   Lucretius' poem was addressed to Gaius Memmius.
I.198.   Major Faubert kept a riding academy between London and Westminster.
I.218.   Origen (186-253) wrote at length on the immortality of the soul, drawing on pagan as well as Christian sources. Theodoret (393-458) was a bishop and theologian with an extensive knowledge of the Greek classics.
I.224.   Theophrastus, who succeeded Aristotle as leader of the Peripatetic School, and Simplicius, who maintained the Neoplatonic tradition in the sixth century, were both responsible for commentaries on Aristotle's *De Anima.* Guillaume Durand (1230-96) wrote extensively on the liturgy and on ecclestastical law.
I.245.   Pierre Gassendi (1592-1655) was a leading critic of the Aristotelian tradition.
I.252ff. The Florio translation of Montaigne's essay 'De l'Yvrognerie' contains the following passage: 'Good fellowes say, that naturall heat is first taken in our feet: That properly belongeth to infancie. From thence it ascendeth unto the middle region, where it is setled and continueth a long time: and in mine opinion, there produceth the only true, and moving pleasures of this corporall life. Other delight and sensualities in respect of that, doe but sleepe; in the end, like unto a vapour, which by little and little exhaleth, and mounteth aloft, it comes unto the throat, and there makes her last bode.' Even as he first states it, Prior's version of the theory is subtler.
I.296.   The fair commonly known as Bartholomew Fair was held, from 1133 to 1855, at West Smithfield.
I.304.   Robert Freind was headmaster of Westminster School from 1711 to 1733. Andrew Snape was headmaster of Eton from 1711 to 1719
I.319.   *Tray and Pointer* hunting-dogs.
I.357.   The phrase 'in cor stillavit' comes from IV.1059-60 of the *De Rerum Natura,* where Lucretius associates love with the heart ('cor').
I.359.   In *Tristia* IV.x.65-6, Ovid declares that his heart has never been 'invulnerable to Cupid's darts'.
I.361.   In *Odes* IV.i.12, Horace refers the pains of love to the liver ('iecur').
I.379.   The bustard *(otis tarda tarda)* used to breed in the British Isles.
I.399ff. Horace's 'recantation' can be found in *Epistles* I.i.1-19.
I.405ff. Lucretius' tribute to Venus as 'the delight of men and gods' comes in the opening lines of the *De Rerum Natura;* and in the texts available to Prior it was immediately followed by a passage about the gods'

indifference to human affairs.

I.418.   Molière's *Les Fourberies de Scapin* was introduced to the English theatre by Otway's adaptation. *The Cheats of Scapin.*

I.441ff.   *Bile* a bitter, brownish-yellow fluid secreted by the liver. It was one of the four humours of early physiology, and is traditionally associated with anger. *Chyle* a white milky fluid which contributes to the process of digestion.

I.483ff.   Achilles withdrew from the Greek army, because Agamemnon had stolen his concubine Briseïs, who was the daughter of a priest named Briseus.

I.484.   *Tall-boy* a character in Richard Brome's comedy *A Jovial Crew.*

I.487ff.   Mark Antony is said to have left the sea-battle of Actium in pursuit of Cleopatra, thus losing his portion of the Roman world to Augustus.

I.491ff.   The Earl of Warwick planned a marriage between Edward IV and a French princess. When the king insisted on marrying the widow of Sir John Grey, Warwick turned against him.

I.497ff.   Henry of Navarre won a military victory at Coutras in 1587. Gabrielle d'Estrées became his mistress in 1592.

II.4.   The argument to the first canto of Butler's *Hudibras* ends with the couplet:

> Th'Adventure of the Bear and Fiddle
> Is sung, but breaks off in the middle.

II.17.   In the dedication to his *Aeneid,* Dryden speaks of 'merry *Andrew* on the low Rope, copying lubberly the same Tricks which his Master is so dexterously performing on the high'.

II.25.   'Clair-obscur' is a French translation of the Italian term 'chiaroscuro'.

II.32.   The royal birthday was an occasion for sartorial display.

II.44.   To furbelow a gown or petticoat is to ornament it with a pleated border.

II.58.   Banstead Down lies south of London, and in Prior's time was entirely rural.

II.60.   *duns* importunes with demands for payment.

II.91.   The story of Poltis is told in Pope's note to *Iliad* IX.450.

II.99.   *Atrides* Menelaus, who was one of the sons of Atreus.

II.131.   *Teague* a stage Irishman in Sir Robert Howard's comedy *The Committee.*

II.161.   *Hack* seems to be used here as a standard name for a bully.

II.199.   It was reported that an iron coffin, containing the body of Mohammed, was suspended in mid-air within the temple of Mecca by means of 'mightie loadstones' in the roof. The image occurs in *Hudibras* II.iii.441-2.

II.200ff.   Prior's argument is based on the story of Buridan's ass, which died of hunger midway between two identical haystacks.

II.216ff.   The two panniers or baskets are suspended from a piece of wood, which is carried on the shoulders. They are called 'tallies' because they correspond to one another.

II.228.   Charles-Jean-François Hénault (1685-1770) was a leading figure in Parisian society. His hospitality was celebrated by Voltaire.

II.231.   *Ombre ... Basset* fashionable card-games.

II.245.   *Attraction* the usual term at this date for Newton's concept of gravitation.

II.254.   *pro tempore* for the time being.

II.255ff.   Nicolini Grimaldi, the famous Italian singer, was in England between 1708 and 1717. One of the operas in which he sang was *Pyrrhus and Demetrius*.

II.257.   Pietro Castrucci was a distinguished musician who came to England in 1715.

II.259.   *Macer* from the Latin, means 'lean', and is therefore appropriate to a hungry parasite.

II.262.   *Bibo* from the Latin verb meaning 'to drink'.

II.278.   *Brocard* an obsolete form of 'brocade'.

II.287ff.   The letters of Abelard and Eloisa were translated by John Hughes in 1713. Pope's *Eloisa to Abelard* appear in his 1717 collection, for which the Duke of Buckingham wrote complimentary verses.

II.318ff.   *Peg ... Madge* both forms of the name 'Margaret', the first being appropriate to a girl and the second to an old woman.

II.320.   *Green Sleeves ... Jumping Joan* popular melodies, the former of sixteenth-century and the latter of eighteenth-century origin.

II.322.   Lincoln's Inn was a centre of legal, Goldsmiths' Hall of commercial society.

II.343.   *Tully* Marcus Tullius Cicero.

II.401.   Peter Heylyn published in 1629 a work entitled *Microcosmus: A Little Description of the Great World*.

II.415ff.   Prior's information about Hottentot and Chinese customs comes *A New Voyage round the World* by William Dampier, but King Chihu seems to be his own invention.

II.431.   *Tonquin* the northernmost part of Indo-China, around Hanoi.

II.432.   The eighteenth century drew much of its information about the Far East from the writings of Jesuit missionaries.

II.441.   Dampier gives an account of 'Jeoly, the Painted Prince', whom he bought in Mindanao.

II.447.   *Oylet-holes* an oillet is a small round hole in a piece of cloth.

II.448.   *Samplar* a sampler is something which has been ornamented with the aid of a needle.

II.452.   To pink a garment or a body is to ornament it with perforations.

II.464.   *Horn-book* strictly, a sheet of paper marked with the letters of the alphabet and protected by a thin layer of transparent horn. It was used, like the gingerbread letters, for elementary instruction in reading.

II.481ff.   *Pagelli* a pagally, according to *A New Voyage round the World,* is 'an innocent Platonick Friend of the other Sex'; but Dampier also asserts that in many places 'the chief Factors and Captains of Ships have the great Men's Daughters offered them'.

II.497.   The reference is to the Pamaunkee Indians of Virginia.

II.516.   *Leman-Lake* the Lake of Geneva.

III.4.   This is a literal translation of a phrase which occurs in, for example, *Iliad* IX.409.

III.20.   *Lucina* the goddess of childbirth.

III.24.   *Cake-bread* bread made in flattened cakes. As cake-bread is smaller than loaf-bread, so the child's face is a miniature of the father's.

III.43ff.   According to Diogenes Laertius, Pythagoras forbade the eating of beans, and expected his disciples to listen in silence for five years.

III.53ff.   Lucretius envisaged material atoms as moving within a void or vacuum. Descartes, having rejected this theory, explained motion by postulating a 'subtle matter' in which bodies were carried. Newton thought of the substance through which the planets move as something 'more elastick and active' than air. Alchemy in Prior's day was evolving into chemistry; but the search for the philosopher's stone had not been abandoned.

III.67.　The two opinions are those previously attributed to Lucretius and Descartes.

III.77.　The three parts of a syllogism are the major term, the minor term, and the consequence.

III.80.　*Cunning-Man*　an astrologer, like Butler's Sidrophel.

III.102.　These terms are associated with the Platonic, Aristotelian and Thomist traditions respectively.

III.104.　The reference here is to the dispute about transubstantiation.

III.127.　*I smell a Rat*　the phrase occurs in *Hudibras* I.i.815, when Hudibras and Ralpho are engaged in a philosophical disputation.

III.128ff. The Pyrrhonists or philosophical sceptics, believing that certainty of knowledge was unattainable, sought rather to correct error than to propagate truth.

III.140ff. An adept is one who is completely skilled in all the secrets of his art, as Shelton will be if he listens to Prior's exposition.

III.154.　*Cerebrum ... Cerebellum*　the anterior and posterior parts of the brain.

III.156.　*Dura... Pia Mater*　the outer and inner envelopes of the brain and the spinal cord.

III.171.　*vimineous*　made of pliable twigs or wickerwork.

III.204.　*Belly-Timber*　a colloquial term for 'food'.

III.214.　*Ammunition-Bread*　the bread commonly supplied to soldiers.

III.216ff. Because she foresaw that he would die in the Trojan War, Thetis disguised her son Achilles as a girl and sent him to the island of Skiros, which is near Thrace.

III.224.　Peter Heylyn (1600-1662) and Gilbert Burnet (1643-1715) wrote extensively on historical and religious subjects.

III.230.　For mohocks, scourers, nickers and sashes, see notes on *Trivia*. III.326, III.314, III.323 and II.142.

III.247ff. In his essay 'Concerning Humour in Comedy', Congreve ascribes the character of the English people 'to their feeding so much on Flesh, and the Grossness of their Diet in general'.

III.252.　*Chicane*　to engage in deceitful negotiations, here as a substitute for fighting.

III.264.　Daniel Quare was a Quaker and a famous watchmaker.

III.277ff. Shelton compares the trigger, wheel and weight of a watch with those foods which promote rhetorical, mathematical and political skill.

III.290.　*Russel*　Presumably an undertaker.

III.295ff. The career of John Rich as the English Harlequin began in 1717 and continued, first at Lincoln's Inn Fields and then at Covent Garden, until 1760. Prior may be thinking of his performance in John Weaver's *The Cheats*.

III.315.　To gravel a ship is to run it aground; hence 'gravel'd' means 'perplexed'.

III.317.　*Hermes*　the god of eloquence.

III.334.　Prior is referring here to a publication of 1717 entitled *A Collection of Papers, Which passed between the late Learned Mr. Leibnitz and Dr. Clarke, in the Years 1715 and 1716. Relating to the Principles of Natural Philosphy and Religion.*

III.341.　*That old Philosopher*　Zeno of Elea.

III.345.　Prior may be alluding to Galen, who denied the propulsive force of the heart.

III.346.　A *quodlibet*　is a scholastic argument.

III.349ff. The arguments of Chrysippus and Epicurus are summarized by Cicero in *De Fato* X.

III.353ff. The Cartesian metaphysician Nicolas Malebranche (1638-1715) maintains that bodies and minds are merely God's instruments, and that only God can be known directly and immediately.

III.360.   *Entre Nous*   between ourselves.

III.364.   *by-Ends*   secret purposes. *crossbite*   to meet someone's deception with deception.

III.368.   In 1713 Humphrey Ditton and William Whiston put forward a scheme for establishing longitude by firing shells. Their method was ridiculed by Swift and Arbuthnot.

III.382.   *Darii ... Bocardo*   mnemonic words related to two types of syllogism.

III.385.   *hic et nunc*   here and now.

III.401.   This image was used by Swift in the preface to *A Tale of a Tub*.

III.422.   Bayes is the dramatist who represents Dryden in Buckingham's burlesque *The Rehearsal*. Act II Scene V begins with the stage-direction: 'Enter four men at one door, and four at another, with their swords drawn ... They all kill one another. Music strikes.' Bayes then informs the audience that the dead men will 'rise up presently ... and fall a-dancing'.

III.423.   Prior is thinking both of Molière's *L'Avare* and of Horace's miser in *Satires* II.iii.111-23.

III.429.   See note on *Trivia* 1.58.

III.435.   See note on II.257

III.439.   *Rarus*   name appropriate to one who collects rarities.

III.443.   *Vento*   name that suggests both 'selling' and 'wind'.

III.447.   *Curio*   name that suggests both 'curiosity' and 'care',

III.464.   *Georgy*   Shelton's son.

III.512.   *Miles*   an English equivalent for 'Michel'.

III.514.   These fictitious names were used to denote the opposing parties in a legal action.

III.515ff. In Act IV Scene I of *The Rehearsal,* when the two kings are about to kill themselves for love of Lardella, the goddess Pallas opens Lardella's coffin to reveal a nuptial banquet.

III.530.   *Hic iacet*   'here lies': the usual beginning for an epitaph.

II.535.   *Clotho*   one of the three Fates who control the threads of human life.

III.546.   Prior had a large collection of paintings, books, coins and medals.

III.560.   *the Box*   a dice-box. *the Main*   the number called before the dice are thrown.

III.566.   Thomas Doily was a linen-draper in the Strand, and 'a great searcher after curiosities'. An advertisement in *The London Post-Boy* for 31 March 1709 declared that books, prints and medals were to be sold by auction at his shop.

III.574.   *Otho's Head*   a Roman coin from the reign of Otho, who was emperor for a few months in A.D. 69.

III.601.   Act V of Addison's *Cato,* which was acted in 1713, opens with the hero 'sitting in a thoughtful posture; in his hand, Plato's book on the Immortality of the Soul; a drawn sword on the table by him'.

III.608.   From 1717 onwards, Prior was a close friend of Harley's librarian Humfrey Wanley.

III.609.   Adrian Drift was Prior's secretary and companion.

III.612.   Prior mentions his servant Jonathan in letters of 1717 and 1718.

NOTES

ALLAN RAMSAY 1684-1758

Ramsay was born in the Scottish mining-village of Leadhills, and spent his childhood in rural surroundings. He settled in Edinburgh in 1700, and earned his living as a wig-maker. In the years between the Union and the 1715 rebellion, he was much involved with literary clubs of a nationalist tendency; and at the same period he wrote the earliest of his extant poems, some in English and some in Scots. Between 1720 and 1730 he published two collections of original verse, a pastoral comedy entitled *The Gentle Shepherd*, a collection of early Scottish poetry, and a collection of Scottish songs. He opened a theatre in Edinburgh in 1736, but was forced to close it after the Licensing Act of 1737. In 1738 he built himself a house on the Castle Hill, from which he had a view across the Forth to the hills of Fife; and about 1740 he withdrew from commercial affairs. His son, Allan Ramsay the younger, was one of the leading portrait-painters of the eighteenth century.

Ramsay was a contemporary of Pope and Gay, and shared their conception of poetry as a social art. He was also a patriotic Edinburgh burgess of the post-Union period, deeply committed to the re-creation of Scottish literary, musical and theatrical culture. Though he is never profound, and none of his non-dramatic poems can be considered a masterpiece, he writes fluently and intelligently on many subjects and in many forms. In the epistles and mock-elegies, which include some of his best work, he develops the stanza of Robert Sempill's 'Habbie Simson' and William Hamilton's 'Bonnie Heck'; and in longer poems he revives and adapts the intricate stanzas of 'The Cherrie and the Slae' and 'Christis Kirk on the Green'. But he works also with lyrical forms, and with the octosyllabic and decasyllabic couplets; and he can be thoroughly Augustan in his tales, fables, pastoral elegies, imitations of Horace, and poetical comments on the stock-market. By his selection of Scottish models and his emulation of contemporary English poets, he created the literary tradition in which Fergusson and Burns were to work.

p. 85. Lucky Spence's Last Advice.

In the early poem entitled 'Lucky Spence's Last Advice', Ramsay converts the traditional mock-elegy into a dying speech through which the speaker reveals her character. The poet's note tells us that Lucky Spence was 'a famous Bawd who flourished for several years' in the Holyrood area, and continues: 'She made many a benefit Night to herself, by putting a Trade in the Hands of young Lasses that had a little Pertness, strong Passions, Abundance of Laziness, and no Fore-thought.' The poem is characteristic of Ramsay's better work in its colloquial energy and its awareness of the social context.

1. *Carline* old woman; *grain'd* groaned; *rifted* belched.
2. *Cod* pillow; *Pow* head.
4. *faun,* found.
5. *shifted* postponed.
7. *maun* must.
8. *Greeting* weeping.
9. *Draunts* sighs; *Droning* moaning; *deave* deafen.
11. *Bairns* children.
13. *mim Mou'd* Ramsay explains: 'expresses an affected Modesty, by a preciseness about the Mouth'.

208

14. *O'er* too.
15. *Sunkots* provisions.
17. *Feg* fig.
19. *fow* drunk.
20. *gar him trow* make him believe.
23. *Jango* liquor.
24. *Syn* then.
27ff. Ramsay comments: 'I could give a large Annotation of this Sentence, but do not incline to explain every thing, lest I disoblige future Criticks, by leaving nothing for them to do'
31. *Cleek* catch.
32. 'Search every pocket from corner to corner'.
33. *truff* steal.
35. *nae deaf Nits* no hollow nuts. Ramsay comments: 'This is a negative manner of saying a thing is substantial.'
37. *whinging* whining.
40. *sweer* loth.
41. The suggestion is that they should be reported to the kirk-treasurer, who will fine them for immorality. Ramsay comments: *'Hale the Dools* is a Phrase used at Foot-ball, where the Party that gains the *Goal* or *Dool* is said to hail it or win the Game, and so draws the Stake.'
43. *dawt* make much of; *scoup* escape.
44. *the Fou of cutty Stoup* a gill of brandy.
45. *To gee them up* if you reject them.
47. *rive* tear; *Brats* clothes; *Doup* backside
51. *Vild Hangy's Taz* the hangman's whip. A 'rigging' is the top or ridge of a house. Ramsay comments: 'If they perform not the Task assign'd them, they are whipt by the Hangman'.
53. *pit* drive; *daft* mad.
54. Ramsay comments: 'The Emphasis of this Phrase, like many others, cannot be understood but by a Native'.
55. *Gear* property
56. *Ilk* every; *Skare* share.
57. *tirl* strip.
58. *gar ye sike* make you sigh.
59. *thole* endure.
61. *Forby* besides; *count upo'* prepare for.
64. 'Collapse utterly'.
67. *well crish'd Loofs* well-greased palms; *canty* merry
68. 'Whenever the men wanted to get at you'.
69. *Taunty Raunty* sexual intercourse.
70. *Coosers* stallions.
73. *Ca'* whistle.
74. Ramsay comments: *'But* and *ben* signify different Ends or Rooms of a House; to gang *But* and *ben* is to go from one End of the House to the other'.
75. *Roun'd* whispered; *Lug* ear.
77. *Spaw* Spa is a health resort near Liege.
78. *unka blate* very timid.
80. *pin* mood.
81. *slade* slipped.
82. *muckle Mense* great discretion.
83. Ramsay comments: 'It was her usual Way of vindicating herself to tell

ye, *When Company came to her House, could she be so uncivil as to turn them out? If they did any bad thing,* said she, *between* GOD *and their Conscience be 't.'*
87.   *Wale* choice.
88.   *sair Snout* sore nose.
89.   *Foul fa'* cursed be; *smoors,* smother. Ramsay comments: 'Such Quacks as bind up the external Symptoms of the Pox, and drive it inward to the strong Holds, whence it is not so easily expelled.'
91.   *Malison* curse; *ilka* every
95.   *want* be without.
98.   *Mutchken* pint; *Jo* dear.
99.   'After that, let Death execute his warrant'.

JOHN DYER 1699-1757

Dyer was born at Llanfynnydd in Carmarthenshire, and spent his childhood at Aberglasney in the same county. He attended Westminster School, and prepared for a legal career; but after his father's death in 1720 he went to London to study painting under Jonathan Richardson. He visited Italy in 1724-5; and in 1726 his first important poem, 'Grongar Hill', was published in a miscellany edited by David Lewis. During the 1730s Dyer lived at various places in the West of England, being responsible for the management of his aunt's estate near Bromyard. He published *The Ruins of Rome* in 1740, and in the following year he entered the church. He held the living of Catthorpe in Leicestershire from 1742 to 1751, and that of Coningsby in Lincolnshire from 1751 until his death. His most ambitious poem, *The Fleece,* was published in 1757.

The two long poems of Dyer's later life belong to the neo-Miltonic blank-verse tradition which was initiated by John Philips; and their rhetorical assertiveness is a reminder of that tradition's epic origins. Their redeeming qualities stem, like those of many eighteenth-century didactic poems, from the seriousness of the author's concern with his subject-matter. In *The Ruins of Rome* Dyer shows the powers of observation and interpretation which were developed by his training as a painter. *The Fleece,* which is a more successful work, reflects both his life-long study of economic geography and his practical experience of farming in Herefordshire. The heroic manner of these poems is partially justified by Dyer's enthusiasm for their themes, which are closely related to those of prose masterpieces by Gibbon and Adam Smith.

p. 88. Grongar Hill.

'Grongar Hill' was written in the 1720s, when Dyer was studying painting under Richardson and was in contact with men of letters like Hill and Savage. The first version was in Pindaric-ode form, but the later and better version is in octosyllabics reminiscent of Marvell and Milton. The poem belongs to the topographical tradition of *Cooper's Hill* and *Windsor Forest,* but differs from most other works of this type in its essentially lyrical character. In celebrating the view over the Towy valley from a hill close to Aberglasney, Dyer stresses not the scene's historical associations but rather the experience of ascending the hill and the emblematic significance of the landscape. Above all, he interprets what he sees by reference to the paintings of Claude and Poussin; and in the final paragraph, recalling his child-hood, he affirms in typically eighteenth-century terms the pleasures of innocence and of tranquillity.

3.   This use of 'van' to mean 'summit' is found in the place-name 'Carmarthen Van'.

11.   *Phoebus* Apollo, the sun-god.

49.   The medieval castles of this area include Carreg-Cenen Castle, Dryslwyn Castle and Dynevor Castle.

57.   The trees are probably those of the Golden Grove estate.

64.   Dyer's umpublished poems include three 'On the Death of Phillis'.

71.   The castle nearest to Grongar Hill is Dryslwyn; but if the grove of line 63 is Golden Grove, Dyer must be looking up the valley towards Dynevor. The old castle of Dynevor, which dates from the thirteenth century, is on a cliff overlooking the Towy.

139.   Zephyrus is the west wind.

146.   The final paragraph recalls the Senecan chorus, 'Stet quicunque volet potens', which was translated by Marvell and others.

RICHARD SAVAGE 1697-1743

Richard Savage may or may not have been the son born to the Countess of Macclesfield as a result of her liaison with Lord Rivers. The Countess, who later married Colonel Henry Brett, maintained that this child had died in infancy; but Savage claimed her as his mother, and convinced most people in the eighteenth century that his claim was justified. At the time of the 1715 rebellion, he composed propagandist verses in the Jacobite interest: and in 1717 he entered the Bangorian controversy with an attack on Hoadly entitled *The Convocation.* He then moved into the theatrical world, adapting two works of Calderón and gaining the patronage of Anne Oldfield; and in 1723 his historical tragedy *Sir Thomas Overbury* was produced at Drury Lane. His literary associates in the 1720s included Aaron Hill, James Thomson, John Dyer and Edward Young. In 1727 he killed a man in a tavern brawl, and was sentenced to death; but the efforts of his friends, including Mrs. Brett's nephew Lord Tyrconnel, secured him a free pardon. He was closely associated with Pope when the first version of *The Dunciad* was being written; and Pope's enemies accused him of acting as a spy for the satirist. His most ambitious poem, *The Wanderer,* appeared in 1729; and in the 1730s he produced a number of occasional poems, including an epistle to Sir Robert Walpole and an attack on the Bishop of London. About 1737 he met the young Samuel Johnson, who had just arrived in London from Lichfield; their conversations provided material for one of the greatest biographies in English, Johnson's *An Account of the Life of Mr. Richard Savage.* In 1739 Savage withdrew from the corruptions of metropolitan life to settle in Swansea; but in 1742 he decided to return to the capital. He stopped in Bristol on the way, and in January 1743 he was arrested there for debt. He was buried a few months later in St. Peter's churchyard, the funeral expenses being paid by his jailer.

The life and character of Savage are of lasting interest, in part because of his friendship with Johnson; and his poetry, much of which offers idiosyncratic responses to personal situation, is of great biographical importance. The visionary poem which he called *The Wanderer* is a confused and derivative work, much less coherent than the poems of Parnell, Pope and Thomson which it echoes; but its extravagant rhetoric communicates a genuine though undirected enthusiasm, and its descriptive passages are full of the new visual awareness created by Newton's *Optics.* There is vitality of a disordered kind, too, in many of his occasional poems: the Jacobite verses, the review of the Bangorian controversy, the epistles to literary friends, the elegy on Mrs. Oldfield, and the celebrations of 'public virtue' which he wrote as 'Volunteer Laureate'. He is an irresponsible writer, both in his thinking and in his craftsmanship; but most of his poems reveal something of the intellectual and imaginative energy to which Johnson paid tribute.

p.93. The Bastard.

'The Bastard', the most personal and most memorable of Savage's works, incorporates in lines 3-46 a defiant celebration of illegitimacy, which was written just before the murder. The poem as a whole, however, was composed when Savage had recently been saved from execution by a royal pardon; and the contrast in mood between the frame and the inset passage conveys the author's character in a highly dramatic way. No less effective as an aid to self-dramatization is the contrast between the mother to whom the poem is inscribed and the queen to whom it ultimately pays homage. Short as it is, 'The Bastard' defines both vividly and clearly the sensational drama which Savage made out of his life; and its couplets are not unworthy, in their sharpness and their authority, of the man who was a close friend first of Pope and then of Johnson.

Epigraph.   This phrase, which is addressed by Hercules to Juno in Ovid's *Metamorphoses* IX.181, means 'One would expect such treatment from a stepmother'.

69.   According to Johnson, Savage admitted at the trial that he had inflicted the fatal wound, 'but endeavoured partly to extenuate it by urging the Suddenness of the whole Action ... and partly to justify it by the Necessity of Self-Defence'.

EDWARD YOUNG 1683-1765

Young was born at Upham near Winchester, where his father was rector, and was educated at Winchester and Oxford. His literary career began in 1713 with complimentary verses to Granville and Addison, and continued in 1714 with didactic poems entitled *The Last Day* and *The Force of Religion.* His first two tragedies, *Busiris* and *The Revenge,* were produced at Drury Lane in 1719 and 1722; and between 1725 and 1728 he published a series of verse-satires under the general title *The Universal Passion.* His lifelong quest for preferment was more assiduous than successful; but Walpole granted him a pension in 1726, and in 1728 he was appointed chaplain to the king. He became rector of Welwyn in Hertfordshire in 1730, and married a daughter of the Earl of Lichfield in the following year. He was impelled towards the writing of his masterpiece by three deaths: these are traditionally identified as those of his stepdaughter and her husband in 1736 and 1740, and that of his wife in 1741. The nine sections of *Night Thoughts* were published separately in the years 1742-5, and a collected edition appeared in 1750. A third tragedy, *The Brothers,* was produced at

Drury Lane in 1753. In 1759 Young addressed to Samuel Richardson a critical essay entitled *Conjectures on Original Composition;* and in 1762 he published his last significant work, a discursive poem called *Resignation.* During the second half of the eighteenth century, his poetry was much admired not only in Britain but also in France, Holland and Germany. One of Blake's most ambitious undertakings was the preparation of a series of illustrations for Young's *Night Thoughts;* and the nine-night structure of that poem is reflected in *The Four Zoas.*

Young was an important figure in the eighteenth-century literary world; but much of his work is uninspired and heavy-handed. The didactic couplets of *The Last Day* and *The Force of Religion* are competent but tedious; and there is much absurdity both in his naval-patriotic odes and in the ballad-stanzas of *Resignation.* The three tragedies are sensational without being fully dramatic; and the most popular of them, *The Revenge,* is heavily indebted to *Othello.* There are merits, however, in *The Universal Passion,* whose authoritative phrasing can often make stock ideas sound like epigrams; and *Conjectures on Original Composition* is a document of great importance to the student of critical theory.

p.95 On Life, Death, and Immortality.

Young's major achievement was the long discursive poem in blank verse which is commonly known as *Night Thoughts.* Read as a whole, this work is intolerably dogmatic and repetitive; and the author's rhetorical skill cannot redeem the simplistic moral tirades of the later nights. In the first night, however, under the title 'Of Life, Death and Immortality', the great platitudes about man's relationship to time are powerfully and convincingly reiterated. The imagery is often theatrical, and the rhythms echo those of dramatic soliloquies; but one can hear the poet committing himself to a deeper knowledge of the selfhood, of suffering, and of the distinction between illusion and reality. Young's talent was not for reasoning in verse, or for the exploration of unusual experience, but for the full apprehension and decisive affirmation of universally-recognised truths.

Dedication. Arthur Onslow (1691-1768) was Speaker of the House of Commons from 1728 to 1761.

67ff. The traditional concept of man's central position on the Great Chain of Being is still important in the poetry of Pope; and this passage recalls *An Essay on Man* II. 1-18. Most poets from Thomson onwards lay more stress on the Newtonian system of natural laws.
115. *vital* from the Latin 'vita', which means 'life'.
179. *it* refers to 'tie'.
213. This appears to be a poetic fiction. The three deaths which are generally thought to have evoked this poem followed one another less closely than Young's phrasing would suggest.
214. *Cynthia* the moon-goddess.
223. *postern* a back door or obscure passage.
284. *terraqueous* of land and water.
321. *Lorenzo* addressed frequently in the later nights, and usually characterized as 'a man of the world'.
344. *Philander* has sometimes been identified as Henry Temple, the husband of Young's stepdaughter.
380. *the Fatal Sisters* the Parcae, who control the threads of human life.
406. *Vails* fees or gratuities.

440. *Philomel* the nightingale.
449. *Maeonides* Homer.
451. The poems of Homer were translated by Pope, who also wrote *An Essay on Man.*

WILLIAM SHENSTONE 1714-63

Shenstone was born at Halesowen west of Birmingham, and was educated in Halesowen, Solihull and Oxford. His friends at Oxford included the novelist Richard Graves and the poet Richard Jago. In 1737 he published a volume entitled *Poems on Various Occasions,* which included an early version of *The Schoolmistress.* His didactic poem *The Judgment of Hercules* appeared in 1741, and in 1742 he re-issued *The Schoolmistress* in a much-expanded text. In 1745 he took charge of the family estate at the Leasowes near Halesowen, and began to lay it out as a *ferme orné* . Many of his poems, including 'A Pastoral Ballad', appeared in the successive volumes of *A Collection of Poems by Several Hands* between 1748 and 1758. From 1757 onwards he was frequently consulted by Thomas Percy about *Reliques of Ancient English Poetry.* His poems, essays and letters were collected after his death by Robert Dodsley, who published along with them a full description of the Leasowes.

Shenstone was the leading figure in a provincial literary circle whose other members included Graves, Jago and Percy. His correspondence reflects the life and thought of that group; and it enables one to follow the gradual transformation of his estate into one of the century's most celebrated landscape-gardens. His prose essays develop a mid-century theory of landscape-gardening with quiet sophistication, maintaining an intelligent awareness of the relationship between abstract ideals and practical techniques. His poetry, though unambitious, gives varied expression to the personal and intellectual qualities revealed in the Leasowes and in the prose writings. 'A Pastoral Ballad' is a triumph of rococo lyricism, calculated to appeal (as Saintsbury observed) 'to all but very superior persons'. The elegies never approach the level of Gray's masterpiece, as Shenstone recognized when the latter was published; but the poet's way of blending artifice with sentiment gives an individual quality both to their pastoralism and to their elegiac quatrains. The distinctive Shenstonian note can be heard again in such major lyrics as the false-Pindaric ode entitled 'Rural Elegance', and in such minor lyrics as 'The Sky-Lark' and 'Written at an Inn in Henley'.

p.107. The Schoolmistress.

The Schoolmistress is a Spenserian burlesque, like Akenside's 'The Virtuoso'; and it originated as a 'deformed portrait' of Sarah Lloyd, who kept a school near Halesowen. As an imitation of *The Faerie Queene* the poem cannot compare with *The Castle of Indolence,* because Shenstone understood and emulated only the superficial aspects of Spenser's art. In 1742 he wrote to Graves: 'I am glad you are reading Spenser: though his plan is detestable, and his *invention* less wonderful than most people imagine, who do not much consider the obviousness of allegory; yet, I think, a person of your disposition must take great delight in his *simplicity,* his good-nature, &c... When I bought him first, I read a page or two of the Fairy Queen, and cared not to proceed. After that, Pope's Alley made me consider him ludicrously;

and in that light, I think, one may read him with pleasure.' Such a reading of Spenser could not produce a wholly successful neo-Spenserian poem; but the writing of a burlesque released Shenstone from certain Augustan inhibitions, enabling him to speak fluently and sympathetically about provincial life and about the sorrows of childhood. Although its archaisms and inversions are often irritating, the poem's treatment of its subject-matter anticipates greater works by Gray, Goldsmith and others.

Epigraph. These lines come from *Aeneid* VI.426-7, and may be translated 'Voices are heard, and loud wailing, and the souls of children crying on the threshold.' Shenstone quotes Virgil frequently in his letters; and in 1755 he told Graves that '*all* the Lines in VIRGIL' gave him 'that Sort of Pleasure which one receives from melancholy Music'.

56.   *Eol*   Aeolus, the god of the winds.
57.   *Libs*   the west-south-west wind; *Notus, Auster* names for the south wind.
98.   'Gill-go-over-the-ground' is a name for Ground Ivy *(Nepeta Glechoma).*
100.   *euphrasy* a plant formerly used in the treatment of eye-disease.
109.   *rosemarine* an early form of 'rosemary'.
119.   Thomas Sternhold and John Hopkins were responsible for a metrical version of the psalms, which circulated widely in Britain from the sixteenth century to the eighteenth. Shenstone is referring here to their version of Psalm 137.
133.   *nould* would not
134.   *lawny saints* bishops, who have sleeves made of lawn.
136.   The reference is to the coronation throne, which incorporates the Destiny Stone brought by Edward I from Scotland.
137.   *eld* old age
146.   This is an echo of Virgil's

'parcere subiectis, et debellare superbos'.

156.   See note on *Alma* II.464.
165.   *Mulla* Spenser's name for the Awbeg, a tributary of the Blackwater which figures prominently in *Colin Clout's Come Again.*
171.   *ermilin* ermine.
242.   Edward Vernon (1684-1757) was the admiral responsible for the capture of Porto Bello in 1739, and for the attack on Cartagena in 1741.
255.   The reference is to the critic John Dennis, who wrote severely of works by Addison, Pope and Steele.
257.   *the 'Aonian field* the Muses were said to frequent Mount Helicon in Aonia.
262.   *Phoebus* the sun-god.
265.   *han* have.
287.   See note on *Trivia* III.125.
294.   *the cath'rine pear* Suckling and Gay associate the red-streaked catherine pear with rosy cheeks.
306.   *Salopia* Shrewsbury. A Shrewsbury cake is flat, round, crisp and biscuit-like.

JOHN BYROM 1692-1763

Byrom was born near Manchester, where his father was a linen-draper, and was educated at Merchant Taylors' School and Trinity College Cambridge. In 1714 he contributed two essays and a poem to *The Spectator.* Because of his Jacobite sympathies, he was unwilling to take the oath required of applicants for public employment. From 1716 to 1718 he studied medicine in Montpellier; and in 1721 he married his cousin, Elizabeth Byrom. About this time he invented a new system of shorthand; and for many years much of his energy was devoted to the exposition and propagation of this art. He became a Fellow of the Royal Society in 1724. In 1729 he met William Law, the author of *A Serious Call to a Devout and Holy Life;* and under Law's influence he became a student of Jakob Böhme. He was in Manchester when the Jacobite army reached the city in 1745; and his daughter's diary gives a lively account of the occasion. Byrom was a considerable linguist, at home not only in Latin and French but also in Hebrew, Greek, Italian and German; and he took an active interest in poor law administration, publishing a small book on the subject in 1755. The main interests of his later life, however, were religious: both his journals and his poems reflect his study of such writers as Law, Böhme, Malebranche and John of the Cross. He died at the age of seventy, after a long illness; and his many friends paid tribute to his 'gentle manners', his 'heart of soft benignity', and his 'copious stores of conversation sweet'.

Byrom's poetry, most of which was printed for the first time in a post-humous collection entitled *Miscellaneous Poems,* is the work not of an aspirant for literary fame but of a man to whom verse came as naturally as prose. Like his journals, the poems reflect both the events of his life and the wide range of his interests; and they are written in a casual and colloquial manner which is usually readable but rarely memorable. He wrote poems about robberies and boxing-matches, about the Jacobite rebellion and the history of Manchester Grammar School; and he wrote poems, some of them very amusing, about controversial points in the text of Horace's odes. In his later life, he engaged in friendly discussion with clergymen and others on theological issues; and he often chose to conduct that discussion in verse. His most successful poems include the pastoral which he sent to *The Spectator,* the verse-epistle which he called *Enthusiasm,* and the well-known Christmas hymn 'Christians awake'. He was also responsible for the epigram on Handel and Buononcini which gave currency to the phrase 'Tweedledum and Tweedledee'.

Byrom's sympathy in the dynastic struggle lay with the Jacobites; but he was disposed, in political as in theological matters, to avoid acriminious controversy. His attitude was concisely expressed in an extempore epigram 'intended to allay the violence of party-spirit':

> God bless the King, I mean the Faith's Defender;
> God bless – no Harm in blessing – the Pretender:
> But who Pretender is, or who is King,
> God bless us all – that's quite another Thing.

p.116. A Dialogue between Sir John Jobson and Harry Homespun.

This, one of three dialogues using the Lancashire dialect, is the work of an unmilitant Jacobite quietly critical of Whig constitutional theory. The disputants are a Hanoverian landlord and a Manchester weaver; and it is obvious that Byrom is in general agreement with the latter.

7.   *Aw whoa* all who.

12. *eem* find time.
50. *lukko me* seems to mean 'believe me'.
58. *winn* will.
60. *mac* sorts.
65. *wurn* were.
68. *mun* must.
79. *waintly* strangely.
88. *getten* been victorious.
91. *Tyke* dog.
92. *ween* we'll
94. *Feight as feight winn* fight who will fight.

JAMES MACPHERSON 1736-96

Macpherson was born near Kingussie in Inverness-shire, where his father was a poor farmer. After attending a local school, he entered King's College Aberdeen in 1753. In 1755 he transferred to Marischal College Aberdeen; and he later proceeded to Edinburgh University, probably as a divinity student. While he was a student he wrote Pindaric odes, blank-verse poems and poems in the heroic couplet; and in 1758 he published in Edinburgh a heroic poem entitled *The Highlander.* After teaching for some time in his native parish, he took employment as a private tutor. At Moffat in 1759 he met the dramatist John Home; and in response to Home's enquiries about Gaelic literature he composed a short prose-poem entitled 'The Death of Oscar'. Encouraged by Home's reception of this work, Macpherson produced others of the same type; and a collection of these was shown to Hugh Blair, who reacted credulously and with enthusiasm. Sixteen of Macpherson's prose-poems were published in Edinburgh in 1760 under the title *Fragments of Ancient Poetry, collected in the Highlands of Scotland, and translated from the Gaelic or Erse language.* Macpherson's attribution of these works to a third-century poet named Ossian was at this stage accepted by David Hume; and Thomas Gray in Cambridge was 'struck with their infinite beauty'. Money was raised in Edinburgh so that Macpherson could record and translate the 'epic poem' mentioned in his preface; and in 1760-61 he made two journeys for this purpose, the first to Skye and Benbecula and the second to Argyll and Mull. Soon afterwards he set out for London; and there in 1762 he published a six-book epic entitled *Fingal,* which he dedicated to the Earl of Bute. Attacks on his work came from Irish scholars, who pointed out its historical inconsistencies; and in England, where Wilkes and Churchill were campaigning against the Bute government, the general reaction was hostile. In 1763 Macpherson published an eight-book epic entitled *Temora;* and Hume, writing from London to Blair in Edinburgh, recommended a thorough investigation of his alleged sources. In 1764 Macpherson became secretary to Governor Johnstone in Florida; but in 1766 he returned to London, where he now worked chiefly as a historian and a political journalist. In 1771 he published *An Introduction to the History of Great Britain and Ireland;* and in 1773 he brought out a translation of the *Iliad,* which was generally condemned. In 1775 his Ossianic poems were decisively rejected by Samuel Johnson in *A Journey to the Western Islands;* and there followed an angry correspondence, in which Johnson answered Macpherson's threats of violence with magniloquent contempt. Macpherson's publications of the years 1775-9 included pro-Jacobite discussions of British history from 1660 to 1714, propaganda for the North government during the American War, and works arising from his role as London agent for the Nabob of Arcot. He became M.P. for Camelford in 1780; and soon afterwards he retired to the Central Highlands, where he bought an estate and was much praised as a benevolent landlord. In 1797 the Highland Society of Scotland undertook an inquiry into 'the poems of Ossian'; and their report, which appeared in 1805, demonstrated that Macpherson's prose-poems were in part original compositions and in part free adaptations of Irish ballads.

Despite the hostility of Johnson, Wordsworth and Scott, the Ossianic poems achieved immense popularity not only in the British Isles but also in France, Germany and elsewhere. Many critics followed Blair in comparing Ossian with Homer; and Macpherson's 'translations from the Gaelic' were rapidly translated into French, German, Italian, Spanish, Dutch, Danish, Swedish, Polish, Russian and Greek. Bonaparte's copy of the French version was carried first to Egypt and then to St. Helena; and Ossian's other admirers included Byron, Hazlitt, Chateaubriand, Lamartine, Klopstock, Herder and Goethe. Macpherson is thus a figure of major importance in European literary history; and his influence on the European image of Celtic culture could scarcely be exaggerated. The wrath which his falsifications have aroused among Celtic scholars is understandable; and there can be no doubt that much of his work is cloudy, pretentious and repetitive. His dream-world, however, has an imaginative power like that of the dream-worlds created by Malory and Tolkien; and in his presentation of that world the concept of a Fall is continually implicit. The un-Celtic twilight which encompasses his tales about Fingal and Morven is the natural mood of a Highland intellectual who was ten in the year of Culloden; and in such passages as the famous address to the sun in 'Carthon' he creates for himself a linguistic medium which is wholly appropriate to his message.

p.119 Oithóna.

'Oithóna', which is one of Macpherson's shorter poems, is characteristic of his Ossianic works in its vaguely-defined setting, its simplified characters, and its generalized rhetoric. It is superior to many of his other poems, however, in the coherence of its narrative scheme; and it is unusual in having no basis, so far as can be discovered, in the ballad-material which he used elsewhere. Like many dramatic works of the classical tradition, it deals with the climactic event in a long story; and the values communicated are in part those of domestic tragedy, the interrelationship of the three main characters being reminiscent of Otway's *The Orphan*. The situation assumed in the poem is defined as follows in Macpherson's note:

> Gaul, the son of Morni, attended Lathmon into his own country, after his being defeated in Morven, as related in the preceding poem. He was kindly entertained by Nuäth, the father of Lathmon, and fell in love with his daughter Oithóna. — — The lady was no less enamoured of Gaul, and a day was fixed for their marriage. In the mean time Fingal, preparing for an expedition into the country of the Britons, sent for Gaul. He obeyed, and went; but not without promising Oithóna to return, if he survived the war, by a certain day. — Lathmon too was obliged to attend his father Nuäth in his wars, and Oithóna was left at Dunlathmon, the seat of the family. Dunrommath, lord of Uthal, supposed to be one of the Orkneys, taking advantage of the absence of her friends, came and carried off, by force, Oithóna, who had formerly rejected his love, into Tromáthon,

a desart island, where he concealed her in a cave.

Gaul returned on the day appointed; heard of the rape, and sailed to Tromáthon, to revenge himself on Dunrommath. When he landed, he found Oithóna disconsolate, and resolved not to survive the loss of her honour. – She told him the story of her misfortunes, and she scarce ended, when Dunrommath with his followers, appeared at the further end of the island. Gaul prepared to attack him, recommending to Oithóna to retire, till the battle was over. She seemingly obeyed; but she secretly armed herself, rushed into the thickest of the battle, and was mortally wounded. Gaul pursuing the flying enemy, found her just expiring on the field: he mourned over her, raised her tomb, and returned to Morven. – Thus is the story handed down by tradition; nor is it given with any material difference in the poem, which opens with Gaul's return to Dunlathmon, after the rape of Oithóna.'

The 'preceding poem' was 'Lathmon', which dealt with Lathmon's attack on Morven and with his defeat at the hands of Ossian and Gaul. Morven, in Macpherson's myth, is a kingdom on the west coast of Scotland; and Fingal, the father of Ossian, is Macpherson's version of the Irish hero Finn MacCumhail. The name 'Tromáthon', according to Macpherson, means 'heavy or deep sounding wave'; and the name 'Oithóna' means 'the virgin of the wave'. 'Oithóna' itself is not a successful poem; but the imaginative potential of its plot was realised in Blake's *Visions of the Daughters of Albion*, where Gaul, Dunrommath and Oithóna reappear as Theotormon, Bromion and Oothoon.

Paragraph 3: The son of Leth is Morlo, whom Macpherson describes as 'one of Fingal's most famous heroes'. He and three others are said to have accompanied Gaul on his voyage to Tromáthon.

CHARLES CHURCHILL 1732-64

Churchill was born in Westminster, where his father was curate at the church of St John the Evangelist. At Westminster School he established a close friendship with George Colman and Robert Lloyd, with whom he was later to be associated as a satirist. He enrolled at St John's College Cambridge in 1748; but after contracting a secret marriage he retired to Sunderland to prepare for the ministry. He obtained the curacy of South Cadbury in Somerset in 1754, that of Rainham in Essex in 1756, and that of St John's in Westminster in 1758. In 1760 he was separated from his wife; and in 1761 the publication of *The Rosciad* established him as one of the leading writers of the day. His other poems of this year were *The Apology,* in which he answered attacks on his work, and *Night,* in which he answered attacks on his way of life. About 1762 he became closely involved with John Wilkes; and in the years 1762-3 he played a leading role in Wilkes' campaign against the Bute government. Early in 1763 he resigned the curacy of St John's; and later in the same year he eloped with Elizabeth Carr, the fifteen-year-old daughter of a Westminster tradesman. His publications of 1762-3 included a long poem in octosyllabic couplets entitled *The Ghost,* which is chiefly remarkable for its attack on Samuel Johnson. His growing involvement in political affairs was reflected in two better poems, *The*

Prophecy of Famine and *An Epistle to William Hogarth;* and in *The Conference* and *The Author* he considered once again the relationship between a satirist's private and public life. Churchill's productivity was maintained in the last year of his life by the publication of a Hudibrastic poem called *The Duellist,* which comments on Wilkes' encounter with Samuel Martin; a moral-didactic poem called *Gotham,* in which the poet imagines himself as ruler of an ideal commonwealth; and four heroic-couplet satires entitled *The Candidate, The Farewell, The Times* and *Independence.* He died at the age of thirty-two in Boulogne, having gone there to meet Wilkes; and he was buried in Dover.

Churchill is least successful as a poet in *The Ghost* and *The Duellist,* where he tries to continue the Butler tradition of low satire in the octosyllabic couplet. His other works, which belong in form and technique to the tradition of Dryden and Pope, are consistently vigorous and accomplished; and all of them contain witty and memorable passages. Comparison with Johnson and Goldsmith, however, reveals the shallowness and harshness of Churchill's sensibility; and there is an incongruity, in his later poems, between the persona which he assumes and the tradition which he inherits. His literary devices are those developed by the great Augustans for satiric poetry of an affirmative kind; yet his creative energy, after *The Rosciad,* seems to arise from a desire to question all firmly-defined systems of value. Although he remained loyal to the heroic couplet even when he abandoned the role of Anglican curate, he is not only a follower of Dryden and Pope but also a forerunner of the great romantic satirists. His schoolfellow and disciple William Cowper commented regretfully on his early death; and one feels that his genius might have been emancipated by a more suitable medium, just as Burns and Byron found their true voices in the 'Habbie Simson' stanza and in *ottava rima.*

p.124. The Rosciad.

The Rosciad is Churchill's most Augustan poem, and is more unified and less idiosyncratic than most of its successors. The narrative framework is a conventional one, which had been used many times for critical surveys of contemporary poetry; and although Churchill owes something to Book IV of *The Dunciad,* he virtually abandons the mock-heroic element of Pope's method. Following the lead given by Lloyd's *The Actor* in 1760, he offers critical assessments of the leading actors and actresses of his day; and by invoking the names of Roscius, Shakespeare and Jonson he defines the cultural standards by which these assessments are informed. His various tributes and criticisms reflect the close study of contemporary acting which he had made from the front row of the pit; and the final enthronement of Garrick affirms the continuing vitality of those values which Roscius and the great dramatists represent. When it first appeared, the poem occasioned a fierce and extended controversy which involved on the one hand Churchill's friends Colman and Lloyd and on the other the dramatist Arthur Murphy and the novelist Tobias Smollett. Its interest for later generations arises partly from Churchill's mastery of verse and language, and partly from what he tells us about theatrical history and histrionic technique. The text printed here is that of the ninth edition, which appeared in 1765 and contained 'large additions'.

Title. As *The Dunciad* was a critical survey of contemporary authors, so *The Rosciad* is a critical survey of contemporary actors.

NOTES

1. Quintus Roscius was the most famous actor of ancient Rome.
26. Fielding's song 'The Roast Beef of Old England' was still popular with theatrical audiences.
27. Robert Clive (1725-74) returned from India in 1760, and was thought to be 'the richest subject in the three kingdoms'.
29ff. Bartholomew Fair was held at Smithfield in August, Lady Fair at Southwark in September. Comedians like Edward Shuter and Richard Yates took booths at these fairs 'for the representation of *drolls* and *pantomimes'*.
33ff. The Licensing Act of 1737 limited the number of theatres in London to two; but Samuel Foote invited the public to 'take tea' with him at the Haymarket. In 1760-61 Foote was acting at the 'Old House' in Drury Lane, while his rival Tate Wilkinson was at the 'New House' in Covent Garden.
46. The *Theatrical Examiner* informs us that John Palmer (1728-68) had 'life and sprightliness'.
48. Spranger Barry (1719-77) was a leading tragic actor, and was 5 feet 11 inches tall.
50. John Coan (d. 1764) was a dwarf, and could be seen at a tavern in Chelsea.
55. Ellis Ackman (d. 1774) was described by John Taylor as 'an inferior performer ... though an intelligent and worthy man'.
61ff. The proposed judges are Samuel Johnson, Laurence Sterne, Thomas Francklin, George Colman and Arthur Murphy. Francklin (1724-84) was Professor of Greek at Cambridge, In 1759 he published a translation of Sophocles, which was attacked by Lloyd.
75. The Scottish lawyer Alexander Wedderburn (1733-1805) was a friend of Murphy and an enemy of Wilkes.
91ff. The Temple and Gray's Inn refused to admit Murphy, because he had been an actor.
107ff. John Hill (1716-75) had a varied career, his activities ranging from the selling of patent medicines to the writing of a daily essay under the title *The Inspector*. The god Proteus was noted for his ability to change shape.
115. Henry Woodward (1714-77) was attacked by Hill, and replied by caricaturing Hill on the stage.
117ff. This is a portrait of Thady Fitzpatrick, whom Garrick satirised as 'Fribble'. Fitzpatrick's persistent hostility to Garrick and Drury Lane contributed to the theatrical riots of 1763.
145. This line is adapted from Garrick's 1761 poem *The Fribbleriad.*
191ff. The arguments Churchill attributes to Lloyd are based on those of Lloyd's poems *The Actor* and *Shakespeare.*
233ff. The reference is to Job XXXII. 4-10.
258: William Murray, first Earl of Mansfield, became Lord Chief Justice in 1756. Sir Michael Foster became a judge of King's Bench in 1745.
259ff. The critical assumptions underlying these portraits of Shakespeare and Jonson stem in part from Dryden's *An Essay of Dramatic Poesy.*
288. *Apollo* the god of poetry.
290. The reference is to William Mason's *Ode to Memory.* The odes of Gray and Mason were parodied by Colman and Lloyd in 1760.
303. *Hautboy* oboe.
310. Churchill implies that Covent Garden was more prosperous than Drury Lane.
315. According to the *Theatrical Examiner,* William Havard (1710-78) had 'the manner and motion of a gentleman' and was a 'very useful' actor.
319. Thomas Davies (1712-85) was not only an actor but also an author

and a bookseller. His wife's beauty is mentioned by Boswell, who first met Johnson at their house.

323. Charles Holland (1733-69) was a pupil of Garrick, and it was said that he 'idolized his great instructor too much to be anything original'.

337. Thomas King (1730-1805) acted the part of Brass in a 1759 production of Vanbrugh's *The Confederacy,* and was later celebrated for his performance as Sir Peter Teazle.

345. Richard Yates (1712-96) was considered 'one of the first comedians of the age', but was 'often imperfect in his parts'. As the angry father in Colman's *Polly Honeycomb* (1760), he covered his failure of memory by repeating the phrase 'Hark ye'.

364. In Farquhar's comedy *The Constant Couple,* the porter Tom Errand exchanges clothes with Beau Clincher.

369ff: Henry Woodward returned from Ireland in 1762. In a Drury Lane production of *Every Man in his Humour,* the parts of Bobadill and Kitely were taken by Woodward and Garrick.

395. Samuel Foote (1720-77) was famous as a mimic, an actor and a dramatist. In his 1760 farce *The Minor* he played the roles of Shift the parson, Smirk the auctioneer and Mrs Cole the bawd.

409ff. Tate Wilkinson (1739-1803) was Foote's rival in the art of mimicry. When Woodward left Drury Lane for Ireland in 1758, his place was taken by William O'Brien (d. 1815). .

416. Master Stephen is a character in *Every Man in his Humour.*

425ff. John Jackson, a native of Westmorland who first acted in Edinburgh, appeared at Drury Lane in 1762. His pronunciation was said to be 'tinctured with something of the provincial'.

451. James Love (1722-74) first acted Falstaff at Drury Lane in 1762.

484. *Dominic* a character in Dryden's *The Spanish Friar.*

485f. *Boniface* in Farquhar's *The Beaux' Stratagem,* he refers to the oldest ale in his cellar as 'Anno Domini'.

493ff. This passage (to line 512) first appears in the second edition, and is a comment on the actors' response to *The Rosciad.*

513. Joseph Austin (d. 1821) was valued by Garrick not for his acting but for the practical experience he had acquired while managing a theatre in Chester.

514. Henry Norris (1665-1731) and Robert Wilks (1665-1732) were major actors of an earlier period. John Hayman Packer (1730-1806) was successful in 'the third rate walks of genteel comedy'.

517ff. Astley Bransby (d. 1789) was very tall,, and was described by the *Theatrical Examiner* as 'a solemn, sententious, and grave person'.

521ff. Charles Blakes (d.1763) was noted for his acting of Frenchmen.

537. John Moody (d. 1812) was noted for his acting of Irishmen.

539ff. Bayes is the dramatist in Buckingham's *The Rehearsal.* Churchill is referring here to Arthur Murphy, who in 1760 hired Drury Lane for the summer. Murphy's company included Richard Yates, Mary Ann Yates and Ann Elliott; and their first play was Murphy's *All in the Wrong.*

560. In 1762-3 Murphy edited a periodical called *The Auditor,* which defended the Bute government against the attacks of Churchill and Wilkes.

582. Murphy first acted Othello at Covent Garden in 1754.

589ff. Murphy was educated at the Jesuit College of St Omer, and later became a clerk in a London Bank.

605ff. These lines recall the enthroning of Shadwell and Cibber in *MacFlecknoe* and *The Dunciad.*

610. The *Public Ledger* was a newspaper conducted by Hugh Kelly.

611. Murphy's friend Thomas Vaughan (d. 1820) engaged in controversy with Colman, who nicknamed him Dapper.

616. In an attack on the Westminster satirists, Murphy referred to 'Mr. Churchill and his little faction'.

625. The *Theatrical Review* accused Luke Sparks (1711-68) of 'uncouthness' and of 'incoherent motions'.

627. William Smith (1730-1819) had 'an agreeableness in his address', and was 'of that size and proportion that pleases the eye'.

629f. David Ross (1728-90) played the part of Alexander in Lee's *The Rival Queens*. The part of Statira may have been taken by George Anne Bellamy.

633ff. Charles Macklin (d. 1699-1979) made his reputation as Shylock in *The Merchant of Venice*. In 1754 he opened an oratorical school in Covent Garden, which he called 'The British Inquisition'.

647. *Cits* citizens.

648. Thomas Sheridan began to lecture on oratory and elocution in London in 1761.

649ff. Edward Shuter (?1728-76) was a comic actor noted for his improvisations.

653. *the placid stream* the New River, which flowed past the Sadler's Wells music-house in Islington and supplied the City of London with water.

657. Richard Rolt (?1725-70) composed songs and cantatas for Sadler's Wells and other establishments, and is said to have planned a collaboration with Shuter.

663ff. John Rich (?1682-1761) was manager of the Covent Garden theatre. His stage name was Lun, and he acted the part of Harlequin in a long series of successful pantomimes.

674. This line is a quotation from *Paradise Lost* II.628.

682. The Salic Law excluded females from succeeding to the French throne.

686. Catherine Clive (1711-85) was famous for her acting of lively maid-servants.

695ff. Jane Pope (1742-1818) acted Corinna in Vanbrugh's *The Confederacy,* Cherry in Farquhar's *The Beaux' Stratagem,* Polly in Colman's *Polly Honeycomb,* and Dolly Snip in Garrick's *Harlequin's Invasion.*

703ff. Mrs. Vincent acted Polly in *The Beggar's Opera* in 1760 John Taylor asserts that Churchill 'was certainly too partial to her talents'.

713ff. Thomas Augustine Arne (1710-78) composed an opera entitled *Artaxerxes,* which John Beard (1716-91) produced at Covent Garden in 1762 as part of his scheme for an 'English opera'. The cast included not only Italian castrati but also English singers like Beard himself and the celebrated Charlotte Brent.

730ff. Mary Ann Yates, the wife of Richard Yates, was said by Francis Gentleman to have 'a good person' but to be 'deficient in tender feelings'.

756ff. Miss Hart and Miss Bride acted for the first time at Drury Lane in 1760, the former in Cibber's *The Provoked Husband* and the latter in Addison's *Cato.*

777ff. Susanna Maria Cibber (1714-66), the wife of Colley Cibber's son Theophilus, was one of the leading tragic actresses of Garrick's time. One of her most famous roles was that of Alicia in Rowe's *Jane Shore.* The scene to which Churchill refers is V.1, in which Alicia raves about the 'headless trunk' of the recently-executed Hastings.

803ff. Hannah Pritchard (1711-68) was described by Edmund Malone as 'a large fat coarse woman, very ordinary if not homely, that from good sense and good feeling played some parts in comedy very well'. The roles mentioned by Churchill are those of Zara in Congreve's *The Mourning Bride*, Lady Macbeth in Shakespeare's *Macbeth*, Juletta in Fletcher's *The Pilgrim*, and Mrs Oakly in Colman's 1761 comedy *The Jealous Wife*.

859ff. Spranger Barry and Henry Woodward opened the second Dublin theatre in Crow Street in 1758. Henry Mossop (1729-73) joined them in 1759, having left Drury Lane after a quarrel with Garrick. In 1760, however, Mossop moved to the old Dublin theatre in Smock Alley, thus initiating the 'mortal fight' to which Churchill refers.

921. James Quin (1693-1766) retired from the stage in 1751, having for many years maintained the histrionic techniques of Thomas Betterton and Barton Booth in opposition to the new naturalism of Macklin and Garrick.

923. *lin'd* supported.

963ff. As Pyrrhus in Ambrose Philips' *The Distrest Mother*, Quin wooed Hector's widow Andromache; and as Horatio in Rowe's *The Fair Penitent* he reprimanded the libertine Lothario. His performance as Falstaff was much praised; and his other roles included those of Sir John Brute in Vanbrugh's *The Provoked Wife*, Cato in Addison's *Cato*, and Dorax in Dryden's *Don Sebastian*.

987. Thomas Sheridan (1719-88) acted at Drury Lane during the 1706-61 season, one of his roles being that of King John in Shakespeare's history. Churchill refers to his scene with Philip in II.1 and to his scene with Hubert in III.3. The part of Philip was taken by Thomas Davies.

1013. *the Nailor* a boxer named Bill Stevens, who was London champion in 1760.

1032. Sergeant Kyte in Farquhar's *The Recruiting Officer* asserts that he that has the good fortune to be born six feet high, was born to be a great man'.

CHRISTOPHER SMART 1722-71

Smart was born at Shipbourne in Kent, his father being steward to the Vane family; and he was reared and educated first in the Maidstone district and then in County Durham. In 1739 he entered Pembroke College Cambridge, where he became a Fellow in 1745. By 1749, when he left Cambridge for London, he had accumulated large debts and had several poems printed in the magazines. The London bookseller John Newbery employed him in 1751-3 on a periodical called *The Midwife*, in which he assumed the role of Mrs. Mary Midnight; and from this there developed a theatrical enterprise called Mrs. Midnight's Oratory, which continued for some years. In 1752 Smart married Newbery's stepdaughter Anna Maria Carnan, and settled at Canonbury House in Islington. In the same year he attacked John Hill in a neo-Scriblerian mock-epic entitled The *Hilliad;* and he also issued *Poems on Several Occasions,* which included odes, fables, tales, epigrams, Latin poems, a masque, and a blank-verse georgic on hop-growing. In the years 1750-55 he won the Seatonian prize five times with blank-verse poems about 'the attributes of the Supreme Being'; and in 1756 he supplemented these with 'A Hymn to the Supreme Being' which resembled the final hymn in *The Seasons.* Other poems, including more fables, appeared in *The Gentleman's Magazine* for 1754; and in 1755 Smart published a prose translation of the works of Horace. He was increasingly affected by mental illness, which he manifested by often 'falling upon his knees, and saying his prayers in the street, or in any other unusual place'. In 1757-8 he spent fourteen months in the curable ward of St. Luke's Hospital; and from 1759 to 1763 he was confined in the private madhouse of George Potter at Bethnal Green. During his confinement he composed the long antiphonal poem known as *Jubilate Agno,* which remained in manuscript until 1939; and he must also have worked on some of the poems which were printed soon after his release. *A Song to David* appeared on 6 April 1763; and in 1763-4 Smart issued various small collections, mainly of secular verse. His most ambitious publication appeared in two parts in 1765, the first part being entitled *A Translation of the Psalms of David* and the second part *Hymns and Spiritual Songs for the Fasts and Festivals of the Church of England.* In 1767 he atoned for his prose version of Horace by translating Horace's complete works into English verse. In 1768, with *The Parables of Our Lord,* he made his first contribution to the eighteenth-century tradition of religious poetry for the young, and in 1770 he followed this with a more interesting book entitled *Hymns for the Amusement of Children.* In the same year he was arrested for debt; and in 1771 he died in the King's Bench Prison.

Smart's secular poetry is varied, ranging from the translation of Horace to the facetious verses of Mary Midnight. *The Hilliad* imitates *The Dunciad* in a rather trivial way, and *The Horation Canons of Friendship* is a clumsy exercise in the epistolary manner; but *The Hop-Garden,* though inferior to John Philips' *Cyder,* has merits as a celebration of Smart's native county. In the fables such characters as the magpie, the scrubbing-brush and the mandrake are well defined by their distinctive modes of speech; and Smart's independent response to natural beauty is apparent in such rural poems as 'A Noon-Piece, or, The Mowers at Dinner'. The secular poems, both original and translated, are the work of an intelligent and versatile writer with a keen visual sense, an Augustan feeling for verse-form, and a lively capacity for original phrasing. The same qualities are present in Smart's religious poetry, but here they are controlled by the poet's overwhelming commitment to the praise of God. His individual blend of boldness and absurdity can already be savoured in the Seatonian poem 'On the Goodness of the Supreme Being', where he writes.

> Bow down, ye elephants, submissive bow
> To him who made the mite;

and in the personal and allusive rhetoric of *Jubilate Agno* he emerges, with all his faults, as one of the most original writers of the eighteenth century. The influences which impelled him towards the realization of his poetic genius included Hebrew poetry as interpreted by Robert Louth and the natural world as interpreted by botanists and zoologists. His great achievement was to communicate, in the religious poems which he published after his release, an intense and ecstatic awareness of the living relationship between the Supreme Being and the minute particulars of His universe. Nothing in the sane and authoritative hymns of the Wesleys is quite as vivid as Smart's superbly idiosyncratic poem about the nativity:

> Spinks and ouzles sing sublimely,
> We too have a Saviour born,
> Whiter blossoms burst untimely
> On the blest Mosaic thorn.
> God all-bounteous, all-creative,

> Whom no ills from good dissuade,
> Is incarnate, and a native
> Of the very world he made.

This decisive and unconventional enthusiasm is equally apparent in other poems, such as the version of Psalm 104 and the hymn for the Feast of St Philip and St James.

p.150. A Song to David.

A Song to David, which is Smart's greatest poem and has often been judged unique in his work, celebrates the author of the Psalms in a rhapsodic manner closely related to that of the 1765 psalm-translations. The poet draws not only on the Psalms and on 1 and 2 Samuel but also on Patrick Delany's *A Historical Account of the Life and Reign of David;* and his poem is among other things a contribution to the controversy about David's character which was initiated in 1760 by Samuel Chandler's sermon on the death of George II. There has been much discussion about Smart's possible debt to cabbalistic or Masonic tradition; and his own account of the poem's contents certainly shows that it was constructed on elaborate rhetorical and numerological principles. After a three-stanza invocation, there follows a stanza setting out 'the excellence and lustre of David's character in twelve points of view'; and in Stanzas 5-16 the twelve virtues ascribed to him are 'proved from the history of his life'. Stanza 17 relates David's wives Michal and Abishag to 'his genius for consolation and edification'; and Stanzas 18-26 list 'the subjects he made choice of', which extend from the Supreme Being through angels and men to 'the works of nature in all directions, either particularly or collectively considered'. Stanzas 27-9 celebrate the triple victory by which David obtained power over evil spirits, subdued the malignity of his enemies, and won the heart of Michal. Stanzas 30-37, whose use of the Greek alphabet has not been conclusively explained, show 'that the pillars of knowledge are the monuments of God's works in the first week'; and Stanza 38 relates this thesis to the poem's theme by celebrating David as 'the scholar of the Lord'. Stanza 39 looks forward to Christ as the fulfilment and realization of such Old Testament wisdom; and Stanzas 40-49, which Smart calls 'an exercise upon the decalogue', re-interpret and amplify the Mosaic commandments in specifically Christian terms. Stanza 49, by calling upon David to maintain his affirmation of 'the genuine word', moves upward to 'the transcendent virtue of praise and adoration', which is celebrated in Stanzas 50 and 51. The song's climactic sequence, from Stanza 52 to Stanza 71, is a rhapsodic assertion that this virtue, supremely manifested in the psalms, is the ideal to which all modes of being aspire. Stanzas 52-63, which Smart calls 'an exercise upon the seasons, and the right use of them', follow this notion through spring, summer, autumn and winter, devoting three stanzas to each. In these stanzas the key phrase 'for adoration' twice progresses from Line 1 through to Line 6; and then in Stanzas 64-71 it is steadily reiterated at the beginning of Line 1. Stanza 64, like Stanza 49, renews contact with the poem's primary subject; and Stanzas 65-9, which Smart calls 'an exercise upon the senses, and how to subdue them', relate the concept of adoration to the senses of touch, sight, hearing, scent and taste. In Stanza 70 the concept of adoration is celebrated in universal terms, and in Stanza 71 it is focused in the person of Christ. Stanzas 72-86, which Smart calls 'an amplification in five degrees', advance towards the Incarnation through five equal groups controlled by an ascending sequence of five adjectives. In each case the adjective has the positive form in the first two stanzas, which refer to the natural world, and the comparative form in the third stanza, which refers to Christ; and the last group is given additional power first by the repetition of the word 'glorious' in Stanzas 84-5 and then by the contrasting expansiveness and alliterative violence of Stanza 86. This five-part amplification, Smart explains, 'is wrought up to this conclusion. That the best poet who ever lived was thought worthy of the highest honour which possibly can be conceived, *as the Saviour of the world was ascribed to his house, and called his son in the body.'* The splendour of *A Song to David* owes much to the accumulating of sensual and biblical details within this intricately-organized scheme.

10.   *To keep* can mean either 'to celebrate' or 'to maintain a record of'.
26.   Compare 1 Samuel, XVI.13.
30.   Compare 1 Samuel, XVI.12.
35.   Compare 1 Samuel, XVII.40. The boaster is Goliath.
38.   Compare 1 Chronicles, XXVIII.
43.   'Judah'h This form of the name 'Dudah' also appears in Smart's psalm-translations.
47.   Compare 1 Samuel, XXIV.
48.   Compare 2 Samuel, XVI.5-14.
69.   Smart's translation of Psalms, LXXVII.70 reads:

> He chose out David from the ranks,
> And plac'd above the world;
> From folded sheep, and from the banks
> Where silver Kidron purl'd.

'The brook Kidron' is mentioned frequently in Kings and Chronicles.
81.   Compare 2 Samuel, I.19-27
83.   Compare 2 Samuel, IX, XVI.1-14 and XIX.24-30
88.   Compare 1 Samuel, XVII.38 and 2 Samuel VI.14
91.   Compare 2 Samuel, XI and XII.
101.   Compare 1 Samuel, XVIII.20-28.
102.   Compare 1 Kings, I.1-4.
111.   *citterns* a cithern is an instrument resembling a guitar.
118.   *briny broad* the sea.
123.   *champaign* level country.
128.   *Gem* here means 'bud'.
140.   *of light escape* probably means 'with the ability to escape quickly'; but other interpretations have been suggested.
148.   *coney* rabbit.
161.   Compare 1 Samuel, XVI.23.
175.   The Seven Pillars of Wisdom are mentioned in Proverbs, IX.1; and 1 Kings, VII, describes the decorated pillars of Solomon's temple. For a full discussion of the Greek letters in this passage see K.M. Rogers, 'The Pillars of the Lord: Some Sources of "A Song to David"', *Philological Quarterly XL* (1961), 525-34.
181.   Compare Genesis I.1-5.
187.   Compare Genesis I.6-8
193.   Compare Genesis, I.9-13.
199.   Compare Genesis, I.14-19.
205.   Compare Genesis, I.20-23.
208.   *foot ... chapitre* the base and capital of the pillar.
211.   Compare Genesis, I.24-31.

217.   Compare Genesis, II.1-3.
235.   Compare Exodus, III.14.
249.   *wilk*   the whelk.
253.   Compare Matthew, XXVI.39.
267.   Compare Deuteronomy, XXII.10.
270.   Compare Deuteronomy, XXII.11.
280.   The New Adam is Christ.
291.   Compare Psalms, CXIX.
310.   Geoffrey Grigson relates these images to the vegetation and geology of County Durham.
316.   *Ivis*   the humming-bird
325.   *spotted ounce*   leopard.
328.   According to Smart, 'there is a large quadruped that preys upon fish and provides himself with a large piece of timber for that purpose, with which he is very handy'.
329.   The halcyon was said to breed in a nest floating on the sea, and to charm the winds so that the sea became calm.
340.   *coasting*   floating downstream in a boat.
341.   Silverlings are fish which resemble small silver coins. The crucian is a species of yellow carp.
352.   *nectarine*   a kind of peach.
354.   *quick*   here means 'pungent'.
356.   'Thyine wood' is mentioned in Revelation, XVIII.12, and has been identified as that of a tree native to Africa.
374.   *holy thorn*   the hawthorn is associated with Christ.
386.   The bullfinch can be taught to imitate a tune.
393.   *Rose*   the constellation usually called Coma Berenices.
397.   *the strings*   of an Aeolian harp.
404.   *bezoar*   a substance found in the stomachs of some animals.
408.   *galbanum*   a type of gum-resin which is obtained from plants native to Persia.
410.   *anana*   a kind of pineapple.
421.   Compare Psalms, LXXXIV.3.
429.   *Hermon*   a mountain west of Damascus.
446.   *glede*   kite.
450.   *xiphias*   the swordfish.
454.   *gier-eagle*   a kind of vulture, which is mentioned in Deuteronomy, XIV.17.
461.   Compare Matthew, VII.7.
467.   *meditated wild*   the planned wilderness of an eighteenth-century landscape-garden.
478.   *conceit*   here means 'conception'
479.   Fish are sometimes referred to as 'the mute creation'.
480.   Compare 2 Samuel, XII.16.
483.   Smart's note refers to 1 Samuel, XXV.18.
485.   *alba*   the 'white stone' of Revelation, II.17.
491.   Compare Leviticus, XXIII.40.
508.   Compare Daniel, VI.23.
513.   Compare Matthew, I.1.

JOHN CUNNINGHAM 1729-73

Cunningham, whose father was a wine-merchant of Scottish extraction, was born in Dublin and educated in Drogheda. In 1747 he wrote a farce entitled *Love in a Mist,* which was performed in the Dublin theatre. He became an actor, and was associated for many years with a company based in Edinburgh. For this company he wrote a series of occasional prologues; and in 1761 he published in Edinburgh a poem modelled on Gray's *Elegy.* Other poems appeared in 1762 and 1765; and in 1766 he put together a small volume entitled *Poems Chiefly Pastoral.* These publications attracted some attention; but Cunningham continued to earn his living as a strolling actor. In his later years he settled in Newcastle, where he died at the age of forty-four.

Cunningham's poetry is unambitious, and is the work of one who regarded Shenstone as his literary master. Like other mid-century poets he writes pastoral-sentimental love-songs often in trisyllabic metres, and composes tales and fables in octosyllabic couplets. He uses the elegiac quatrain for meditative and didactic poems, and echoes 'A Pastoral Ballad' in lamenting Shenstone's death. His rural-descriptive poems in the octosyllabic quatrain, the best of which is 'Day: A Pastoral', invite comparison with similar works by Alexander Hume and John Clare. His other poems include epigrams, drinking-songs and imitations of Anacreon.

p.167. Newcastle Beer.

'Newcastle Beer' is the most ambitious of Cunningham's drinking-songs; and its patriotic energy, like the elegiac and sentimental notes sounded in his other verses, is typical of the age. The military victories which it celebrates are those of the Seven Years' War.

2.   Olympus is the dwelling-place of the gods. 'Gallic' means 'French'.
3.   *Mars* the god of war. *Mercury* the messenger of the gods.
5.   *Comus* the spirit of revelry.
13.   *Moor's* a Newcastle tavern.
14.   *Stingo* strong ale or beer.
22.   The fountain associated with the nine Muses was at the foot of Mount Helicon.
31.   *Alcides* Hercules, the grandson of Alcaeus.
40.   *quantum* a specified amount.
43.   *probatum* here means 'infallibly'.
52.   *bolus* a large pill.

MARK AKENSIDE 1721-70

Akenside was born in Newcastle as the son of a Unitarian butcher, and acquired a permanent limp through an accident in his father's shop. His first poems, which appeared in *The Gentleman's Magazine* for 1737, included imitations of Spenser, Milton and Pomfret; and his later contributions to the same journal included an attack on the Jacobites and a tribute to Young. Between 1739 and 1744 he studied medicine at the the Universities of Edinburgh and Leyden. In the latter year he published a blank-verse didactic poem in three books called *The Pleasures of Imagination* and a political satire in heroic couplets called *An Epistle to Curio;* and these were followed in 1745 by a small collection entitled *Odes on Several Subjects.* In 1746 Akenside became the editor of Dodsley's periodical *The Museum;* and in 1751 he was satirized by Smollett in

NOTES

Peregrine Pickle. A number of his poems, including 'A Hymn to the Naiads' and six inscriptions, were included in Volume VI of Dodsley's *Collection* in 1758; and in the same year he reasserted his Whig principles in *An Ode to the Country Gentlemen of England.* In 1759 he became physician to St. Thomas' Hospital, and in 1764 he published a medical treatise with the title *De Dysenteria Commentarius.* In his later years he undertook but did not complete a revised version of his most famous poem, which he now called *The Pleasures of the Imagination;* and this was published with other posthumous works, in 1772.

Akenside is a serious, versatile and accomplished writer; but with all his talents he never attains a poetic individuality like that of Shenstone or Fergusson. *The Pleasures of Imagination,* which was much admired in the eighteenth century, draws its philosophical arguments from Addison, Shaftesbury and Hutcheson, its style and didactic method from Lucretius and Virgil's *Georgics,* and its versification from Milton, John Philips and Thomson. The odes are unremarkable in content, their moral values being expressed mainly through Whig clichés about liberty; and their impressive craftsmanship is directed above all towards establishing English equivalents for the lyrical manners of Pindar and Horace. *An Epistle to Curio,* which drew extravagant praise from Macaulay, employs a weighty Ciceronian irony to enforce platitudinous assertions about political ethics. 'A Hymn to the Naiads' and the best of the inscriptions convey the poet's feeling not about their professed subjects but about the linguistic texture of ancient Greek verse. Akenside resembles Collins in his uncritical devotion to the Whig ethos, and in the quality of his admiration for classical literature; but his work reveals no qualities comparable with Collins' emotional sensitivity and mythopoeic version.

p.169. The Pleasures of the Imagination.

The Pleasures of the Imagination is less coherent than the 1744 poem, not only because it is unfinished but also because the various layers of its argument sometimes contradict one another. Akenside's desire to revise his masterpiece seems to have arisen from dissatisfaction with its aesthetic theory; and the pretentiousness of his didactic manner is somewhat modified by his continuing search for truth. The finished portion of the revised poem consists only of Book I, Book II and a part of Book III: but Akenside also drafted, and his friend Jeremiah Dyson decided to print, 'the Introduction to a subsequent book, which in the manuscript is called the fourth, and which appears to have been composed at the time when the author intended to comprize the whole in Four Books; but which, as he had afterwards determined to distribute the poem into more books, might perhaps more properly be called the last book'. Lines 1-30 of this passage, which profess to introduce a new division of the subject, depend too much on echoes of Latin poetry and of *Paradise Lost* IX.1-47; but Lines 31-57 advance, in a manner that suggests Cowper and Wordsworth, from self-conscious exposition to the egotistical sublime. The eighteenth-century didactic manner reasserts itself in Lines 58-130; but even here Akenside affirms with some eloquence, from an essentially Platonic standpoint, the value and importance of artistic creation.

14.   *If* here used in Miltonic fashion, and means 'to see whether'.
19.   *apt to be conceiv'd of* capable of being understood by.
32ff. The castles of Prudhoe and Dilston are on the Tyne between Newcastle and Hexham; and the valleys of the North and South Tyne, which

could be explored from Akenside's birthplace, contain other medieval fortresses.
40.   The town of Morpeth, which Akenside visited as a boy, stands on the River Wansbeck.
47.   *The graver tasks of manhood* include those of a physician at St. Thomas' Hospital.
121.   *obsequious* here means 'obedient'.

THOMAS CHATTERTON 1752-70

Chatterton was the posthumous son of a Bristol schoolmaster who had been closely associated with the church of St. Mary Redcliff. In 1767, after seven years at Colston's Hospital, he was apprenticed to an attorney named John Lambert; and in 1768, after submitting to *Felix Farley's Bristol Journal* a prose extract 'from an old Manuscript', he made the acquaintance of a surgeon named William Barrett and a pewterer named George Catcott. He convinced Barrett and Catcott that he had discovered a large store of medieval manuscripts in the Treasury of St. Mary Redcliff; and in 1768-9 he produced transcripts not only of historical documents but also of poems and dramatic pieces, most of which he associated with a Bristol contemporary of Lydgate named Thomas Rowley. One of the Rowley poems was printed in *The Town and Country Magazine* in May 1769; and Chatterton tried unsuccessfully to persuade first Robert Dodsley and then Horace Walpole to bring out a complete edition. Several of his acknowledged works in English were accepted by periodicals; and in April 1770 he left Bristol for London, intending to make his living as a writer. He wrote fluently for the London press in support of Wilkes, and had a burletta accepted by Drury Lane; but on 24 August 1770 he committed suicide at his lodgings in Brooke Street. The Rowley poems were fully edited in 1777 by the Chaucerian scholar Thomas Tyrrwhitt; and all competent authorities quickly recognised them as original compositions by Chatterton.

Chatterton's acknowledged poems include African eclogues reminiscent of Collins, vehement political satires modelled on Churchill, and plaintive elegies which recall Gray; and his imitative precocity is further manifested in Hudibrastic satires, poems on astronomy, mock-heroic poems, abusive epistles, mythological burlesques, religious poems and conventional love-lyrics. As a group, his poems in modern English appear the work of a clever, self-confident and morally irresponsible adolescent; and although their fluency and variety are astonishing, they rarely suggest a deeply poetic intelligence. Chatterton became a poet only when he entered, under the influence of St. Mary Redcliff and the lexicographers, the imaginary fifteenth-century Bristol of Thomas Rowley and his patron William Can-ynge. The most ambitious of the Rowley poems, the 'tragycal enterlude or discoorseynge tragedie' called *Aella,* has a plot analogous to those of *Othello* and Macpherson's 'Oithóna'; but Rowley, who shares Chatterton's interest in his native city, sets the action in Bristol at the time of the Danish invasions. The various rhyme-schemes employed recall Chaucer, Spenser and Milton; and the dialogue, with its eighteenth-century idiom and fifteenth-century vocabulary, unites philological absurdity with a touch of linguistic genius. Especially memorable is the 'minstrelles songe', whose dramatic function is like that of Desdemona's 'The poor soul sat singing by a sycamore tree'. The penultimate stanza was a favourite with Keats:

> Comme, wyth acorne-coppe and thorne,
> Drayne mie hartys bloode awaie;
> Lyfe and all yttes goode I scorne,
> Daunce bie nete, or feaste by daie.
> > Mie love ys dedde,
> > Gon to hys death-bedde,
> > Al under the wyllowe tree.

The more interesting of the shorter pseudo-medieval poems include the eclogue called 'Elinoure and Juga', where 'twa pynynge Maydens' share their anxieties about lovers fighting in the Wars of the Roses, and the ballad called 'Bristowe Tragedie or The Dethe of Syr Charles Bawdin', which uses techniques learnt from Percy's *Reliques* to celebrate a Lancastrian martyr of Edward IV's reign. As a literary confidence-trickster Chatterton was less skilful and less successful than Macpherson; but his Rowley, as Wordsworth and Coleridge recognised, was a better poet than the author of *Fingal*.

p.173. An Excelente Balade of Charitie.

If 'An Excelente Balade of Charitie' was a new composition when Chatterton submitted it to *The Town and Country Magazine* on 4 July 1770, it must be one of the latest of the Rowley poems. Whether it was written in London or in Bristol, it probably reflects the young poet's feeling about the responses of Walpole and others to his appeals for help. The plot is a fifteenth-century Bristol equivalent for the parable of the Good Samaritan; and the influence of Spenser, Thomson and Chaucer is apparent in the descriptions of the pilgrim, the storm and the two ecclesiastics. The verse-form, which is rhyme-royal with an alexandrine in the seventh line, comes from Milton's poem 'On the Death of a Fair Infant'. The notes marked 'C' in the following commentary were copied by Tyrrwhitt 'from MSS in the hand-writing of Thomas Chatterton'.

Title. 'Thomas Rowley, the author, was born at Norton Mal-reward in Somersetshire, educated at the Convent of St Kenna at Keynesham, and died at Westbury in Gloucestershire.' *C*

1.   *Virgyne* Virgo, the sign of the zodiac which the sun enters about 21 August. *sweltrie* oppressively hot.
2.   *mees* 'meads'. *C*
3.   *rodded* 'reddened or ripened'. *C*
4.   *mole* 'soft'. *C*
5.   *chelandri* 'pied goldfinch'. *C*
7.   *dighte* 'drest or arrayed'. *defte* 'neat or ornamental'. *aumere* 'a loose robe or mantle'. *C*. *eke* also.
9.   *welken* 'the sky or the atmosphere'. *C*
10.   *arist* 'arose'. *C*
13.   *Hiltring* 'hiding or shrouding'. *attenes* 'at once'. *fetive* 'beauteous'. *C*.
14.   *swolne* swelled.
15.   *holme* oak.
16.   'It would have been *charitable,* if the author had not pointed at personal characters in this Ballad of Charity. The Abbot of St. Godwin's at the time of the writing of this was Ralph de Bellomont, a great stickler for the Lancastrian family. Rowley was a Yorkist.' *C*

18.   *ungentle* 'beggarly'. *C. weede* clothing.

19.   *bretful* 'filled with'. *C*

20.   *almer* 'beggar'. *C*

22.   *glommed* 'clouded or dejected. A person of some note in the literary world is of opinion, that *glum* and *glom* are modern cant words; and from this circumstance doubts the authenticity of Rowley's Manuscripts. Glum-mong in the Saxon signifies twilight, a dark or dubious light; and the modern word *gloomy* is derived from the Saxon *glum.*' *C*

23.   *forwynd* 'dry or sapless'. *C*

24.   *church-glebe-house* 'the grave'.   *ashrewed* 'accursed or unfortunate'. *C*

25.   *kiste* 'coffin'. *dortoure* 'a sleeping room'. *C*

26.   *Cale* cold. *gre* grow.

27.   *elves* people.

30.   *forswat* 'sun-burnt'. *smethe* 'smoke'. *drenche* 'drink'. *C*

31.   *pall* 'a contraction from *appall,* to fright'. *C. ghastnes* horror. *do* does.

33.   *flott* 'fly'. *C*

34.   *levynne* 'lightning'. *C*

35.   *smothe* 'steam or vapours'. *lowings* 'flames'. *C*

36.   *clymmynge* 'noisy'. *C*

37.   *Cheves* 'moves'. *embollen* 'swelled or strengthened'.*C*

38.   *dispended* dissipated.

39.   *gallard* 'frighted'. *C*

40.   *swanges* sways noisily.

42.   *braste* 'burst'. *C. stonen* hail.

45.   *chapournette* 'a small round hat, not unlike the shapournette in heraldry, formerly worn by Ecclesiastics and Lawyers.' *C. drented* soaked.

46.   *pencte* 'painted'. *C*

47.   *He ayneward tolde his bederoll* 'he told his beads backwards; a figurative expression to signify cursing.' *C*

49.   *mist* 'poor or needy'. *C*

50.   *cope* 'a cloke'. *C*

52.   *autremete* 'a loose white robe, worn by Priests'. *C*

53.   *a loverds* 'a lord's'. *C shoon pyke* shoes with piked toes.

56.   'I believe this trade is still in being, though but seldom employed.' *C.* The world 'horse-milliner' could still be seen in 1776 above a shop-door near Colston's Hospital.

63.   *crouche* crucifix.

66.   *faitour* 'a beggar or vagabond'. *C*

69.   *shettynge* shooting. *glairie* bright.

70.   *eftsoones* quickly

74.   *jape* 'a short surplice worn by Friars of an inferior class and secular priests'. *C*

75.   *Limitoure* a priest licensed to beg within a limited area.

82.   *halline* 'joy'. *C. mister* poor.

83.   *eathe* 'case'. *C*

84.   *nete* 'nought'. *C*

85.   *unhailie* 'unhappy'. *C*

86.   *Scathe* scarcely.

87.   *semescope* 'a short under-cloke'. *C*

89.   *aborde* went on.

90.   *gloure* 'glory'. *C*

91.   *mittee* 'mighty or rich'. *C*

NOTES

ROBERT FERGUSSON 1750-74

Fergusson's parents came from Aberdeenshire; but he was born and brought up in Edinburgh, where his father was a clerk in a lawyer's office. He attended the High School in Edinburgh and the Grammar School in Dundee; and in 1764 he visited his maternal uncle, who lived on an Aberdeenshire farm. From 1764 to 1768 he was a student at St. Andrews University; and about 1765 he wrote a mock-elegy, in the 'Habbie Simson' stanza, on the Professor of Mathematics:

> He could, by *Euclid*, prove lang sine
> A ganging *point* compos'd a line;
> By numbers too he cou'd divine,
>   Whan he did read,
> That *three* times *three* just made up nine;
>   But now he's dead.

In 1769, after another visit to Aberdeenshire, Fergusson settled in Edinburgh as a clerk in the Commissary Office; and he quickly formed connections with Edinburgh musical and theatrical society. In 1771 he published some English poems in *The Weekly Magazine or Edinburgh Amusement*. Most of his Scots poems appeared in the same periodical between January 1772 and December 1773; and enthusiastic correspondents greeted him as 'Allan risen frae the deid'. In October 1772 he became a member of the Cape Club, which met in a tavern off the High Street; and during the summer of 1773 he spent a month in Dunbar and made an excursion to Dumfries. A serious illness in the autumn was followed by fits of religious melancholy; and in July 1774, after a fall on a staircase, he was carried home delirious. Because his mother was unable to look after him, he was 'at last removed to the Bedlam of the city of Edinburgh'; and in October he died in his cell, and was buried in the Canongate Churchyard. Robert Burns was given permission, thirteen years later, 'to lay a simple stone over his revered ashes'.

Fergusson's poems in English include Popean eclogues, Shenstonian elegies and lyrics, octosyllabic tales and fables, and mock-heroic narratives in neo-Miltonic blank verse. Being closely related to his experience of Edinburgh society, they are often lively and informative; but in management of verse and language they are consistently inferior to their southern models. The Scots poems, which renew and develop the eighteenth-century vernacular tradition created by Ramsay, use established forms and conventions in a more authoritative and individual way. Fergusson's observation of nature and understanding of rural life are apparent in the 'Ode to the Gowdspink' and in 'The Farmer's Ingle'; but he is primarily a poet of the city, and his vivid rendering of the urban scene in 'Auld Reekie' recalls Swift and Gay. He makes effective use of colloquial octosyllabics in the 'Mutual Complaint of Plainstanes and Causey' and in less ambitious poems like 'On Seeing a Butterfly in the Street'; and the command of Scots heroic couplets which he shows in 'The Ghaists' and the pastoral elegy on Wilkie suggests that his planned version of Virgil's *Eclogues* and *Georgics* might have been a worthy complement to Douglas' *Aeneid*. Much of his best work, however, is in two of the Scottish verse-forms which had been revived by Ramsay; the stanza of 'Habbie Simson' and the stanza of 'Christis Kirk on the Green'. In the former, he excels Ramsay with such energetic yet serious poems as 'Braid Claith', 'The Daft Days' and 'Elegy on the Death of Scots Music';

and his work in the latter advances, in a characteristically eighteenth-century manner, from antiquarian pastiche to original poetry of contemporary life. Fergusson is a considerable poet in his own right; and the 1782 edition of his poems provided the example and stimulus for Burns' major creative achievements of 1784-5.

p.176. Hallow-fair.

'Hallow-fair', which is the earliest of Fergusson's poems in the 'Christis Kirk' stanza, follows its late-medieval predecessors in celebrating a popular festival; but the poet is alive not only to the convention within which he is working but also to his local and topical subject-matter. In 1772 Edinburgh's annual Hallowmas fair began on 26 October, at a site just west of the city; and Fergusson's poem appeared in *The Weekly Magazine* on 12 November. It traces the fair's progress from morning to evening, noting the various motives, behaviour and language of those who attend it. The young people's search for pleasure is contrasted with the fortune-tellers' search for profit; and there are fuller portraits of an Aberdonian stocking-seller and a noisy recruiting-sergeant. The dramatic climax is a mock-heroic account of Jack Bell's encounter with the warlike Highlanders of the City Guard. This poem, along with its successors 'Leith Races' and 'The Election', provided the literary inspiration for Burns' 'Halloween'. 'The Holy Fair' and 'The Ordination'.

1. *Hallowmas*   normally the first week of November.
2. *starnies*   stars.
3. *fock* folk. *bang* overcome.
4. *hap-warms* wraps.
5. *there hads* is held.
6. *wat* know.
8. *cap* drinking-bowl. *stoup* wooden flagon.
10. *ilka* every. *lum* chimney.
11. *keek* peep.
12. *trig made* smartly dressed.
13. *joe* sweetheart.
14. *browsters* ale-wives.
15. *yale* ale. *gantries* wooden stands.
16. 'And don't grudge an allowance'.
17. *kebbucks* cheeses.
18. *saut* salt.
20. *eke* also. *clais* clothes.
21. *rokelay* cloak.
22. *sappy* moist.
23. *coof* fool.
24. *gab* mouth.
25 *criesh* grease. *loof* palm.
26. *fairin* a present bought at a fair.
28. *chapmen billies* pedlar fellows.
29. *bonny wallies* fine goods.
30. *gleg* glibly. *aff hand* on the spur of the moment.
32. *cairds* beggars.
33. *horse-coupers* dealers in horses.
34. *spae-wives* fortune-tellers. *fengying* feigning or pretending.
35. *siclike* such. *landloupers* vagabonds.
37. Before the Industrial Revolution, Aberdeen was the principal centre

in Scotland for the making of hosiery. Sawny's speech is in the Aberdeen-shire dialect.

38.   *fa* who
39.   *brawest* finest. *shanks* legs or stockings.
40.   *guid* good. In Aberdeenshire speech the word rhymes with 'need'.
41.   *wyt* know. *protty* pretty.
42.   *weyr* wire or knitting-needles. *leem* loom.
43.   *rug* bargain. *pose* savings or purse.
44.   *ain* own. *teem* empty.
46.   *gang* go.
47.   *hooly* cautiously.
48.   *lowns* fellows.
49.   *fegs* indeed. *spulzie* rob.
50.   *fairn-year* last year.
51.   The accent in 'mischievous' falls on the second syllable.
52.   *scaw'd* worthless.
55.   *dinlin* rattling.
56.   *screechs* yells.
59.   *gie* give.
62.   *soum* swim or float.
64.   *cussers* stallions. *nicker* neigh.
65.   *our* over. *ley-rig* grass field.
66.   *carls* fellows. *bend* drink. *bicker* drinking-cup.
67.   *wud* mad.
68.   *sic* such. *yellowchin* yelling.
69.   *wee-anes* children. *gablin* chattering.
70.   *true* believe.
73.   'When Phoebus lies in Thetis' lap', i.e. when the sun descends into the sea.
74.   *Auld Reikie* a familiar name for Edinburgh, which means literally 'Old Smoky'. *gi'es* gives.
75.   *cadgily* gaily. *cap* drinking-bowl.
76.   *ca* drive or pass. *helter-skelter* cheerfully and quickly.
77.   *gaed* went. *friaks* tricks.
79.   *stark* strong. The Lochaber axe carried by members of the City Guard is described in Chapter III of *The Heart of Midlothian* as 'an ancient weapon ... with an axe at the extremity, and a hook at the back of the hatchet'.
80.   *clamihewit* severe blow.
81.   *sair* sore.
82.   *ohon* alas.
83.   *bagnet* bayonet. *stickit* stabbed.
85.   *sic* such. *nicket* cut.
86.   *straik* blow.
88.   *gar'd* made. *feckless* feeble.
89.   *reikin* smoking.
91.   *peching* panting. *cawsey* street.
92.   *saird* supplied.
93.   William Creech asserts in 1788 that 'The city-guard seem to preserve the purity of their *native Gaelic tongue'*. *aith* oath. *ga'e* uttered.
94.   The feminine pronoun is part of Fergusson's imitation of Highland speech. *maun* must. *he see* go and see. *guard* guard-house.
95.   *weirlike* warlike.
96.   *pring* bring. *ta* the.

97. *trail'd* dragged. *ben* to the inner room. *saul* soul.
98. *drunken groat* fine for drunkenness.
99. *neist* next.
100. *fock* people.
101. *Bide yont* keep away.
102. *nae sic* no such.
106. *wanruly* unruly. *fellin* striking.
109. 'A small quantity of drink serves very well'.
110. 'To keep up the spirits'.
111. *canny chiel* happy man.
112. *steeve* upright. *shoon* shoes.
113. 'But if a man's too well supplied'.
114. *gars* makes. *stammer* blunder.
115. *pleys* arguments.

JOHN LANGHORNE 1735-79

Langhorne, whose father was a clergyman, was born at Winton in West-morland and attended schools in Winton and Appleby. His father's death made a university education impracticable; and he therefore worked first as a private tutor near Ripon and then as an usher at a school in Wakefield. In 1759 he became tutor to the Cracroft family at Hackthorn near Lincoln; and in the years 1761-8 he was successively curate at Dagenham in Essex, curate at St. John's in Clerkenwell, assistant preacher at Lincoln's Inn, and rector of Blagdon in Somerset. He married Ann Cracroft, the sister of his former pupils, in 1767; but she died in the following year, and Langhorne went to live with his brother William in Folkestone. Their joint translation of Plutarch's *Lives* was published in six volumes in 1770, and has since been frequently reprinted. In 1772 he married the daughter of a Westmorland magistrate, and went on a tour of France and Flanders. On his return to Britain he settled once again at Blagdon, where he become a Justice of the Peace. His second wife died in 1776.

Between 1759 and 1778 Langhorne published many volumes of prose and verse, most of them characterized by modest learning and genteel morality. His prose works included, besides the translation of Plutarch, a collection of sermons and a discourse called *The Eloquence of the Pulpit;* and he also edited, in 1765, the poems of William Collins. His own poems include translations from the Greek of Bion, the French of Gresset, and the Italian of Petrarch and Milton. His earliest surviving work, *Studley Park,* is a topographical poem based on *Cooper's Hill* and *Windsor Forest;* and its successors include a pastoral entitled *Genius and Valour,* which was composed as a reply to Churchill's *The Prophecy of Famine.* Langhorne emulates Shenstone in his elegies and inscriptions, Lyttleton in his monodies and didactic epistles, and Pope in his monologue for the Duchess of Mazarin and his 'Verses in Memory of a Lady'. He shows more originality in two works, *The Fables of Flora* and *Owen of Carron,* which appeared in 1771 and 1778 respectively; but even these novel mutations of the beast-fable and the popular ballad are marred by unintelligent sentimentality.

p.180. The Country Justice.

Langhorne's best poem, *The Country Justice,* appeared in three parts between 1774 and 1777. The first part, which is dedicated to the author of a legal work called *The Justice of the Peace and Parish Officer,* discusses the Justice's role mainly in historical and theoretical terms. The second part, which is dedicated to Langhorne's former pupil R.W. Cracroft, is largely concerned with 'Protection of the Poor'. The third part, which is dedicated to a Somerset doctor named Thomas Smith deals with the suppression of crime and the punishment of immorality. The poem is less unified than its stylistic model, *The Deserted Village;* but its blend of expository precision, humanitarian concern and judicious satire looks forward to *The Village and The Borough.*

5.   As tutor to the Cracroft family, Langhorne introduced them to moral philosophy and classical literature.

11.   Langhorne contrasts this socio-didactic poem with earlier works like *The Visions of Fancy.*

17ff.   This idyllic picture of rural Essex is based on Langhorne's memories of Dagenham.

21.   Langhorne's first years as tutor to the Cracrofts were spent at Hackthorn near Lincoln.

33.   Langhorne's doctor was Thomas Smith of Wrington in Somerset.

37.   Part I concluded with a passage about gipsy fortune-tellers and their pernicious influence on rural life.

40.   *Tame* Thames.

43.   Langhorne's note informs us that 'the Mahometan Princes seem to have a regular System of Begging'.

44.   *Prussia's sturdy Beggar* Frederick the Great.

60.   The seventeenth-century Dutch painter David Teniers the Younger was celebrated for his winter-pieces.

64.   Compare Mark VIII.2-3.

113.   *meet* here means 'fit'.

169.   *Augusta ... Gallia* London and France.

186.   The quotation is from Line 56 of Gray's *Elegy.*

189.   Sea-bathing was becoming popular at this time, and Brighton was developing into a fashionable resort.

190.   *the Margate-Hoy* a hoy was a small vessel used to carry passengers. About 1806, J. Beresford speaks of 'a coach as long and as crowded as the Margate Hoy'.

198.   The earliest citation for 'Venetian blinds' in the O.E.D. is dated 1791.

200.   *Blood* according to Johnson, 'a hot spark, a man of fire'. *Maccarone* a macaroni is a fop who imitates continental fashions. *Cicisbeo* the recognized lover of a married woman. *Rook* a dishonest gambler.

203.   The most celebrated of these gaming clubs was that of William Almack in Pall Mall.

204.   Charles James Fox gambled heavily, and borrowed from Jewish money-lenders to cover his losses. In 1773 the money-lenders refused to give him further credit; but his debts, which amounted to £140,000, were paid by his father.

220.   Compare John V.2-4.

221.   Elizabeth Linley, the famous singer, had married R.B. Sheridan in 1773.

227.   Garrick was nearing the end of his career; he retired in 1776.

263.   The officer wants to ensure that his parish will have no legal obligation towards the child.

271.   See note on *The Rosciad,* L.258.

272.   Francis Conway, Marquis of Hertford, became a member of the Privy Council in 1763.

280.   See note on *The Schoolmistress,* L.119.

Index of First Lines